Yip Harburg

HARRIET HYMAN ALONSO

Yip Harburg

Legendary Lyricist and Human Rights Activist

WESLEYAN UNIVERSITY PRESS Middletown, Connecticut

Wesleyan University Press
Middletown CT 06459
www.wesleyan.edu/wespress
2012 © Harriet Hyman Alonso
All rights reserved
Manufactured in the United States of America
Typeset in Miller types
by Tseng Information Systems, Inc.

Wesleyan University Press is a member of the Green
Press Initiative. The paper used in this book meets
their minimum requirement for recycled paper.

Library of Congress Cataloging-in-Publication Data
Alonso, Harriet Hyman.
Yip Harburg: legendary lyricist and human rights
activist / Harriet Hyman Alonso.
     p. cm.
Includes bibliographical references and index.
ISBN 978-0-8195-7128-1 (cloth: alk. paper)—
ISBN 978-0-8195-7124-3 (ebook)
1. Harburg, E. Y. (Edgar Yipsel), 1896–1981.
2. Lyricists—United States—Biography. I. Title.
ML423.H313A46 2012
782.1′4092—dc23
[B]   2012012525

5 4 3 2 1

FRONTISPIECE
Yip at work in his New York City apartment, 1970s.
Photo by Ken Golden. Courtesy of the Yip Harburg
Foundation

For my sister Carolyn,

with love

this book was enabled by the generosity of
Jewish Federation of Greater Hartford

Contents

Illustrations

Preface

When I began working on this book, friends and colleagues asked me what it was about. In response to my enthusiastic "Yip Harburg," I received one of two retorts: (1) "What a great subject! He was such a wonderful songwriter and what a guy. His politics were right on," or (2) "Who?"

For those who knew about him, E. Y. "Yip" Harburg stood for two things: first, beautiful or catchy song lyrics and shows, and second, more profoundly, the courage to use his creativity to speak out for human rights. His was one of the voices that came out of the 1930s and reverberated through the land well into the post–World War II years; his was the era of Irving Berlin, George and Ira Gershwin, Cole Porter, Harold Arlen, Vernon Duke, Richard Rodgers, Lorenz Hart, Oscar Hammerstein II, and a host of others who wrote Broadway and Hollywood tunes and popular hits. This was a precious age in theater and film music, a period that produced songs we still consider classics today.

Yip was unique in his commitment to supporting human rights, world peace, and social justice. Fans see in Yip a kindred spirit, whether they identify with his women of Cicero Falls who wear bloomers and campaign for the vote, or with the runaway slave who steals his freedom in the mid-nineteenth century in *Bloomer Girl*; whether they cheer on the poor sharecroppers who fight the racist senator in *Finian's Rainbow*, or even identify with the need for courage, heart, and intelligence to run the world in the late 1930s of *The Wizard of Oz*.

For those who looked at me with puzzled expressions, I only needed to respond, "Oh, you know him very well. He's the one who wrote the lyrics for 'Brother, Can You Spare a Dime?'—the anthem of the Great Depression."

"Oh."

"And 'April in Paris'—that song that brings romance to your heart (or memory, as the case may be)."

"Yes."

"Or try 'Over the Rainbow.' In fact, try much of the story and song integration and all the other lyrics in the 1939 film *The Wizard of Oz*. Did you know that a 2001 poll conducted by the Recording Industry Association of America and the National Endowment for the Humanities declared the Oscar-winning song as performed by Judy Garland the number-one recording of the twentieth century? Or that in 2004, the American Film Institute ranked it as number 1 of its 100 Greatest Film Songs?"[1]

"I know him!"

And of course, I could add over 500 other song titles; the names of Broadway productions, such as *Bloomer Girl* (1944), *Finian's Rainbow* (1947), *Flahooley* (1951), *Jamaica* (1957), and *The Happiest Girl in the World* (1961); and a host of movie titles for which Yip wrote the lyrics for one or many songs.

"But why haven't I ever heard his name?" they persist in their effort to understand why Yip Harburg deserves being written about.

The answer to that is a bit obvious, and yet complex. First, the average music listener tends to remember the names of composers rather than lyricists, often not understanding the difference between the two. Yip himself often described that difference, as in this example from a presentation he gave in 1970 at the 92nd Street YM-YWHA in New York City: "Words make you think thoughts, make you think a thought. Music makes you feel a feeling. But a song makes you feel a thought. Together, they stand ready to soothe not only the savage breast, but the stubborn mind. Barriers fall, hostilities melt, and a new idea can find a soft spot even under a hard hat."[2] For him, the music and lyrics form a powerful bond.

But Yip and others have also commented on the secondary role that listeners often assign to the lyricist. In 1972 at the same 92nd Street Y, Yip humorously stated, "Music, which is an extension of our emotions, comes naturally. It is the vested interest of the heart, an ancient organ. The word must be worked at and memorized, for it is the vested interest of the frontal lobe, a rather recent development. And you can see how much farther along in evolution music is than words if you compare Beethoven's 9th Symphony with [then Vice President

Spiro] Agnew's latest speech. That perhaps answers the question why the composer is always known while the lyricist is a ghostly figure."[3]

The backseat given the lyricist is easiest to grasp when considering a famous story, the validity of which is often questioned. It seems that one evening at a party, Dorothy Hammerstein overheard a fellow reveler gush, "I just love Jerome Kern's 'Ol' Man River.'" Eager to protect her lyricist husband Oscar's reputation, Dorothy chimed in, "Jerome Kern did not write 'Ol' Man River.' My husband wrote 'Ol' Man River.' Jerome Kern wrote, 'Dum, dum, dum, dum; dum, dum, dum, dum, dum!'"[4] Indeed, as Denny Martin Flinn, the author of *Musical! A Grand Tour*, noted, "A lyricist's notoriety is almost inversely proportional to the fame of his musical partner."[5] Wilfrid Sheed echoed this sentiment in his best-selling book *The House That George Built*: "A lyricist is a musician too, one who arranges tunes for the human voice so that you can 'hear' them for the first time. But once the lyrics have done that, and made you laugh or cry two or three times at most, they fade in importance. Again and again, people will request a favorite song while knowing only its tune."[6]

Second, the public seems to prefer the team approach, remembering duos as a single unit. Note how in all but one of the following cases, the composer's name is listed first: Rodgers and Hart, Rodgers and Hammerstein, Lerner and Loewe, Bock and Harnick, and Kander and Ebb. Richard Rodgers is remembered as one part of two teams, but often not on his own. Yip wrote with several composers, including Harold Arlen, Vernon Duke, Arthur Schwartz, Johnny Green, Burton Lane, Jule Styne, Sammy Fain, and Earl Robinson, and therefore was not identified with any one alone. In fact, he preferred it that way. As he said more than once, parodying his own song from *Finian's Rainbow*, "When I'm not near the composer I love, I love the composer I'm near."[7] And in the end, Yip collaborated with at least fifty-eight accomplished tunesters.[8]

Third, although he was known for innumerable individual songs, except for *The Wizard of Oz* and perhaps *Bloomer Girl* or *Finian's Rainbow*, Yip Harburg's name is not connected in public memory with a host of complete scores. This can be explained by the fact that the bulk of his work consisted of writing parts of scores for Hollywood films and Broadway shows, especially during the 1930s and 1940s, when revues were a popular form of entertainment on the Great White Way. His own entirely written Broadway musicals were primarily staged from the late 1930s into the early 1960s. Yet, who can deny that his songs have stuck in our minds and given us hours of pleasure? Consider just a few: "April in Paris" (1932), "It's Only a Paper Moon" (1932), "Brother, Can You Spare a Dime?" (1932), "I Like the Likes of You" (1934), "Let's Take a Walk Around the Block" (1934), "Lydia, the Tattooed Lady" (1939), "Over the Rainbow" (1939), and of course, "If I Only Had a Brain (a Heart; the Nerve)" (1939). These are only 10 of the 537 songs listed in Harold Meyerson and Ernie Harburg's book celebrating Yip's work, *Who Put the Rainbow in The Wizard of Oz?*—and the list keeps growing as researchers continue to discover more items.[9]

Fourth, innumerable people identify songs with the artists who perform them and not with those who wrote them. Bing Crosby had a major hit with "Brother, Can You Spare a Dime?", Groucho Marx with "Lydia, the Tattooed Lady," Rosemary Clooney with "What is There to Say?", Doris Day with "April in Paris," Tony Bennett with "Fun to Be Fooled," Frank Sinatra with "Last Night When We Were Young," and of course, Judy Garland with "Over the Rainbow."

Finally, another possibility for Yip Harburg's semi-invisibility may be that from the 1930s through the 1950s when his popularity (and income) most soared, his political beliefs were more progressive than the norm, at times more radical. He was one of the first (if not *the* first) Broadway and film lyricists to place human rights at the center of his work. One can certainly cite Oscar Hammerstein II's lyrics for *Showboat* (1927, with Jerome Kern) for pointing out the tragic results of racism; or, in the same vein, his *South Pacific* (1949, with Richard Rodgers); or their *Carousel* (1945) for its sad portrayal of domestic abuse (however romanticized). Yip's lyrics, however, went further, commenting in a critical but humorous way on governmental and societal discrimination on the basis of race, gender, and class; and on the dangers and folly of war and the nuclear arms race, while at the same time offering alternatives to rectify these injustices.

As the political climate of the late 1940s and 1950s grew more conservative, Yip found that financial backing for his work became more difficult to obtain and audiences less likely to line up at the box office to purchase tickets. In addition, in the early 1950s, Hollywood, in its infinite wisdom, decided to blacklist Yip for his supposedly subversive activities, none of them ever proven. In spite of personal hard times, Yip always stood by his political belief in human rights. As he stated in 1980 (and many other times in similar words), "See, I was always politically aware and conscious of what was going on, and my main concern in writing was to hook up real life with the humor of it and maybe the betterment of it."[10] In another interview that same year, he was even more explicit: "My songs try to point out through laughter, through humor or through emotion that life should be taken humorously, hopefully, philosophically, and that underneath all our mistakes that there is a purpose to life and the purpose, as [George Bernard] Shaw says, is evolution, the ascent of man to get out of the animal stage into the civilized age . . . and that the mark of civilization is . . . brotherhood, laughter, un-neuroticism and the therapy of good will."[11]

This book is a study of the lyrical world of Yip Harburg, as told largely by Yip himself through interviews, speeches, song lyrics, and poems. In it, I hope you will journey with me through Yip's life and art, but especially through his political expression. His words reflect what was most important to him and also how he wanted people to understand his work long after his days on this earth had ended. His was a pioneering vision in the worlds of musical theater and film, one that presaged the successes of the women's, civil rights, and peace movements. And his words still have meaning. One needed only to hear audiences roar with laughter and stand in ovation at the Broadway revival of *Finian's Rainbow* in 2009, or to hear over our modern airwaves the new and older versions of "Brother, Can You Spare a Dime?" to know that Yip's words are still relevant and as irreverent as they were during his lifetime. His is the story of dedication to human rights, and he, a person we could sorely use today.

A Note to the Reader

As Yip Harburg said many times, "When something is set to music, you have a more powerful force of communication because then you have not only the words, which give destination to the song, but the music which gives wings to the words."[12]

Unfortunately, this book can present only one-half of the equation: the lyrics. So I urge you to seek out the songs—lyrics and music—which are readily available on solo and original cast or other recordings, on film, and online. I particularly encourage you to listen to *Yip Sings Harburg* (Koch International Classics, 1996) and *E. Y. Harburg: American Songbook Series* (Smithsonian Collection of Recordings), and to view *A Visit with E. Y. "Yip" Harburg: A Life in Concert* (DRG Records and Sony Fox Production). A list of the works I used for this book appears in the bibliography. A complete discography can be found on the Yip Harburg Foundation website at www.yipharburg.com.

In addition, you may find that the printed lyrics here have different line breaks than those you have seen elsewhere. This is because many lyrics are presented here as they appear in the unpublished sources I used, including interviews, librettos, random sheets of paper, and so on. In the same vein, the labels for verses and choruses also appear as they appeared in the sources and only when the entire lyric is quoted.

On another note, you will notice the use of parentheses ( ) and brackets [ ] within excerpts from Yip's interviews. The parentheses denote their original use in interview transcriptions. The brackets indicate something that I added for clarity, to provide important information, or to point out an inconsistency in Yip's stories.

Yip Harburg

1 | What's in a Name?

Before taking a look at Yip Harburg's life and work, we need to briefly consider the evolution of his rather unusual name.[1] In addition, we need to keep in mind that as people age, their memories sometimes get fuzzy, so I will note some inconsistencies or possible inaccuracies throughout our journey. According to research carried out by his family, when Yip was born on April 8, 1896, in New York City, he was most likely given the name Isidore Hochberg. In fact, this is the name listed for him in the Thirteenth Census of the United States and seems to be confirmed by his credit as "I. Hochberg" when he worked as contributing editor for Townsend Harris High School's newspaper, *Academic Herald*. So why the "E. Y. Harburg" in later years?

In May of 1980, when Yip appeared at an oral history luncheon hosted by Martin Bookspan, he gave this tongue-in-cheek rendition of his parents' immigration from Europe and his naming: "Well, my parents came over on the S.S. Steerage, third class . . . They were very poor. They had one child after another. They had about eleven children and as one was born, the other died, and another born and another died. The only one that survived was an elder brother of mine and I was the tenth child and just before me, that child died and I was born. And as the eleventh child was being born, my folks had the superstition that I was going to die, so they wrapped me up in a dirty old sheet and ran me through the streets, with a crowd following behind. I got very sick and they came to a rabbi . . . a big Vilna rabbi named Itzok El Zoneh and after throwing some magic water on me, he said, 'There's only one thing to do with this kid.' He said, 'You gotta change his name.' And they changed it to Itzok [Yip may have meant Isidore here] El Zhoneh, and that's what the 'E' is for. I never tell anybody what El Zhoneh is because [it's] a rather hard . . . Teutonic name to pronounce so I usually say the 'E' is for 'evocative.'"[2]

That "E" became somewhat fluid, as did the spelling of his first name, Isidore. The final "e" on his name was mysteriously dropped, as his City College of New York transcript indicates, and the initial "E" morphed into Erwin. That document, dated in early 1914, lists Yip as Isador Erwin L. Hochberg.[3] There seems to be no information on the "L." It may have reflected his father's name, Louis, or the El of the rabbi he mentioned earlier.[4] Further changes followed. In 1926, Yip's name was listed as "Erwin I. Hochberg" on his son Ernest's birth certificate, but three years later, his professional name, as a lyricist, became "Edgar Y. Harburg" and then, simply "E. Y. Harburg." There seems to be no known rationale for either Erwin or Edgar. The official change to Edgar Y. Harburg came on a court order dated October 16, 1934.[5]

The nickname "Yip" also has an interesting history. It's a name that he remembered having from his earliest years. As he told Studs Terkel, "The nickname Yip, well, it's one of those funny things that stick to you for the rest of your life. My people were immigrants. They came from Russia. And *yipsl* was the [Yiddish] term for a squirrel and evidently I was quite a flighty kid. I moved fast and went from one thing to another and I clowned a lot and I sort of was a maverick in the family. They were all frightened people. I tried to lift them up all the time with games and fun and running. And I was very good at athletics; I won all my four prizes for high jumping, for running, for baseball and so the word *squirrel* became part of it, and it was 'yipsl' to the kids around the block."[6]

Although current Yiddish dictionaries and speakers of the language do not equate *yipsl* with "squirrel," Yip evidently remembered that his parents' vernacular did. And the nickname stuck with him throughout his life, becoming the only name he truly identified with. "I don't know," Yip told Michael Jackson in an interview in the late 1970s. "It just clung to me from the ghetto days. I think my people called me 'Yipsl' and then it turned into 'Yip-i-anny,' and I began writing for Frank P. Adams, sending in little squibs and things under the name of Yip, and then people just hung onto it and I couldn't change it, no matter what I did."[7] Add to that "Yipper," as he was known by several of his friends and collaborators.

With this history of his name in mind, we move on to Yip's life and work. To make things manageable, I will use his chosen names: Yip, or E. Y. Harburg.

2 | Early Years

At one o'clock in the morning on April 8, 1896, Isidore Hochberg (our Yip Harburg) was born to a poor Jewish family on Manhattan's Lower East Side. His parents were recent arrivals from Russia; his father Louis, mother Mary, brother Max, and infant sister Anna all disembarked in 1889. They were but a speck among the 26 million immigrants, many from Eastern Europe, who came to the United States between 1870 and 1920. These immigrants gave a big boost to the number of Americans living in cities, to the number of industrial workers—and to the number living in poverty. And although US cities gained a diversity among ethnic and racial groups unlike anything in their previous experience, there was tension and separation into ghettos and isolated neighborhoods. There was also generational conflict, as children learned English and melded into American society while their parents remained locked within their Old World practices, beliefs, and languages. The children of recent immigrants often became the mediators between their parents and US institutions. They also became sources of income, as well as lifelines to a strange and seemingly hostile environment. All of this is reflected in Yip's story.

For most of his young life, Yip lived, played, and learned on the crowded streets of the Lower East Side of Manhattan—Allen Street, Hester Street, East Ninth and East Eleventh Streets, and the "alphabet" avenues, A, B, C, and D. When he was around the age of fourteen, his parents moved the family to the Bronx in order to be near medical treatment for his older brother, Max; still, the key influence on Yip's life of suffocating poverty, ethnic tension, and hard work was the Lower East Side. Yet this was also the place where he was introduced to education, literature, poetry, and the strong and popular Yiddish culture: theater; newspapers such as the *Forward, Yiddishes Tageblat*, and the *Morning Freiheit*; and writers such as Shalom Aleichem. Yip spoke about his early years in several interviews he gave as an adult. Through them, we can get a clear picture of his feelings about his parents, his neighborhood, and his great love for learning. We can also see how important it was for Yip to have people understand something about the roots of his great passion for human rights.

Let us journey first into Yip's remembrances of his youth, as told in 1959 to an interviewer from the Popular Arts Project through the Columbia University Center for Oral History: "I'm Yip Harburg. My initials are E. Y. Harburg, for literary purposes. Now, you want to know how I started?

"I think I more or less repeat the history of most of the immigrant people who came to America. My father and mother were Russian refugees. They were fleeing from another Russia, at the time, Czarist Russia. They landed in New York with a lot of other immigrants, and were sort of lost in the vast new society, couldn't talk the language, and were rather frightened and insecure. When I came along (I was born here, down on the East Side, in New York City), and learned to talk English probably at the age of three, they were stunned. They never learned for the forty years that they were here; they never seemed to catch on to English. Either they didn't want to or they had a block or something. So I became a hero immediately—I was set up as a model and hero. Their amazement at my being able to talk I think gave them an exaggerated idea of my prowess, and so they looked upon me as a great litterateur, right there and then, you see, and expected great things of me. In fact, I think it was this silly little incident—putting me on a pedestal at that age—that made me feel kind of important.

"It did two things: it made you feel important, and it also made you feel insecure, because these people were so insecure that here they were depending on you to help them out, to help them get along, and they let you know it at a very early age. Not that they meant to. They were lovable and very sweet and loving, and I got a lot of affection, especially from my father. But he always gave me the feeling that it was I who had to support him. Finally, later on, it was I who had to go out in this new land that was mine and not his."[1]

In 1980, Yip provided more information about his Yiddish-speaking father: "My father was what they call a *schneider*. A *schneider* is a fellow who's looking for work, never gets it, when he does he's in the workshop, and so he has an awful lot of children whom he expects to support him when he grows up. So all I heard was, 'Sonele, [pronounced son-el-eh] you're going to be a great man and . . . because you speak English . . . you're going to support me when I get older.' So he was a charming Santa Claus of a man, a little fellow with a very good sense of humor and with a little pot belly—plenty of herring—'Son,' he says, 'all my good friends should be worth what it has cost me, all my enemies should possess what it is worth.' Well, this one little anecdote will give you an idea of the kind of atmosphere I grew up with . . . no matter what the conditions were, and they were terrible because we were half of the time out in the street not being able to pay the rent, [he] had a wonderful sense of humor and . . . read Shalom Aleichem to me. He'd sit on one end of the table, I'd sit on the other with a samovar in between and he used to consume about fifteen glasses and at the age of eight or nine I'd get about eight or ten glasses with, of course, a lump of sugar."[2]

"As you can see, that left a big mark on me. There was no authority, there was no big father image, really. There was love, but there was no security. So there was a double conflict all the time—having to go out and make a living in a society, which I was not equipped to do at the time, being six or seven; and at the same time, not wanting to let them down, and their impression of me."[3]

Being Jewish was, of course, a large part of Yip's identity. Yet, surprisingly, religious practice itself was not as big an influence as one would expect, especially because Yip was a boy. As he told Bernard Rosenberg and Ernest Goldstein, "My parents were Orthodox Jews, though not as strict as the Hasidim. To some extent they were tongue-in-cheek Orthodox. My father did go to *shul* (Orthodox synagogue) regularly and I usually went with him. Whatever religious feeling I had evaporated when I was about fifteen in the face of a devastating personal crisis. I had an elder brother, Max, twelve years my senior—my hero—my inspiration. He was the first born. Max and my sister Ann[a] survived nine others who died before I, number ten, was born. Max became a famous scientist. At the age of twenty he got a B.S. from City College. We never knew exactly how he did it. He was a quiet, taciturn youth, tiptoeing in and out of the house like a mysterious stranger. A superb physicist and mathematician, with a law degree and a master of science degree from NYU and a Ph.D. from Columbia. I remember his having written a thesis on the weight of the earth, news of which was all over the papers. We were too naïve to encompass all this but we had the feeling something important was happening. My parents were mystified. I was a kid; he was my god. Wonderful people started coming to the house—scientists, mathematicians, physicists. It was a world apart. And then, at twenty-eight, he died of cancer . . . The tragedy left me an agnostic. I threw over my religion. I began seeing the world in a whole new light. My father was shaken, but something in him had to carry on . . . He [had] . . . a darling, loving disposition. I told him I was not going to *shul* anymore. '*Papa, Ich gehe nicht.*' We talked in Yiddish. He said, 'Well, sonele, I don't blame you. I can understand. But I'm an old man. I need insurance.'"[4]

Although Yip's father, mother, and—because child labor was a fact of life—his sister Anna and even he himself worked in a ladies' garment sweatshop, his family's poverty was so extreme that by the age of twelve, Yip took a more regular job as a lamp lighter for the Edison Electric Company, founded in 1880. His route ran from East Eighth Street to East Twenty-Fifth Street, up Third Avenue, down Second Avenue, then up First Avenue to East Twenty-Third Street again, and finally down to the docks on the East Side. As he told one interviewer, "I must have been about twelve years old at the time and I lived in New York City, in the slums, down on the east side. And of course if you wanted to get through high school, you had to work your way through at the time. It was a different age. And among the many, many jobs a kid used to have at that time while going to school, one of the first jobs I had was with the Edison Company lighting the street lamps at night. At that time there were no general switches that lit up the whole city or sections of the city. You went around lighting each switch separately.

"And I'd have to light the lamps at sundown and walk about, oh, I think it was about three miles, two and a half, three miles, and it was full of a lot of gangster kids, tough little Irish kids, one section, up in the Twenties. Down around Fourteenth Street there were the Italian gangsters, and they were all looking for the little Jewish boy who was lighting lamps, and we wore blouses at the time with cords. So I had my blouses filled with cigarettes which I picked up . . . butts around the block, distributed them so that I didn't get a bloody nose.

"Then I'd have to get up in the morning . . . just before sun up, summertime, it was around three-thirty, three o'clock, then later on about four or five o'clock, in wintertime just before going to school, put 'em out. And my weekly munificent pay from the Edison, as I remember exactly, three dollars and six cents a week."[5]

Yip learned early on that education was the key route out of his poverty. He benefited greatly from having dedicated teachers who directed him to good books to read and who expected excellence in the classroom. And he also learned from being with the children in his neighborhood, and from programs at the Henry Street Settlement House and the Christadora Settlement House. But perhaps most important was the example of his older brother, Max, and the fun instilled in him by his father. Besides turning Yip away from a firm religious belief, Max's early death gave him a yearning for a good, well-rounded, liberal arts education: "There went the mainstay of the family, you see. He was our rock. That was a real turning point for me. He had inspired me with the idea of learning and literature, the idea that it was important. My father and mother of course would never have that idea. They knew that education was important—all immigrant parents knew one thing, that education was a sort of savior for them. In fact, most of them came here because they couldn't get any education in Russia. It was forbidden, especially for Jewish people. The history of the race was always that: education was the foremost important thing, so they looked forward to that as the panacea, for some reason or other, for life.

"So, poor as we were, and we certainly were, I must have education. My father was a garment worker in the Seventh Avenue section, ladies' garments. He had arthritis—he had terrible hands—and that always worried me and made me feel very sad. It was a funny kind of a paradoxical childhood; and really I think [he] had great literary feeling, and would take me to the Jewish theatre every Saturday. He'd never let my mother know, because first of all, we couldn't afford the quarter for the show, and secondly, he was supposed to be in the Synagogue. So he'd run off with me. He loved the theatre; at that time, there were plenty of them on Second Avenue, Third Avenue, the Bowery. I was just a little snip of a kid, and we'd go off, his hand in mine. I loved the theatre. Of course, I got a great love of it from him."[6]

For Yip, his father's introduction of Yiddish theater meant every-thing. Louis wanted his son to appreciate this art form that had come to New York with the same migration that had brought him, and that had spread to many cities as the Jewish population also spread. Origi-nal comedies and dramas, as well as Yiddish versions of the classics, enchanted audiences. The works of George Bernard Shaw, Henrik Ibsen, and, especially, William Shakespeare, were all adapted into im-mensely popular plays. Among Yip's favorite actors were Boris Thoma-shefsky and Leni Liptzin, the superstars of the time. (Later, Yip likely misremembered Liptzin as "Madame Lipsik.") As Yip related, "The House of God never had much appeal for me. Anyhow, I found a sub-stitute temple—the theater. Poor as we were, on many a Saturday, after services, my father packed me up and told my mother that we were going to the *shul* to hear a *magid* (itinerant preacher). A *magid* was a super rabbi who usually came over from Smolna or Slutsk or some unpronounceable place. But somehow, instead of getting to the *magid* from Slutsk we always arrived at the Thalia Theater where the great Madame Lipsik or Thomashefsky was performing. These excursions were an adventure not only in art but in mischief, for we never told the mamma. As far as she knew, it was the holy Sabbath; we were out soaking up the divine wisdom of a *magid*.

"Everything in the Yiddish theater set me afire. The funny plays had me guffawing; they were broad and boisterous. And the tragedies were devastating. When Thomashefsky paced up and down at the end of the second act, and his daughter came into the room pleading with him to come back to mamma, to cease living with that whore, his mistress, his exit was exquisitely dramatic, followed by his Jovian outrage of guilt. There he was pacing up and down. Beating his chest, until the moment he uttered his mighty last words: '*Mir Kennen Leben, Aber Mir Lasst Nicht!*' ('One can live, but they won't let you!') Such scenes stay with you forever. I look back on them with great delight.

"The Yiddish theater was my first break into the entertainment world, and it was a powerful influence. Jews are born dramatists, and I think born humorists, too. Yiddish has more onomatopoetic, satiric, and metaphoric nuances ready-made for comedy than any other lan-guage I know of. Jewish humor was the basis for so much great vaudeville, my next passion. Whenever I could rake up a quarter, I would spend weekends in the gallery of the Palace Theatre watching these most wonderful performers: Al Jolson, Fanny Brice, Willie Howard, Ed Wynn, Bert Lahr. Memorable names! Saving up the quarter, walking maybe five miles to the theater, going up to the 'pit' in the third gallery, reveling in the great artists. I was hooked."[7]

Yip attended P.S. (public schools) 64 and 36, both located at that time near his homes. He later told interviewer Max Wilk that the schools were better than in later years. "Great teachers—they were aware of the poverty conditions of the kids they were teaching. I had an English teacher—his name comes back to me as though it was yesterday: Ed Gillesper. I'd write something for the school newspaper, or a composition, and he'd read it and see something funny in it and say, 'Harburg, come up here and read it to the class.' I'd read, and there would be twenty-odd kids laughing out loud, and, by God, that was really something. I'd tell myself, 'I want to repeat *this* experience!'"[8] (Yip's memory played tricks on him here, or else Wilk decided to simplify things for his book, as Yip's last name at the time was, of course, not Harburg.)

In his interview with Rosenberg and Goldstein, Yip revealed more about his talent for acting and public performance, a gift he would later use to bring his political messages to eager audiences: "As for myself, my passion to be an actor was consuming. Luckily, the public school I attended, P.S. 64, had a lovely stage. When the teachers found that I was a talented reciter and actor, they had me on all the time. I experienced the whole gamut of roles, from the high tragedy of the death of Cromwell to the whimsy of Jack Frost and Peter Pan. There wasn't a play I didn't get the lead in. I won prize after prize for acting and reciting.

"I liked school because of the acting, the drama, and the recitation. Basically, I loved the English language, the poetry. We had inspiring teachers. I was a whiz at 'The Village Blacksmith' and 'The Wreck of the Hesperus.' Once I invited my folks to a recitation contest. I won a prize that evening with 'Spartacus and the Gladiators.' They wept at my 'Gunga Din,' and Tennyson's 'Lady Claire.' Those were the beginnings, the roots of my passion for rhymes.

"My passion for humorous verse and stories goes all the way back to Mother Goose. My father, too, delighted in good satire. It was one of his great joys to sit at night and read me funny articles by great Yiddish writers from the columns of the Jewish press—stories by Shalom Aleichem and others that tickled and delighted us both."9

During his younger years, Yip also loved going to the public library in his neighborhood. As he told musical theater historian Deena Rosenberg, "You see, I spent my time, a lot of my time, trying to keep warm. We lived in a very cold-water flat on the east side, a little coal stove for three rooms and so if I had to do any homework I had to go to the library and there was a dear one on Tompkins Square, 10th Street facing the park, and there were some lovely librarians there, blonde hair, that made a very important impact on me and they were always more than willing to do something for slum kids and I was more than willing for them to do it and so there was a lot of that first, faint identification with sex attraction there, you know.

"[I was about] seven, eight. But more than that, I was very interested in their speech. I mean, they had beautiful accents. They didn't talk like us kids on the east side and it hit my ear, and they would put books out for me and I became at a very early age acquainted with O. Henry, made a big impact on me, and then finally I got to the light verse section—Carolyn Wells and so on. And I evidently had a natural genetic pull toward versification, and especially versification of a satiric nature, the fact that I liked O. Henry and [W. S.] Gilbert and that point of view of life. And it was a warm place with clean tables and so I could do my homework and so I began reading a lot of things in that library. I couldn't work at home, as I said, we were poor, cold, we had no room for anything. Well, so my poverty turned into a piece of rather good luck. I mean, otherwise I'd probably be doing other things. I never would have gotten in touch with W. S. Gilbert. So that when Ira [Gershwin] came into my life and he had this phonograph and he had all the records of all the Gilbert and Sullivan shows, which we played over and over again.

"The next great big impact that . . . I remember which had some connection with my work was a very sweet lady, a Miss Weisand, also blonde hair, at public school 36 on 9th Street and Avenue C, who took me, took three kids in the class because we were the top of the class, to see Maud Adams in *Peter Pan*. And I think that had something to do with my point of view of fantasy and my love for fantasy and my love for people that were a little larger than life . . . *The Wizard of Oz* came naturally to me. *Finian's Rainbow* came naturally to me. In fact, I'm much more at home, much more at home with people that are a little larger than life . . . who represent symbols of life, rather than people . . . I can't deal with dialogue or lyrics even that are bread and butter lyrics, with cliche lines, with ordinary everyday lines of 'I love you.' It must be something that has some rose petals in it or stardust or something."[10]

But all was not peaceful for Yip. There were the threateningly tough kids in the neighborhood who inspired him to seek out the services of the Henry Street and Christadora Settlement Houses. These were safe havens, unless the youth involved were enjoying themselves on the street. Henry Street, in particular, had a big influence on Yip and his peers. Founded in 1895 as the Nurses Settlement, within a few years it grew from a program offering home nursing classes and services to immigrant families into a full-fledged settlement house. Lillian Wald, its creator and leader, came from a long line of Jewish Americans who had immigrated in the aftermath of the multiple 1848 upheavals in Europe. Raised in the Midwest, Wald came to New York to study nursing and then medicine, in the process discovering her life's mission in fostering civic, educational, social, and philanthropic work in New York's Lower East Side. It was Yip's good fortune that this woman and her allies were particularly committed to the welfare of poor children, for the opportunities that Henry Street offered him through his high school years helped in Yip's intellectual and political formation.

Christadora House was a tinier venture, but no less remembered and appreciated by an older E. Y. Harburg. It dated back to 1867, when it was established to provide social services for Russians, Poles, Ukrainians, and other Slavic immigrants, though not, at least at that time, for Jewish immigrants. As the Lower East Side neighborhood changed, so did the Christadora House clientele. One of the institution's claims to fame was that it purportedly hosted George Gershwin's first public recital. It was also the place where Harry Hopkins—future New Deal leader and close friend and colleague of Franklin D. Roosevelt—worked in 1912 and 1913, the years when Yip was in high school. Yip joined the Christadora's Hawthorne Club, a group that introduced him to much good literature.

As Yip explained to Rosenberg and Goldstein, "Among the kids there was plenty of friction. The enmity was supposedly residential—block by block—but we Jews were always aware that the *goyim* [non-Jews] were after us. Since they came in gangs we formed gangs too. We fought the 14th Streeters who were Italian, we fought the Irish—and both of them fought the Jews. They had big gangs. Battles fought with vegetables and rocks were frequent. I remember using my mother's washtub boiler top—huge, oval, tin-plated—as a shield; it looked like a replica of Greek armament. We all had shields to guard against the rocks and battled.

"Our folks didn't know much about all this. A kid was automatically independent at the age of eight, surely by the time he was ten. The street, not the home, was your life. Your parents spoke Yiddish. That alone made you a displaced kid. The older generation of men and women brought their Russian and Jewish culture with them. They spoke no English. Down on the street you were being Americanized, but in a special ghetto way. Parents were very proud of children who spoke English and could interpret for them. This put the parents in an inferior position.

"The drama of life was enacted within a context of poverty. You lived from month to month. But youngsters didn't feel the sting of it because everyone else was poor too. We knew no other way of life, and it didn't mean much to a kid who turned the street into an exciting playground. You could swipe your sweet potatoes from the grocer, light a bonfire, and eat 'em right there at midnight. The potatoes tasted a hell of a lot better than those your parents bought baked, and forced you to eat at a table, on top of having to wash your hands. What adventure! We'd have lookouts on different streets to warn us that the cops were coming; then we'd squash out the bonfire and beat it."[11]

As Yip told Wilk, "I came from a rough area, right there on the East Side—the East River, with all the derelicts, docks, lots of sailors and gangs. There wasn't any such thing as an East River Drive down there. This was before World War I. Italian gangs on Mulberry Street—we used to play them in baseball. I was on the Tompkins Square Park team; we won the New York State championship. And then there were the Irish, a little further up on 14th Street. Plenty of gang fights. Those of us who were a little more sensitive and didn't care for that so much were directing ourselves to the settlement houses, like the Henry Street Settlement. Wonderful places. They took the kids under their wing. They had wonderful social directors. They had clubs, athletic clubs, literary clubs. I belonged to a literary dramatic club. We were putting on plays, and that excited me.

"We'd do shows at the settlement house, or in school, and I'd usually get parts. I found I had the ability to act and to write my own stuff. Scrounging around for costumes, putting on shows—it was great. We were poor, always out on the street with our furniture, and never knowing if the next rent would be paid. But I had an exciting time. More fun than I ever had in Hollywood. It was real. If you wanted to play a basketball game, you had to make the equipment yourself. No basketball, no bat or ball—you made everything, improvised."[12]

As he grew up, Yip realized the importance of receiving a good education. It was his ticket out of poverty, but it was also the way for him to follow his dreams into a more sophisticated literary world. Once he finished his elementary education, he attended Townsend Harris High School, then located a good twenty blocks from his home. The school was highly selective and offered a superior education for "gifted" students who might also be poor. At the time, a three-year education at Townsend Harris led directly to a four-year program at the College of the City of New York (now known as the City College of New York, CCNY, or just plain City). City College was founded by Townsend Harris in 1847 as the first free institution of higher education in the United States. When Harris sought its charter from New York State, he described the school as a place where rich and poor young men could study together with no evident class distinction. It became a tremendous source of hope and upper mobility for young men who might otherwise have no way to achieve a college education. As Yip later remembered with gratification, "You didn't have to pay any fee, you didn't even have to pay for textbooks. A wonderful place . . . More Ph.D.'s come out of City College than probably Harvard and Yale, and this was all free."[13] But getting in was not that easy. As Yip remembered, "There were tough competitive entrance exams—you had to be a masochist to attempt to get in—and those admitted were an elite group, real studious kids from the Lower East Side. Grind or not, I *had* to get in, to finish school as fast as possible, and get to work full time . . . Most of my fellow students were also the sons of immigrants, all of us pursuing an education as though our salvation depended on it. 'Get that degree!' was the aim of life. We were driven. At the same time, the education was terrific."[14]

While in high school, Yip became a contributing editor of the school's newspaper, *Academic Herald*, for which he co-edited a column called "Much Ado" with a classmate named Isidore Gershvin (later known as Ira Gershwin). It was here that he began signing his columns "Yip" while Ira signed his "Gersh." Their partnership carried over into City College, where "Yip and Gersh" co-wrote the column "Gargoyle Gargles" for the *Campus* newspaper. The name of the column reflected on the famous City College gargoyles (or grotesques) that were situated on the college's Gothic-style buildings. After Ira left the college, Yip also edited the column "Silver Lining: A Chronicle of Our Own Wit and Other People's Folly." As Yip later explained, "We had something special in common, Ira and I. Among other things, we both hated algebra, he more than I, so one day in class we started a little paper called *The Daily Pass-It*. We wrote verse and he did some cartoons, which we passed around the room, giving our classmates a real chuckle. Our rag was 'printed' on Townsend Harris toilet paper to make it real establishment stuff. Soon we wrote for the official high school paper; our column was called 'Much Ado.' It was an imitation of 'The Conning Tower,' Franklin P. Adams' column in the *Daily World*. [At this time, the column was actually in the *New York Tribune*. It moved to the *New York World* with F.P.A. in 1922.] We were living in a time of literate revelry in the New York daily press—F.P.A., Russell Crouse, Don Marquis, Alexander Woollcott, Dorothy Parker, Bob Benchley. We wanted to be part of it."[15]

Yip further described to Deena Rosenberg how his and Ira's admiration for these great satiric writers led to their own satiric work: "Then we both became editors of the *Townsend Harris Herald*, which was, naturally, the high school paper. And we ran a column that imitated Frank P. Adams, with humorous light verse and paragraphs and Ira was a very good draftsman, a very good cartoonist, so I would write captions, he would do the cartoons and we each wrote little bits of verse . . . And of course that gave us a lot of fame around the school with everybody. And then when we got to college, CCNY, why, we began running a column in the *Mercury* and then there was a new newspaper started called *The Campus* and we ran a column there called 'Gargoyles.' So Yip and Gersh became an inseparable team."[16]

As Yip told an interviewer from Columbia University, "When I got to City College, I found I had a great love for all the columnists at the time. It was a lovely age, as I look back on it, from my point of view—the *New York World*, the wonderful Pulitzer paper, with [Alexander] Woollcott and Heywood Broun and Frank P. Adams. These people were really inspiring; at that time, it seemed that the kids who were going to college were terribly interested in reading that daily column ["The Conning Tower"]. It was a sort of a Sam Pepys' Diary, you know, and worthwhile. Lovely things were discussed. It wasn't rock and roll, and it wasn't Westerns, it wasn't all the shenanigans of today. It was the light verse, it was the French forms, it was who could write a *villanelle*? Suddenly people would love to write for F.P.A., and only a very few would be accepted. It was an honor to be accepted, and the standards were high, higher than anything I know of today. Frank P. Adams was a great force in making people aware of versifying. He was a purist. Then names began to appear in the column, like Dorothy Parker and Sam Hoffenstein and G.S.K. [George S. Kaufman], and Marc Connolly and Deems Taylor and Howard Dietz. And of course, I joined the procession with a 'YIP.' I was just flabbergasted the day my first trial appeared at the top of the 'Conning Tower' when I was just finishing high school. Then I knew that somebody thought I was all right—I mean somebody with some standards, you see.

"That started me off, really. If there had been no F.P.A. column, I don't think I would have had the confidence to know any of the inner turmoil, the inner quakings in me, for rhyme. We went in for really nice things then, for really good rhyming, good ideas. It was a fine age. From that, I went to editing some of the humorous columns in the City

College magazines. I wrote a lot of light verse, instigated by F.P.A.; since I was accepted there, of course everybody accepted me then.

"The college was a great impetus, because just getting a magazine out and writing for it was a great reward. Not monetary, but it was glory of the most thrilling kind, naturally."[17]

In spite of all the time he spent on studying and writing, Yip still had to work throughout his high school and college years, which might be why his grades at CCNY, especially in math and science, were not exceptional. He sold newspapers and groceries in Macy's grocery department, and took any other job he could find. That is how his family survived and how he himself remained in school. "Then in the summertime of course we'd get jobs. I mean, there was no such thing as a vacation, and no such thing as seeing a tree or anything like that, or taking a swim—not until I was way grown up. Not till you were out and you got the diploma."[18]

Yip also learned that college by itself was not the way to economic prosperity. "When you got the diploma, it didn't mean a damn thing either. Now, what do you do with that? You see?—The funny thing is, the values that we thought education would give us: that it would give us a job, that it would mean monetary release—turned out to be wrong. It didn't mean that at all. It was a general foundation for a person adjusting himself to a life that was tough in a jungle that was rough—however, you look back and you say, 'Thank heaven for that education,' because none of the things that happened would have happened without it, even though it didn't appear palpable at the moment. At graduation, everybody said: 'Well, now you've got your diploma. Now eat it. Put mustard on it.'"[19]

Much is made of the generation of composers and lyricists who came out of the immigrant Jewish population that produced Yip Harburg, but one of the most interesting stories is the early friendship that evolved between Yip and Ira Gershwin. Yip spoke about this friendship in innumerable interviews—about their immediate closeness, their similar interests in Gilbert and Sullivan and operettas in general, and of course, their interest in writing. In fact, it was W. S. Gilbert's book of light verse that opened the door to their lifelong friendship. As Yip told it, "Well, I found myself going to Townsend Harris Hall, . . . and

I found myself, 'H,' Harburg [actually Hochberg], sitting next to a guy named Gershwin, 'G.' See? And once I brought the *Bab Ballads* into class and was reading under a news[paper], and Ira turned around and said, 'You know the *Bab Ballads*?' And I said, 'Yes, I think I know most every one of them by heart.' He says, 'They're great.' He says, 'Do you know that the fellow who wrote those had music put to them?' I said, 'They have?' He says, 'Wanna come up to my house? I live on Second Avenue.' Now Second Avenue was very high-class stuff at the time.

"Yeah, I lived toward the East River, the Drive, you know? With the Dead End Kids. Well, I went up to Ira's house on Second Avenue, and there was a Victrola, and that was class status at that time, and he put on [*H.M.S.*] *Pinafore* and there it was . . . ["The Queen's Navee"] . . . Well, that opened up every possibility.

"I had no idea there was melody. And then I think that Ira, who had some money, blew me to the first Gilbert and Sullivan show, with the Wolf opera, which was *The Mikado* . . . I saw *Mikado* and of course, my eyes popped and they've been popping ever since."[20]

"Now, they were pretty wealthy, the Gershwins. They were all right. They had restaurants, a chain of restaurants called the W. and G. Restaurants. Ira used to invite me to come to the restaurant and eat. Really, that was my first introduction to baked apple, and I'll never forget the moment that baked apple came. He said, 'You know, you can have cream on it, too.' I said, 'Could you?' He said, 'Yes,' and he called the waiter and put some cream on it. Well, that was about the end, I think. That was one of the high moments. The fellow who climbed Mt. Everest never hit the high spot I did at that time I discovered baked apple and cream."[21]

"By the time I met them they were middle class. Mr. Gershwin, Gershwin's father, was a pixie sort of a little fellow who . . . was good at both business and pinochle . . . so they were able to have a flat on . . . Fifth Street and Second Avenue, and it had a little stoop, and Mrs. Gershwin, in order to keep the status going, said 'We've got to have a piano.' She said, 'If you want to be able to confront your neighbors at all, you've got to have a piano.' And she said, 'Since Ira is the scholar in the family and George is a loafer . . .' George ran around town, quit Stuyvesant High School where they tried to teach him accounting. [Again, Yip's memory was incorrect. George actually attended the High School of Commerce.] That was the silliest thing I ever heard of—double-entry bookkeeping for George Gershwin. So he quit. And Ira loved reading. Ira was an omnivorous reader, and Mrs. Gershwin thought she'd buy the piano for Ira, and sure enough, Ira was pretty sick about that. He said, 'There goes my mother again, there she goes! Who the hell wants to play the piano?' And, anyhow the piano was hoisted up at that time through the window, it was an upright, and there Mrs. Gershwin stood in a fox fur and she was directing the operation of the piano to see that there were no scratches on [it]. They came in and when George came up from the street where he was loafing around Second Avenue, he sat down at that piano, two hands, and played [an] Irving Berlin [tune] . . . He just played it.

"Well, we found what happened. There was a piano store in the neighborhood and any time they wanted an errand run, like call somebody for a telephone, we had no telephones, so Mrs. Moskowitz had to be called to the telephone and she lived two blocks down, and they'd call George and he'd get the person to the telephone, and his reward was not three cents or five cents, but ten minutes at the piano. And so in the piano store where there were a number of pianos, he'd be allowed to play for ten minutes, but he (noted) it all out by himself, like Mozart . . . I understand, I don't know whether he did or not, or whether it was his parental biography, but I understand . . . well, I've seen kids do that."[22] Within six months, George was so good at playing that he got a job in Tin Pan Alley, the row of publishing houses that ran for the two blocks of West Twenty-Eighth Street between Fifth and Sixth Avenues (with Broadway in between) and which produced most of the nation's sheet music and popular songs.

Meanwhile, Ira, the reader and constant learner, dropped out of City College after a year, leaving Yip on his own, at least in school. Yip missed him sorely, but he continued the writing that the two had so enjoyed doing together. "When Ira left college, I suffered on with the goddamn trigonometry and differential calculus. But I did take some very good courses in Shakespeare with a professor named Coleman. Another teacher who influenced me greatly was Professor Otis. He recognized something in me and made me wait after school one day, saying, 'I want you to continue writing, especially humorous pieces.' I once wrote a parody of Marc Antony's speech at the burial of Julius Caesar: 'Friends, Romans, countrymen . . .' It was a satire on the teachers in which I had them kill each one of the students after an exam. Otis loved it, and I became his pet pupil. He strongly encouraged me to write.

"I began submitting little poems for publication. A magazine called *The Parisian* was the first to buy a poem from me, for ten dollars. After that came *Judge* and *Puck*, ten dollars, fifteen dollars here and there. It was evident that you couldn't make a living this way. At this point I never thought of writing poems as a career. As for songs, I had no idea how they were written, let alone that they could mean anything to me. I thought words and melodies sprang more or less full-blown like Athena from Zeus' head . . . When Ira began writing words to George's music in the twenties, I became aware of lyric writing as a possible profession."[23]

Yip was supposed to graduate from City College in 1918, but he did not. Instead, with only about twenty-one credits to go, he accepted a job that a wealthy alumnus offered him to work in Swift and Company's Uruguay office. This turned out to be a serendipitously fortunate decision, as Swift was considered part of the nation's defense effort, so Yip was kept safely away from the horror that was World War I. In fact, he might have been on the side of those who opposed that unfortunate global conflagration. As John Lahr pointed out in his portrait of Yip for the *New Yorker*, Yip wrote in his column "Silver Lining," "What should I fight for? I don't own anything. Let the millionaires fight."[24] His words echoed that of a majority of the US population from the time war broke out in Europe in 1914 until the country finally joined the war in 1917.

As Yip later told Deena Rosenberg about the benefits of working for Swift, "It was the first time I was able to support my mother and father which was what I wanted. They were poor, pathetic people and I felt awfully guilty about them. I was able to send back money. I became a big shot down there. I got to be head of a department and I was written up in all the papers, so I was for the first time becoming a man. And I realized that was important for me. Because I was a frightened little

Yip's passport photo, 1920.
Courtesy of the Yip Harburg Foundation

kid all the time, and I began feeling like a man, real grown up. I had the image of my father always in mind. They [my parents] frightened me that they were loose screws in the world and that I would be like that too. This trip helped me to grow up.

"When you're alone in a foreign country and you have to work for yourself, you become a man damned quick. Also the experience. I began feeling the triumph of being a leader, of making decisions, of having five hundred people under me and being a big shot. I stayed another year after the war finished. Two years. I was afraid to come back, afraid of not getting a job. I had such a good job down there.

"I kept in touch with the Finley Club [a writing group started in college]. My friends and Ira's . . . were all together . . . I would write them poems back home, and I was even writing poems for the *Montevideo News* in English. It was an English paper, so I became sort of a top guy in the English community there. Then we put on some American plays. I was a very good actor and we put on some three-act plays. You can't imagine when you're living in an isolated country where the handful of Americans are all homesick and you give them an American show. You become like Merlin. And so wherever I went I was always given respect—no matter if I was a lost kid in space."[25]

Three years later, Yip returned to New York and, ironically, got a job with the Consolidated Gas and Electric Company, but he was not required to walk around the city throwing light switches on and off. In his spare time, he attended evening classes at City College and composed light verse, which appeared in the column "The Conning Tower" and in other publications. He married Alice G. Richmond on February 23, 1923; on August 12 of the following year, they had their first child, daughter Marjorie. Another child, Ernest, arrived on September 7, 1926. Between the two births, Yip and his City College friend, Harry Lifton, started their own business headquartered in nearby Brooklyn, the Consolidated Gas Iron Company, which sold electrical appliances. There, Yip even invented a few gadgets, including an ironing board that was easy to open and a small dryer for baby clothes that its owner merely had to attach to the apartment's steam radiator. Why did Yip become a businessman? Well, as he later explained, "Harry got the capital. He liked me; my verses in the college papers gave me a following and a popularity which Lifton confused with genius in every department of life. So when Harry Lifton, a go-getter extraordinaire, said 'Come on, let's go into business,' I went along with him."[26] Yip stopped attending his college courses in the spring of 1922, with only three-and-one-half credits left to complete.

As he described this part of his life, "This was in the twenties. The twenties was a booming period, and I borrowed some money, he [Lifton] borrowed some money, and it [the business] did very well.

"It was going big, but I was very unhappy in it. I was unhappy unless I was writing, and you couldn't both write and attend to the business. I had a partner who'd made me sign a contract that while doing the partnership, I would not try to write, because he knew I would get off days and go to the library and try to write light verse. So they had me signed down to a contract where it was forbidden to waste time on that sort of shibboleth.

"However, we were making a lot of money, and it was being put back in the business all the time. The business was growing, as everybody told you. The accountants told you you were making money, you were getting very wealthy and rich. I said: Well, I'm going to work ten years and then sell out, and then go into the writing business. Because that was what I always had my eye on. I didn't know whether I could do it. I had no confidence, really. But luckily, I had a classmate of mine by the name of Gershwin."[27]

That friendship would save Yip when the stock market crashed in 1929, putting an end to a business worth about a quarter of a million dollars.

3 | Brother, Can You Spare a Dime?

Yip Harburg might be the only person in the United States to claim that the Great Depression was the best thing that ever happened to him. As he told the great oral historian Studs Terkel, "I never liked the idea of living on scallions in a Left Bank garret. I like writing in comfort. So I went into business . . . And a thing called Collapse, bango! Socked everything out. 1929. All I had left was a pencil.

"I was relieved when the Crash came. I was released. Being in business was something I detested . . . When I lost my possessions, I found my creativity. I felt I was being born for the first time. So for me the world became beautiful."[1]

Although in hindsight after a most successful career in show business, Yip could find humor in his enormous business loss, at the time it must have been devastating. After all, he was a family man with growing financial responsibilities. And nationally, the effects of the crash of 1929 and the onset of an economic depression that lasted until 1941 were profound. Just in the first four years of the crisis, more than 100,000 businesses failed besides Yip's. Thousands of banks closed and, before the Federal Deposit Insurance Corporation (FDIC) was created, millions of people's savings disappeared into thin air. By 1933, about one-quarter of the possible work force was unemployed. Those lucky enough to find some work were usually faced with part-time or low-paying positions. The president at the start of the Depression—Herbert Hoover—made a few efforts to help the bankers, farmers, and businesses, but the situation called for more drastic measures than either he or Congress were willing to take.

Over the years, Yip portrayed what he considered his great good fortune in losing his livelihood with his usual humorous take on life. In 1961, he told radio interviewer Jack Stirling, "Well, I was romancing a few hundred thousand dollars . . . We got up to about two hundred and fifty thousand. I said . . . 'Get two hundred and fifty thousand, I'll sell, get out and start writing.' Well, I thought writing was for dilettantes, the fellas who were just lazying around. You don't make money writing.

You make money in business, you know . . . Of course, as I've said before many times, that proved to be a big dreamer's idea, this business. The real business is in the arts. I mean, that's where you really make money. Not in business . . . We went down with 1929 when all the other fellas . . . went outta the window. What I did was get into the musical comedy field. So I was courting suicide by the slow way."[2]

Finding himself not only broke, without an income, and in debt for about $50,000 because of contracts he signed without ever reading them, Yip decided to seek help from his close friend, Ira Gershwin. As he later related, "So I went to Ira for some money and some advice. He put me in touch with a composer . . . and a $500 check, enough to see me through for three or four months. I sent my wife and two kids off to California, assuring them, 'I'll break into this new business somehow.' I rented a little back room four flights up in a house on Eighty-fifth Street, from a Russian friend living with her mother. Her name was LaLa—not a show girl, but a sober secretary with a literary bent.

"One day LaLa told me, 'I have a good friend who's married to a composer. Maybe I can get you two together.' 'Fine. I'll phone him.' Meanwhile Ira had called Jay Gorney . . . Luckily, Jay's lyricist, Howard Dietz, had just teamed up with a new composer, Arthur Schwartz, and Jay needed a new collaborator. He asked who I was. Ira answered, 'Well, he hasn't written song lyrics, but you'll know him from "The Conning Tower." He signs himself "Yip."' To which Jay responded, 'Oh, Yip from "The Conning Tower"!' Ira made a date for me. LaLa also made a date for me with her friend who was married to a composer, and *he* turned out to be the same Jay Gorney!"[3]

It was fortunate that Yip and Gorney had some things in common. They were both born in the same year—Yip in April, Gorney in December—and both had Russian Jewish heritage. Unlike Yip, though, Gorney was born in the Old World and had witnessed Russian anti-Semitism and pogroms firsthand. His family immigrated to the United States in 1906, settling in Detroit. In Michigan, Gorney thought he would pursue a career in law and started working his way through school, but World War I intervened. After a stint in the navy, he decided to move his family to New York and take up songwriting, an art he had been working on for some time. In fact, he had already had some success before he and Yip hooked up.

As Yip recalled, "We clicked. I worked at the Sterling Watch Company in the daytime and wrote with Jay at night. We wrote a dozen or so songs together, right off the bat. Just then, Earl Carroll had a new theater with a turkey in it called *Fiorito*, which flopped. Jay and I caught him on the rebound and played him our songs. 'Great,' he said, 'These'll make my new revue.' The show was called *Sketchbook*— an immediate hit. Around that time, J. P. McEvoy, the satirist, was writing another show, *Americana*. He was looking for a lyric writer, and we happened to meet at Gorney's house. He'd seen our revue and thought the songs were cute. Did I want to write his new show for him? 'Sure.' So the Shuberts hired me on his say-so and I went to work with Vincent Youmans, the composer they'd hired. But after we wrote the opening song, Youmans took his $5,000 advance, got drunk, and disappeared. The show had to open in a couple of months. Catastrophe! What to do? The only way to do it is to call in several composers and let them all feed me. When good tunes set me off I work fast. That was okay with the Shuberts: 'You select the composers you want to work with.' So I grabbed a few tunes from Jay and a few from a then little-known guy named Harold Arlen, and one from a complete unknown named Burton Lane. That's how the show was written."[4]

Yip had actually worked on several projects between 1929 and 1932, including some with Gorney. He wrote lyrics for various radio plays, stage revues, feature films, animated short films, film shorts or featurettes, and stage musicals, but the concept and lyrics he wrote for *Americana* marked the first time he forayed into the world of social commentary, and there was no turning back. Although he continued writing all sorts of lyrics with an eye toward enhancing script stories and producing a popular and therefore lucrative hit, he also used his art form to foster a spirit of human rights advocacy. As a revue, *Americana* (which opened on October 5, 1932) was designed to bring together a series of skits and song numbers meant to entertain. There was much humor, vaudeville antics, short skits, and song and dance to make an audience (especially during the Great Depression) guffaw. However, the show was not a great hit, running ten weeks before being shuttered. Yet it produced one of the greatest American songs ever written: E. Y. Harburg and Jay Gorney's "Brother, Can You Spare a Dime?"

Yip felt deeply about two aspects of the Depression that he wanted the show to comment on. First was the image of "the forgotten man," a term which at the time of the production, Democratic presidential candidate Franklin D. Roosevelt had popularized. The forgotten man referred to the veterans of World War I, who many in our society felt had become unjustifiably invisible. In particular, these men received no special consideration for the Depression era poverty forced upon them, even though they had sacrificed both mind and body for the nation during the war. After 1919, Congress had agreed to pay these veterans a bonus, but not until 1945. When certain members of congress put forth a bill to authorize the money ($2.4 billion) immediately, 15,000 unemployed veterans and their families decided that an effective way to lobby for it would be to go to Washington themselves. With the label the Bonus Expeditionary Force (a wordplay on the World War I American Expeditionary Force), they set up tent camps and settled in unused government buildings.

Although President Hoover supported the bonus bill, the Senate voted it down, and though many of the campers then left town, several thousand remained over the summer. As the heat of June and July made tempers short, Hoover turned against the veterans and refused to meet with them. The army, too, was sent to confront them. Using tanks and bayonet-rifled soldiers, the military chased men, women, and children, tear-gassing them and setting their possessions and housing on fire. The incident infuriated the public, and pretty much helped to ensure that Hoover would be defeated in his 1932 re-election bid. For Yip, the forgotten man became a powerful symbol of what was wrong with the country.

The second phenomenon that Yip wanted to emphasize was the presence of the breadlines, a scene that took place in every part of the country each and every day. Yip understood on a very personal level what it meant to lose everything because of the economic collapse, and his heart went out to the people waiting in long lines for something to eat. As he explained in 1980, "The American Dream Train was derailed. People who loved liberty more than life had flocked to this democracy, this paradise of opportunity where they could get political freedom and time for education and imbibe the ideals of Franklin and Jefferson. The branches of that tree of knowledge grew as wide as the land was wide, but an economic system based upon gluttony, in time, produced a citizen who thrived upon greed. The big apples from the tree of knowledge were ravaged, shaken down, machine-mashed into applesauce, sodium monoglutenate added, canned, labeled 'Excelsior' and exported for profit, and people who came to till the soil and build the homes found themselves in Wall Street, tangled in ticker tape in a strangled economy. Those who failed to leap out of their skyscrapers did the more rational thing. They joined the breadline, still reading [Norman] Vincent Peale's bestseller, *The Power of Positive Thinking*. The man in the breadline was not angry, but bewildered. How could this happen to this great infallible country, still overflowing with riches?"[5]

One of the skits in the *Americana* revue led to Yip and Gorney's creating what has become the anthem of the Great Depression, "Brother, Can You Spare a Dime?" Yip explained the impetus for the song to Studs Terkel. One day, as he was walking near Columbus Circle in Manhattan, he observed a large truck owned by publisher William Randolph Hearst dispensing hot soup and bread to desperate men living in Hoovervilles and wearing burlap sacks for shoes. For a sketch in *Americana*, Yip decided to pit Mrs. Ogden Reid of the *Herald Tribune* against Hearst to see who could have the best breadline. Yip's intention was to present a satiric view of the instant poverty of the Great Depression. As he told Terkel, "On stage, we had men in old soldiers' uniforms, dilapidated, waiting around. And then into the song. We had to have a title. And how do you do a song so it isn't maudlin? Not to say: my wife is sick, I've got six children, the Crash put me out of business, hand me a dime. I hate songs of that kind . . . I don't like songs that describe a historic moment pitifully.

"The prevailing greeting at that time, on every block you passed, by some poor guy coming up, was: 'Can you spare a dime?' Or: 'Can you spare something for a cup of coffee?' . . . 'Brother, Can You Spare a Dime?' finally hit on every block, on every street. I thought that could be a beautiful title. If I could only work it out by telling people, through the song, it isn't just a man asking for a dime."[6]

While Yip was mulling over the concept for the song, he heard Gorney playing one of his tunes that already had a lyric. "It was a torch song," Yip later recalled, "and went this way:

> I could go on crying
> Big blue tears
> Ever since you said we were through.
> I could go on crying
> Big blue tears—

Well, I said, 'Jay, is that lyric wedded to this tune?' And he says, 'Well, we can get a little divorce,' he says, 'if we have the right tactics.' And so [I said], 'I've got a title for it.' And then it came: 'Brother, can you spare a dime?' And that's how the thing was written and that's how the thing was gotten into the show."[7]

Yip also felt that the song "flowed naturally" out of the theme of the forgotten man. And it affected how the rest of the show developed, as a satire as well as a social commentary on the times. "We cut out all the usual tap dancing and hired the Humphrey and Weidman dancers and José Limon. The first show to have ballet. Mucho advance for Broadway.

"It was clear to me from the start how much skill goes into writing a whole show. Much more complicated than writing single songs for Tin Pan Alley, where a good titillating jingle does the trick. But in good musicals, each song is a whole scene; you need to soak yourself in character, motivation, mood, tempo, everything. You're advancing plot, you're extending dialogue, using music and lyrics to make the statement explosive and emotional. Each song has a different problem, or many problems. Each one has to be fitted, guided, placed.

"'Brother, Can You Spare a Dime?' called for a lyric to identify the fellow in the breadline, just back from the wars. A bewildered hero with a medal on his chest ignominiously dumped into a breadline. I wanted a song that would express his indignation over having worked hard in the system only to be discarded when the system had no use for him. The lyric required political, economic, and sociological knowledge to prevent maudlinity. I wanted to avoid, 'Please mister—I've fought your country's war. I did my part—can't you spare a dime?' This is sentimental, tear-jerking, on the surface—second rate."[8]

The song that Yip created with Jay Gorney had these lyrics:

Verse
They used to tell me
I was building a dream
And so I followed the mob
When there was earth to plough
Or guns to bear
I was always there
Right on the job

They used to tell me
I was building a dream
With peace and glory ahead
Why should I be standing in line
Just waiting for bread?

Chorus
Once I built a railroad,
Made it run
Made it race against time
Once I built a railroad
Now it's done
Brother, can you spare a dime?

Once I built a tower
To the sun
Brick and rivet and lime
Once I built a tower
Now it's done
Brother, can you spare a dime?

Once in khaki suits
Gee, we looked swell
Full of that Yankee Doodle-de-dum

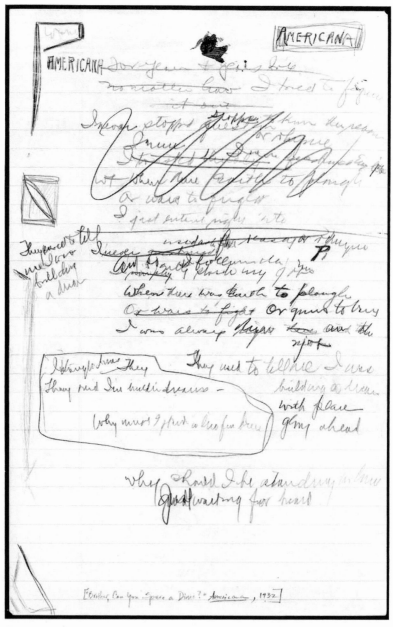

Section of Yip's 1932 worksheet for "Brother, Can You Spare a Dime?"
Courtesy of the Yip Harburg Foundation

Half a million boots went sloggin' thru hell
I was the kid with the drum

Say, don't you remember?
They called me "Al"
It was "Al" all the time
Say, don't you remember
I'm your pal
Buddy, can you spare a dime?[9]

Yip considered the song to be very political in questioning the inequities of the capitalist system. "Why should this man be penniless at any time in his life, due to some fantastic thing called a Depression or sickness or whatever it is that makes him so insecure?"[10] In fact, as Harold Meyerson and Ernie Harburg have pointed out, Yip drafted out several other possible lyrics for the song, one aimed at the oil magnate John D. Rockefeller:

Once you drilled an oil well
Made it gush
How Socony did climb
Once you drilled an oil well
Now I'm flush
Brother, here's a brand new dime.[11]

Yip decided not to be so specific in the lyrics. As he explained his intention, "My analysis started with an awareness of the injustice of a society in which the man who produces, who builds towers, makes railroads, farms the land, is left empty-handed. Why doesn't he share in the wealth his sweat and skill have produced? So much for analysis. How to say all that poetically, dramatically, and with lasting emotional impact, to make the song neither pitiful nor sentimental but an intelligent dramatic statement?

"Well, it was a situation many were going through, so the title, the central phrase, had to be popular. Wherever you went you heard, 'Brother, can you spare a dime—Brother, can you spare a dime?' The people who pleaded weren't begging. They had dignity as human beings; they'd accomplished things in their lives and were proud of it. Thus: 'Once I built a railroad, made it run, made it race against time . . .' He's not sighing about it—he's feeling his strength, and brings that strength into the song. But suddenly he looks at himself and stops short, puzzled: 'How the hell did I get into this position, where I find myself saying, "Brother, can you spare a dime?"' The dramatic juxta-position of this phrase with the upbeat of what went before—'I *built* that railroad'—makes a powerful rhetorical statement, put in a lyrical way for greater impact."[12]

The song was not greeted as enthusiastically as one would expect. As Yip told radio interviewer Paul Lazarus in 1980, the song had to pass muster with the show's producers, J. J. and Lee Shubert: "The Shubert brothers, who were living apart for the last twenty-five years—one of them lived over the top of the Shubert Theatre; the other lived over Sardi's—and they hadn't spoken for twenty-five years. They had a system. The medium was not the message at that time. It was notes and [saying to someone] 'Tell him to come over and tell him to listen to some songs.' J. J. Shubert had to corroborate and verify all the songs that Lee was doing at that time and he came over and we sang. He says, 'Tell him to listen to this song for this show.' And so J. J. listened and we sang 'Brother, Can You Spare a Dime?'—we sang our hearts out—and his face fell. It hadn't very far to fall and he said, 'Tell him I don't like it.' And so Lee said, 'Ask him why.' And so J. J., drawing himself up to his full, splendid dictatorship and compounding his outrage, said 'Be-cause it's too sorbid [*sic*].' But Lee was the senior partner and we got it in, and the rest is history."[13]

And then there was the outside resistance. "What the complicated socio-economic treatises could not convey to us, this song crystallized in this simple statement: 'I produce—why don't I share?' The then-establishment tried to ease it off the radio . . . The question it pro-pounded brought forth some national soul-searching. The search pro-duced a president with a sense of history, a sense of humor and a sense of humanity. His twinkling initials were F.D.R., and in the sphere of politics, he was an artist. An artist is essentially a person in search of beauty. He cannot abide ugliness either in a bad script or in a bad society. He is always willing to rewrite even if his subject is the social system. In other words, he is always the rebel. He is a re-evolutionist.

He re-evolves. When you re-evolve, you release new creative forces, and so in spite of oppression, he gave us inspiration, new life that gave the people Social Security, old-age pensions, unemployment insurance and that sweet new feeling of togetherness . . ."[14]

Of course, as everyone knows, "Brother, Can You Spare a Dime?" became a great hit, heard throughout the decades to the present day. As Yip recollected to Studs Terkel, "Everybody picked the song up." Before he knew it, bands were playing it live on radio and in dance halls, and recording artists were requesting to sing it. When Roosevelt was a candidate for president, the Republicans became so concerned about its message that they tried to persuade radio show hosts to suppress it. "But it was too late. The song had already done its damage."[15]

"Brother, Can You Spare a Dime?" became especially popular through recordings by Bing Crosby and Rudy Vallee. John Lahr surveyed its various adoptions into US culture, noting that the title was used by cartoonists and became such a catchall for the times that satirists played with it and some entities even stole it. Lucky Strike cigarettes, for example, ran an ad asking, "Brother, Can You Spare a Light?" Lahr also related that some years later, Lee Shubert greeted Jay Gorney with, "I'm glad to see you. Do you have another song like, 'Mister, Can You Spare Me Ten Cents?'"[16] In 1974, even Yip himself parodied his song, when he sent "Anthem for a New Depression" to the *New York Times*:

Once we had a Roosevelt,
Praise the Lord,—
Life had meaning and hope,
Now we're stuck with Nixon,
Agnew—Ford,
Brother, can you spare a rope?[17]

What made Yip Harburg take the leap into writing songs with a message of human rights? Perhaps some inkling of the impetus can be found in these 1971 thoughts: "Always the climate, the political climate, the social climate, affects the writer. The writer, he is not ever living in a void. He's always living in a live, vibrant, vigorous world. And he tries to reflect that world around him. Now of course you must have some predisposition to react to that world. There were many chaps in 1930 who were still writing about castles in the air or palaces in Long Island. There are many, I mean, you go through the list of songs and the list of shows that were done during that era, most of them just kept right on with parties at the Fitzgeralds' and little, puffy love plots.

"But I think I had a predisposition to feeling for the underdog. I grew up in the slums. I know what it is to work in a sweatshop, I know what it is to have your father come home from the sweatshop after working twelve hours a day and greeting you. I know what it is for a neighbor to come and ask for a piece of bread, or what it is to have your rooms emptied by the sheriff and put down because you can't pay the rent.

"So that I grew up with very poor people on the east side and I knew what they went through. When you know that, you also start thinking about causes, what is the cause for those things. Then you get interested in reading and if you have a chance to go through school and college, which I did only because I was able to fight my way through and work my way through, struggle my way through, then you begin taking courses that will give you an insight into the reason for this poverty, for this thing.

"Well, when you come out, then if you're an artist of any kind you're certainly going to apply the thing that affected you most as a child and that you've seen around you, and the thing that impressed you when you went to college, so that you make a hook-up between cause and effect . . . And if you're a writer you'll apply it. Naturally it'll work inside of you. Your creative juices will be working around the thing that either has aggravated you or made you hostile or made you so philosophical and wise that you want to educate others about it, or that you want to laugh at it. There are many . . . several ways that you can react to this thing, especially if you're a man with words, if you're a writer."[18]

4 | A Pause for Jay Gorney

As Yip himself said about the power of combining words and music, "The reason a song is an important communicative effort is because words make you think thoughts. Music makes you feel a feeling. A song makes you feel a thought. To think a thought is an intellectual process. To feel a feeling is an emotional process. But to feel a thought is an artistic process. That is getting to the heart of people." He also felt deeply that together, music and lyrics—a song—was "the most powerful method of communicating to people because it is ubiquitous, because a song follows you wherever you are, in your elevator, in your dentist's chair, in your shopping center, and whether you know it or not, you, your children are listening to words, are listening to language, which is the important tool of communication . . . You have the responsibility as a song writer, as much responsibility as the guys sitting in Congress who are making laws. A song is more powerful than a law."[1]

So it is enlightening to hear at least a little something about a few of the composers (and in one case, a choreographer) who collaborated with Yip during his lyric-writing career. What did they have to say about the process? Are their memories the same as Yip's, or different? In this first instance, let's hear from and about Jay Gorney, the composer for "Brother, Can You Spare a Dime?" The song, after all, is as much Gorney's as it is Harburg's. According to Sondra Gorney, Jay's wife and author of the book *Brother, Can You Spare a Dime? The Life of Composer Jay Gorney*, her husband was also a close friend of Ira Gershwin's. So when his partnership with lyricist Howard Dietz ended, Gorney asked Ira if he knew someone with the nickname of Yip. Ira then introduced them. The two began working together in 1929 when Gorney was commissioned to do a CBS radio program, the *Ever Ready Radio Hour*. Yip apparently wrote scripts and lyrics for three of the shows, but was never credited for the work. The two also created film songs for Paramount Famous Lasky Corporation (or Paramount, as it was commonly called), including their *Glorifying the American Girl*, in which Helen Morgan sang "What Wouldn't I Do For That Man?" As

Sondra Gorney notes, the two Jewish songwriters were horrified when the song was later used in a foreign documentary film praising Hitler.[2]

In 1958, Gorney related his version of how he and Yip came up with the idea for "Brother, Can You Spare a Dime?" As we can see, the two versions, while similar in spirit, differ somewhat in specifics.

"In 1930 conditions in the country were very tough. It was the period of the Depression; people were out of work, men were selling apples in the streets, people were struggling to survive. And it was not possible to be satirical in writing material for a musical revue.

"It was the time of the torch song made popular by Helen Morgan and Libby Holman. I had a melody which Yip liked, but we couldn't get a title. The melody was rather masculine in mood, and we thought we would write a torch song about a woman who had lost her man, but that wasn't news anymore. The melody had a plaintive note in it, and we wondered what a man would be sad about losing which he would sing about.

"We found no answer to the dilemma, so we went for a walk in Central Park to clear our minds. All of a sudden, a young man, nicely dressed but with his coat collar turned up against the cold and his hat pulled down over his eyes, stepped up to us and asked, 'Buddy, can you spare a dime?'

"'That's it,' said Yip. And we went right home and he wrote the lyric in about two hours."[3]

It's interesting that Gorney described the melody as being masculine because he also claimed that it derived from a Russian Polish Jewish lullaby that his mother had sung to him when he was a child.

We have already reviewed Yip's remembrance of his and Gorney's performance of "Brother, Can You Spare a Dime?" for J. J. and Lee Shubert. Gorney's own story includes the brothers' difference of opinion about how the song should be presented. As he told it, Lee Shubert wanted to hire an opera singer for the job and called in the writers to hear the singer perform: "It was a very cold morning and the singer appeared on the stage in all his opera regalia. He wore a coat with a fur collar and a beaver hat. He sang the song with all the phony dramatics of an operatic solo."[4] Gorney convinced Shubert to hire Rex Weber, a more down-to-earth performer from the vaudeville circuit . . . and he was a great success. As Gorney recalled, "When *Americana* opened on Broadway on October 5, 1932—at the bottom of the Depression, with nearly one-quarter of the work force unemployed, and only one month before the Hoover-Roosevelt presidential election—'Brother' stunned its audience. It was the first theater (or film, or pop) song to treat the wreckage of the Depression seriously."[5]

The collaboration between Gorney and Yip was a good one, but each liked to work with other artists, and each had plenty of opportunity to do so. When Gorney signed a contract with Fox Studios in 1934, he left New York for Hollywood, turning over his apartment in the Hotel Des Artistes to his—and his wife, Edelaine's—good friend, Yip. As things turned out, the threesome's close friendship had an unhappy result for Jay Gorney.

As Yip's son, Ernie, related in 2010, "Yip and my mother, Alice Richmond, split up in 1932. She simply disappeared. Since Yip was 24/7 doing Broadway shows that year, he left my sister, Marge, and me in the care of his beloved sister Anna and her husband Phil, who had five other children. In 1934, Yip and Alice were divorced.

"In 1939, Marge went to Los Angeles to live with Yip. In 1941, Yip brought me west to join them; to this day, I recall the memorable drive across the US! Jay Gorney had bought a house in Beverly Hills where he lived with his wife Edelaine [Eddy] and their son Roderic. We all stayed with them temporarily, until Yip had a house of our own built. Jay and Eddy's nineteen-year marriage had its ups and downs, and in 1941, Eddy decided to leave Jay—for Yip! The tensions in the house among Yip, Eddy, and Jay and we three young teenagers reached such a high point that Jay, in a joint meeting with Eddy and Yip, issued an ultimatum. He would grant Eddy her divorce as long as Yip agreed to marry her. In 1943, Yip and Eddy married. Soon after, Jay married Sondra Karyl. Eddy used to joke that she had never married anyone who hadn't written 'Brother, Can You Spare a Dime?' Years later, the two couples became friends again."[6]

In 1976, during a time when Jay Gorney was suffering from illness and general decline, Yip wrote him a letter from Hawaii, where he was vacationing. Sections of it reflect the deep connection he still felt for Gorney from the time the two had written "Brother, Can You Spare a

Yip and Edelaine Gorney, who married in 1943, riding bikes, 1935.
Courtesy of the Yip Harburg Foundation

Dime?"; the guilt he continued to hold deep in his heart; and the respect he always carried for his fellow activist, a man who wrote "not only the music of the theater, but the music of Human Rights."[7] The letter read,

> Dear Jayster—
>
> To live on a beach and look at the stars thru the tropical trees of Kiahuna is to turn the camera eye on many flashbacks in one's life and try to relate the mysteries of accidents and incidents that bring me to this moment of contemplation.
>
> Uppermost in my thoughts—now—is the lucky day that Lola Weisman [the formerly noted LaLa] and Ira Gershwin put me in touch with—to quote them—"a grand guy and a fine composer, Jay Gorney, who was looking for a lyric writer."
>
> We met and thru your experience and expertise, a light versifier became a lyricist . . .
>
> "Brother, Can You Spare a Dime?" has earned me several thousand dollars. Without this perfect tune I could not have gotten that head start I did. I was luckier than you since there was always a dearth of lyricists and a plethora of composers. Let me mend the break by a tenth of an inch of recognition.[8]

5 | Yip's Path to Show Business Success

Yip Harburg might be one of the few people who felt lucky that the Great Depression had come his way. He also might be in the minority of folks who gained both monetary and professional success during the era. Broadway, a booming center of entertainment in the 1920s, suffered greatly in the 1930s. It may be hard for twenty-first-century theater enthusiasts to believe that in the 1929–1930 season, 239 shows opened on the Great White Way. This number dropped to 187 the next year, to 100 in 1938–1939, and to 72 in 1940–1941.[1] For musicals, this translated into a drop from 34 in 1929–1930 to only 13 in 1933–1934.[2] There was simply no money for investment and brave speculation. In addition, the advent of "talking pictures" in 1927 with *The Jazz Singer* literally stole audiences away from live theater.

Because of the Depression's effects on people's wallets, the lack of money for large productions, and the popularity of films, Broadway performers, writers, and other creative artists left New York City in the thousands for Hollywood. Yip was one of them—a commuter of sorts—writing many hit songs in both places. While he continued to write primarily for Broadway revues, which were not faring so well, Yip expanded his contributions to Hollywood musicals, where money was no object. One only has to look at the big Busby Berkeley musicals of the thirties, sing and dance along with Fred Astaire and Ginger Rogers, or gaze at any number of other types of films to know that Hollywood prospered in spite of the national economic crisis.

From early 1929 through the end of 1937, Yip wrote lyrics for no less than fifty-six projects. As John Lahr reported, "During the 1932–33 season, *Billboard* announced that William Shakespeare was the most prolific playwright, Harold Arlen wrote the most music, and E. Y. Harburg turned out the most lyrics."[3] But Yip's interviews later in life indicate that out of this tremendous creative output, several specific ventures stood out for him, and he used these to build his public persona and to please his fans. "Brother, Can You Spare a Dime?" certainly served as a spur for Yip's career. After *Americana*, for which

Yip with daughter Margie (left) and son Ernie (right)
in Brooklyn, New York, 1932.
Courtesy of the Yip Harburg Foundation

he was the only listed lyricist among a plethora of composers, he received many offers. As he later stated, "The reaction was tremendous. After that song, I had no trouble getting jobs, one show after another: *Walk a Little Faster*, with music by Vernon Duke, which had a lovely score, including 'April in Paris,' and charming performers—Bea Lillie, [Bobby] Clark and [Paul] McCullough; Sid Perelman did the skits; all in all another smart show. An edition of the *Ziegfeld Follies, Life Begins at 8:40*, with Ira [Gershwin] and Harold Arlen, starring Bert Lahr, Ray Bolger, Luella Gear—we had nothing but fun."[4] Because initially the film work came out of Paramount's studio located in Astoria, Queens, part of New York City, Yip was able to work simultaneously on film, radio, and Broadway productions.

One of Yip's favorite songs was "If You Believed in Me"—later called "It's Only a Paper Moon." The song first appeared in a play by Ben Hecht and Gene Fowler, *The Great Magoo*, which opened on December 2, 1932, and closed eleven performances later. The composer for the song was Harold Arlen, who Yip had met in 1930 while working on *Earl Carroll Vanities*. Arlen, like Yip, was born in the United States, in his case in Buffalo, New York, in 1905. The two shared the same immigrant Orthodox Jewish upbringing, the difference being that Arlen's family was not dirt poor, and later, Arlen took a somewhat apolitical view of life.

In 1932, Yip and Arlen wrote one song together for *Americana*, "Satan's Li'l Lamb." Yip admired Arlen's style—his mix of Jewish and African American rhythms derived from his youth as a cantor's son, his love of jazz, and his work as composer and musician at Harlem's famed Cotton Club. As Yip related to radio personality Jonathan Schwartz, the Broadway producer Billy Rose "was doing . . . *The Great Magoo* . . . and it needed one song about a barker in a circus, or rather in a Coney Island joint, and he wanted a song for that barker who was a man disillusioned with the world. And he . . . finally fell in love. And how do you write a song for a man who was disillusioned in love and who is a barker? And he called me up and says, 'Have you got any kind of a song that would fit that situation?' Harold had a tune; he had the whole tune . . . And I got the idea, 'Well, here's a guy [who] sees the lights of Broadway, thinks that the whole world is that, and that the moon is a paper moon and everything is a Barnum and Bailey world.' So I got that title and fitted the first line, first two lines, 'It's only a paper moon / Sailing over a cardboard sea.' I brought it to Billy Rose. Harold and I brought it. He says, 'Gee, that's great, just right, just what we want. C'mon, let's sit down and do it!' Well, when Billy Rose says 'Let's sit down and do it,' he's the producer of the show, he's paying you the advance, you're a neophyte. What do you do? You sit down!"[5]

As it happened, Billy Rose worked a bit with Yip and Arlen and then decided to take credit on the song as one of the lyric writers. Yip understood the situation precisely. "Well, but I will say one thing about Billy Rose. I must give him due credit. He was a great editor . . . Don't forget that I was writing poetry and free verse at the time and I had to make that terrible, terrifying transition from light verse to lyricism, to lyric writing, and he really helped me come down from Olympus to Broadway. So his editing did a lot of good for me. I was always grateful for it."[6]

The lyrics to "It's Only a Paper Moon" were very significant to Yip, and during his later lectures, he loved to perform them and speak about their deeper meaning. The words, as we can see, fit the carnival setting perfectly:

Say, it's only a paper moon
Sailing over a cardboard sea
But it wouldn't be make believe
If you believed in me

Yes, it's only a canvas sky
Hanging over a muslin tree
But it wouldn't be make believe
If you believed in me.

Without your love
It's a honky-tonk parade
Without your love
It's a melody played
In a penny arcade

It's a Barnum and Bailey world
Just as phony as it can be

But it wouldn't be make believe
If you believed in me.[7]

Yip explained in 1979, "Well, the paper moon is something that belongs in a Disney studio, makes everybody believe it's real, and, all
right, I apply it to the world. What makes the song, I think, important is because it becomes a cosmic song, because really all our lives
are . . . really fleeting, evanescent, and we find that moon was made of
rock anyhow, it wasn't made of Puck's star dust at all, and so you see,
real life proves the point of the poet . . . that everything is fleeting, dis-
appearing, that we're all here in a little mythological thing called the
world, we all give it up, and this is what makes it universal in its appeal. I mean, bigger, more . . . better poets than I have said that in a
more pompous and sumptuous way. Shakespeare said plenty of things
like that, but he said it in a lot of golden words. All I do is take those
fellows and melt them down to popular form and give it my own twist.
And so does Harold, and this is what I think our contribution was."[8]

"It's Only a Paper Moon" became a big hit for Yip and Arlen, a song
that made them money then and is still a popular standard now. In
1975, Yip addressed its great success: "Now, [a] big hit song, and it was
popular because it was done popularly. It was done so you could tap
your toesies to it . . . Sure, it had all those elements. We know all those
tricks. But behind the tricks, behind the artifice, is art, the art of honesty, the art of being responsible for your craft . . . As I walked along the
streets of MGM which were big lots, acres and acres and acres of lots,
and I'd see a whole city built. There was an elevator, there was a bank,
there was Switzerland, all in front of me. Behind them were props.
Tomorrow they would be struck and come down. But while I was walking through those streets I was very excited. I was full of creativity. I
wanted to write songs. And they were real for that moment. I didn't
care that there were props behind them and that there [were] men
ready to strike those sets. The courage was in having fun, in having ex-
citement and living that moment. And that moment is made livable
when there is a feeling of camaraderie, that another person is on your
beam, that is equal to you, that there is a thing called love. And love,
of course, . . . it doesn't have to be just that one thing, the two things

that the boy and girl do. It has all sorts of qualities and definitions, and as long as there is love and life, and it's always there, our friends and people communicating with [one] another, I think this is what makes it palpable.

"And this is why the song, I think, is a hit . . . and why it lasts. And it's been in six different pictures now and in *Streetcar Called Desire* [*sic*]. And outside of the royalties which have always been good and helpful in sending kids to college and buttering your bread with jam and so on and so forth, that wasn't the big thrill. The big thrill is that it's lasting, that it has . . . and for some reason or other, people get an honest kick out of singing that song. It isn't just a momentary thing. So, that goes into, I think, everything that I try to do or that the good musician tries to do or that the good librettist tries to do. Tries to do something that'll have a quality that is connected with life and that is meaningful and that gives you courage, that gives you laughter and that helps you continue to live this sort of fleeting life which is full of all kinds of dangers, stumbling blocks, a lot of sorrows, lotta sadness, but also a lot of good things because of the struggle. And I think all art aims to give people hope. Yeah."[9]

With "If You Believed in Me," Yip and Arlen came together in a partnership that would last until 1962, and a friendship that never ended. The song, in fact, helped to move the friendship along. It quickly reappeared in 1933 in a feature film called *Take a Chance*, where the title was changed to "It's Only a Paper Moon," the name we know today. However, although Yip loved writing with Arlen, he also continued to create with other songwriters. Indeed, at the same time that he was working with Arlen on *The Great Magoo*, Yip was also writing with Vernon Duke, a classically trained Russian musician/composer seven years his junior. Together, they collaborated for four years (until 1934) on various projects, including another of Yip's standard songs, "April in Paris," written for the 1932 revue *Walk a Little Faster*. This show starred two of Broadway's funniest comics: Bobby Clark and Beatrice Lillie.

As Yip told Max Wilk, "I met Vernon Duke through George Gershwin. After Gorney went to California, I started writing with various composers, and I began to realize different types of songs that existed.

It was fine for me because it allowed me to learn my own abilities. Vernon had just come over from Europe. He was a Russian—his real name was Vladimir Dukelsky—and he was very far advanced in his music. Very serious composer. As Dukelsky, his symphonic works were performed in concert halls. In Europe he'd worked with Diaghilev, writing ballets, and he was very avant-garde for this period, the mid '30s. George Gershwin was very impressed with Duke's music. I suppose you could say he learned a lot from Vernon.

"I liked Vernon's facility. He was fast and very sophisticated, almost too sophisticated for Broadway. *Walk a Little Faster* had some very smart stuff in it. In fact, that's when I bounced out of the bread-and-butter stage into sophistication. My light-verse background popped up to reinforce me, and I could write much easier with Vernon than I could with some of the others. It was light, and airy, and very smart.

"Vernon brought with him all of that Noel Coward/Diaghilev/Paris/Russia background. He was a global guy with an ability to articulate the English language that was very interesting. A whole new world for me. He could drive you crazy, and he could also open up a new vista. Maybe it was a little bit chi-chi and decorative, but with my pumpernickel background and his orchid tunes we made a wonderful marriage. Maybe we were a strange mixture. We didn't compromise with each other. I applied the everyday down-deep things that concerned humanity to his sense of style and grace, and I think it gave our songs an almost classic feeling, along with some humor. We came together at a certain point, and for a while, it was fine. He satisfied my sense of light verse and the need for sophistication.

"Later I felt that his music lacked the essential theatricalism and the histrionics that writing for shows demanded—the drama, the emotions. So gradually I gravitated more and more to Harold Arlen."[10]

Yip took great pride in "April in Paris" and its famous chorus, which included these lyrics:

April in Paris
Chestnut in blossom
Holiday tables under the trees

April in Paris
This is a feeling
No one can ever reprise

I never knew the charm of Spring
Never met it face to face
I never knew my heart could sing
Never missed a warm embrace
Till,

April in Paris,
Whom can I run to?
What have you done to
My heart?[11]

As he related to an audience in 1973, "On page 189 in the autobiography of Pola Negri [an early film actress], there's a funny little paragraph. It says, 'If the French government has not already given the man who wrote "April in Paris" the Legion of Honor, it should, because a more flattering picture of the city in that month could not have been written.' Well, I never was in Paris when the song was written. What happened was that Courtney Burr was producing a show called *Walk a Little Faster* with Bea Lillie and [Bobby] Clark & [Paul] McCullough and there was a young man who'd just come over from Europe. His name was Boris Aronson, and he was in love with Paris. He came to Paris by way of Kiev, when Stalin got in. And he really designed one of the most beautiful, sensitive sets that was ever seen, and of course the producer involves the lyric writer and says, 'We need a song for that set.' So I went down to Cook's Tour and got some brochures to see what it was like and most people think I was at the Café de Jou-Jou looking at the Eiffel Tower when it was written, but I was really at Lindy's looking at the marquee of the Winter Garden. Anyhow, I find that writing songs about places I haven't been, people I haven't seen are the most exciting because, after all, beauty is what you in your spirit and imagination invest in a place or invest in a person, and so it came out."[12]

As Yip further explained, Duke also had a history with Paris that helped him out. "Vernon Duke, who had also lived in Paris for a while, and he was imbued with the atmosphere of Paris, he came up with a tune, the whole tune, 'April in Paris,' and he said, 'Here's a tune,' he said 'that I started while I was in Paris.' And I said, 'Well, . . . what does it connote to you?' He says, 'Well,' he says, 'spring in Paris.' There were so many spring songs. And I was born in April so I thought I'd celebrate myself by saying 'April in Paris.'"[13]

Walk a Little Faster ran for 119 performances, and "April in Paris," like "It's Only a Paper Moon," became a popular choice for cabaret singers and pleased the ears of the general public. Its haunting melody and lovely lyrics made it so appealing that in early 1935, Universal Studios asked Yip to produce a film of the same name.

In 1933, Yip and Duke worked on their final show together, *Ziegfeld Follies of 1934*. Like the others, the show was a revue in the style of the original Ziegfeld productions, which were now produced by the Shubert brothers. Also like the others, it was a lightweight production that did not offer Yip the opportunity to delve into his political ideas, as he had with "Brother, Can You Spare a Dime?" However, the production's history is interesting because in a rare surviving interview from January 25, 1934, celebrating the show's opening, we get an idea of the playfulness that Yip demonstrated in public, even though he was still at the beginning of his lyric-writing career. The interview took place with the popular music critic and broadcaster Deems Taylor on the *Kraft Program*. Here is a small selection of the interchange between interviewer and interviewee:

DT: Mr. Harburg, do the words or the music come first?

YH: As a rule, the check comes first.

DT: Oh, you don't write grand operas? How did you get your start?

YH: I started by writing verse for FPA's [Franklin P. Adams's] column in the *New York Tribune*.

DT: Oh yes?

YH: But that didn't discourage me. From there I began writing on fences.

DT: Yes?

YH: And did I give up?

DT: Did you?

YH: No, sir. I worked my way right down to sidewalks.

DT: And then?

YH: The rest was easy. I began writing songs.

DT: Do you attribute your success to hard work?

YH: No, no. Just . . . just talent. . . .

DT: And what do you write about, Mr. Harburg, when you run out of ideas?

YH: Exactly what happened to me in the *Follies*. I ran out of ideas, so I wrote this [Yip speak-sings to accompaniment of the Paul Whiteman Orchestra]:

This is not a song,
There's no waterfall or cottage small
Where love comes along.
This is not a song.

This is not a torch,
No one breaks your heart,
Or wants to part,
No one does you wrong.
This is not a song.

Cabin in the cotton,
What! No cabin in the cotton?
Say, who the deuce wrote the words?

Pettin' in the moonlight.
What! No pettin' in the moonlight?
No tea for two?
No skies of blue?
Phew!

This is not a song,
This is not a tune
To learn to croon,
So don't get me wrong,
This is not a song.[14]

In later years, the song that Yip liked to talk about and perform most from the *Ziegfeld Follies of 1934* was "I Like the Likes of You." He claimed in 1980 that the then-younger generation most identified with this song: "Implicit sometimes in satire is a sense of prophecy, to sense the future in the instant, the instinct to see a little ahead of your time is what gives the satirist the funny point of view on the present and so this next song, which was written for the *Follies of 1934*, happens to accommodate the youth of today, who have reduced the English language to two phrases and a catchall adverb—like. I mean like when the producer says to the lyricist he should, you know, like, I mean, write a song, like I mean it should, you know, like, communicate the lack of communication."[15] He then sang "I Like the Likes of You," which he wrote with Vernon Duke.

Verse
Lady, last Saturday, or was it yesterday?
I was rehearsing a speech
Really, I think it's a peach
Hope you don't think it a breach
Of, recognized etiquette
I'm from Connecticut
You see the state that I'm in,
I mean I'm in a mess,
What was that speech
Oh, yes . . . yes . . .

Chorus
I like the likes of you
I like the things you do
I mean, I like the likes of you

I like your eyes of blue
I think they're blue, don't you?
I mean, I like your eyes of blue

Oh, dear, if I could only say what I mean
I mean, if I could mean what I say

That is, I mean to say
That I mean to say that

I like the likes of you
Your looks are pure de-luxe
Looks like I like the likes of you.[16]

Most of the songs that Yip worked on during the early to mid-1930s were satirical or romantic. But two shows that he wrote in the mid- to late 1930s allowed him to begin to build his political repertoire and reputation. They included *Life Begins at 8:40* (1934) and *Hooray for What!* (1937), an antiwar musical that he wrote with Harold Arlen. Aside from a few individual songs, such as "Last Night When We Were Young," these were the works he enjoyed talking about because they showed his early self-identification as an activist.

In this start to more consistent political writing, Yip relied on humor and satire, no matter how serious the subject matter. As he told radio personality Paul Lazarus in 1980, "I think every writer has some theme that runs through everything he does. I think you can recognize it in [George Bernard] Shaw, you can recognize it in [W. S.] Gilbert. You can recognize it even in some of our lyric writers like Cole Porter and [Ira] Gershwin and each one contributes his own hallmark and I don't think they can be compared as to who is the better. Each one has his own technique and his own contribution. What moves me, of course I'm very conscious of social injustice and the use of satire and humor as a weapon against these follies and foibles, but I suppose, like everybody else, I think that basically we all go around trying to find out who we are . . . And I think we all want to know how we're related to the universe and how we are related to people."[17]

The revue *Life Begins at 8:40* came on the heels of the *Ziegfeld Follies of 1934.* As Harold Meyerson and Ernie Harburg point out in their biography of Yip, the lyricist was exhausted by this time, and somewhat at a loss with the breakup of his marriage and the end of his collaboration with Vernon Duke. His main comfort came from the community of musical artists he had come to know over the past years, and who had come to appreciate his talent. As his biographers reported,

Yip once said, "I write for my peers. In fact, our tribe of songsmiths always wrote for our peers. We were very much ashamed of ourselves if we wrote anything clichéd, if we took an idea from another person. By 'our tribe,' I'm talking about Cole Porter, Ira Gershwin, [Lorenz] Hart, [Howard] Dietz, all those people who got together every week . . . and we would more or less compare the things we were working on.

"All the songwriters got together regularly at the Gershwins in the twenties and thirties. Something like Fleet Street in Samuel Johnson's time—an artistic community where people took fire from each other. We'd hang around George's piano, playing our latest songs to see how they went over with the boys. We were all interested in what the other fellas were up to; we criticized and helped each other. There was great respect for each other's work and the integrity of our own music and lyrics. Sometimes, we would hear a whole great score before a show opened, a new Gershwin show, or Rodgers and Hart. We ate it up, analyzed it, played it over and over. You wouldn't dare write a bad rhyme or a clichéd phrase or an unoriginal or remotely plagiarized tune, because you were afraid of being ripped apart by your peers. This continuous give-and-take added to the creative impulse. It worked as incentive, opened up new ideas, made it necessary to keep working and evolving.

"Everyone you could imagine came to the Gershwin parties on weekends, not only songwriters, but all kinds of people—performers, critics, actors, novelists, choreographers—the likes of Moss Hart, Oscar Levant, Harpo Marx. Wherever the Gershwins happened to be living, whether on Riverside Drive [in Manhattan] or in Beverly Hills, when we all went out west writing for the movies, their house was always crammed with creative people. Those were exciting, inspiring days."[18]

When the Shuberts asked him to take on the lyrics for a new revue, Yip turned to Ira Gershwin as a collaborator. Because his brother and usual partner, George, was busy composing the music for *Porgy and Bess*, Ira happily accepted. The composer was to be Harold Arlen, who Yip had come to respect for his ability to delve into any musical landscape and lose himself in it. As Yip told Max Wilk, "You know, a lot of George Gershwin rubbed off on Harold. George was Harold's deity, he really was. George, you must see, changed the whole face of chords and music and development. He brought to American music a combination of his own Semitic background and melded it to the Negro jazz. Put them together, made new rhythms. It was really a melting pot of America, a great contribution to music.

"But later Harold went off in a different direction. True, his background was much more of the cantor, and also, Harold had a completely different psyche from George's. That's another thing that matters deeply, a fellow's psychological equipment. Harold is a very, very melancholy person. Inside, deeply religious. But he's very superstitious. When he gets to the piano, it's a feeling of witchcraft. He'll spit three times and almost talk to the chords, talk to God. He does it humorously, but behind the humor are all sorts of superstitions and beliefs.

"Behind every song that Harold writes is a great sadness and melancholy. Even his happy songs. You take a song like his rousing hit, 'Get Happy.' Sing it slowly. Examine it. It's painful! Everything he does, he's never liberated from that . . . *thing* hanging over him." At this point, Wilk asked Yip if he found it difficult to write his light lyrics to Arlen's music. "Not for me," he responded. "Because I realize that the best of humor has pathos in it."

Then Yip continued describing the specific experience of collaborating with Gershwin and Arlen on *Life Begins at 8:40*: "It was a joyous experience. John Murray Anderson was producing the show for the Shuberts, and I loved Murray. He was a very smart man. Had such class, style, taste, sophistication—everything. Always put on such beautiful sets and décor. It was my big chance too . . . So the three of us got together with Murray Anderson and said we'd do the show for him.

"We had this darling notion for the opening—that life begins at 8:40 p.m. A parody on a current best-seller by a man named Walter Pitkin; it was called *Life Begins at Forty*. Our idea was that life begins when the curtain of the show goes up. We had this big Munich clock onstage, and out of the clock came all the characters that would appear in the revue. The husband, the lover, the wife, the blues singer, the comedian, the dancers, and so on. And in the words for the opening we said, '*At exactly eight forty or thereabouts, this little playworld not of the dayworld, comes to life.*' And then out came all the people who were working in the theatre itself, show-business types, who said we're *not* the average run of people who sleep all [night] and work all day. We reverse the process.

"Ira would come in with one idea. I'd come in with something, then Harold would come up with a tune. It was a very happy few months there, and we got a great score out of it."[19]

The show opened on August 27, 1934, to excellent reviews. Among its stars were Ray Bolger and Bert Lahr, two established Broadway performers, the first a dancer, the second a comic. They would become essential to Yip later on as the Scarecrow and Cowardly Lion in *The Wizard of Oz*.

Yip once told Deena Rosenberg and Mel Gordon that, as he saw it, *Life Begins at 8:40* was "a political show, done with great charm . . . It was such a good-looking show . . . And Ira and I had a point of view. We were going to write a satiric show and more or less cover the field. We weren't focusing in on one thing; we were just covering the field . . . it started off with the theatre. We started kidding the theatre. The fact that we called the show *Life Begins at 8:40* already tells you that we had tongue in cheek . . . Then we said, what is in a show? A typical revue. A funny man begins throwing people into the aisle. A little ingénue . . . A husband, lover and wife, the typical gag. They came as a team. The clown, the guy with the funny man, came. Everything that was in a revue, so it was a delicate kind of take off on every revue, including ourselves . . ."

The song "What Can You Say in a Love Song?" Yip continued, was "kidding love songs. It started on the stage with candlelight. There was a little stage, a little revolving stage, and a boy and girl dressed in Renaissance clothes came out [Yip sings] . . .

Mmm, mmm mmm
So sweetly
Mmm mmm mmm
Completely
Mmm mmm mmm
Je vous adore.
What can you say in a love song
That hasn't been said before?

And then the stage turned around and disappeared and the gaslights came on and you got the boy and girl dressed a little further up the line [sings] . . .

> Mmm mmm mmm
> Completely
> Mmm mmm mmm
> So sweetly
> Mmm mmm mmm
> Je vous adore
> What can you say in a love song
> That hasn't been said before?

> You are my true love
> Old and new love
> I live for you, love
> You are my guiding star.

Then another thing turned around and it was modern, you see, with electric lights [sings] . . .

> Lovers long before us
> Sang the same old chorus
> If it worked in days of yore
> Why should I say in a love song

Then the whole chorus came out with different costumes, you know? . . . It was a beautiful score. Tender, sweet and gentle satire . . . and that was the first time that dirty books were starting to come out like *Lady Chatterly's Lover*. We had Boccaccio, Rabelais, DeMaupassant and Balzac all dressed up, came out, and all bewailing the fact that they were passé. And of course [Bert] Lahr, who was the boisterous one, had the Balzac, you know, at the end. There was a verse saying how they'd become passé now. Let's see [sings] . . .

> Rabelais, DeMaupassant, Boccaccio and Balzac
> Babes in the woods are we.
> The dirt we used to dish up, sad to say,
> Wouldn't shock a bishop of today."

As Yip continued, he explained that the scenes were not connected, but the feeling of the show was: "You know that each thing was a little bit of a satire on something in our lives. That connected it . . . It was all songs, rhymes. Oh, there were skits, oh yes, by [David] Freedman. Very funny skits. There would be a skit, a song, a skit and a song, and maybe two songs and a skit. The skits were very funny. Bert Lahr being called up by Internal Revenue, income tax, for something he hadn't paid. Terribly funny . . . I mean, these people were hilarious. We don't have those kind of comics any more . . . And there was a big audience for it. Lovely audience. If a show ran six months it was a big hit. If it ran a year, it was a terrific hit . . . So what kept it together was not only the beautiful scenery and costumes and the great clowns and the fun, but also the marvelous dancing. The [Charles Weidman] dancers . . . So the accumulation of all these things added up to a great night, of not only fun but charm and lovely music, lovely lyrics, adroitly done, and something to think about. Each one had a little point of view. We had a finale which was simply stunning.

"That was the time of Franklin Roosevelt and Eleanor Roosevelt, and of course, they were the two grandest, most loved people . . . it was a world, it was a country that had leadership, that had two great humanitarian people that you never saw the likes of since and probably never will any more. They were both great, educated, philosophic, wonderful, humanitarian people who were out to do beautiful things for the world, and everybody recognized it and they were loved. And Eleanor worked harder than Roosevelt. She went around all over the world. She was on a plane always. I remember all the big fun we used to have calculating how many miles she covered, where she was, you know. So we had a funny skit on her. She'd go every place where a new thing was being done, like opening a housing project or a school or a college or an athletic field and Mrs. Roosevelt was always there. She was the symbol of the new age . . . so we had a take-off on her.

"And then again we had a wonderful mayor [Fiorello] LaGuardia, who was just a charming, cute character . . . used to get on the radio every morning, every Sunday morning; everybody would tune in on Mayor LaGuardia, and he'd read the funnies. And there isn't a thing that he wasn't interested in. Wherever there was a crime, wherever there was a bad subway something, he would be on the fire engines going to see what caused the fire. He was interested in people and . . . he had a terrific personality, just great. Anybody could see him at any time. He'd come to *shul* with you, you know. It was a real people's country. So we had a wonderful take-off on him, and all he was trying to do was beautify the city. So we got the conception, a little exaggeration . . . the ferry boats that were going to Staten Island were kind of ugly and didn't become a city like New York and that he was going to put in gondolas to Staten Island . . . So we were launching the first gondola, and Mrs. Roosevelt came to help us launch the gondola and the lyric was delightful, about all the funny things. What we did was, we tied up the whole show. We took all the songs in the whole show like 'Walk Around the Block' and 'Fun to Be Fooled'—everything that was in the show—and we got every character into some connection with the gondola. Jimmy Walker [a former corrupt mayor of New York City] was coming back; he was smuggled back to be with the gondola—he was in exile at the time. And of course, Mrs. Roosevelt, Eleanor Roosevelt . . . [Luella Gear] did an imitation of Eleanor Roosevelt and she sang the song, 'At seven o'clock this morning in Poughkeepsie I opened a . . .' She did it in her voice. She had to open a bridal path, then she had to fly to Cincinnati to open a Turkish bath, and all the things she did that one day, then 'Here I am to launch a gondola,' and everybody sang and it was fun—sheer laughter, sheer fun, and also there was a tenderness, too, about the whole thing, you know, the joy of having these people doing these cute things and the lyric was very funny.

"One night, she [Eleanor Roosevelt] was there, and . . . oh, God, it was a great night. She laughed. And it was just a take-off on her bushy-buzhy, busy-busy things she was doing all around . . . [What] you got out of the thing [was that] there was no line, there was no plot, there was no book, nor anything except skits, but it did have a theme . . ."[20]

To get a sense of the lighthearted spirit of *Life Begins at 8:40*, let us consider one of the songs that became a major hit, "Let's Take a Walk Around the Block." (The other top sellers were "Fun to Be Fooled" and "You're a Builder Upper.") As Yip explained, "Well, this whole period of writing was for me a reflection of the glow of this one man's [FDR] humanity cast over the nation, and this glow was mirrored . . . in songs which—remember, although they were all written in the Depression and about the Depression, had in them the sorrows of life, but the humor of living. Humor is essential for survival.

"Well, the system may have fallen apart, but not the dream, while that blithe spirit in the White House kept it together with his vision and personality. With FDR in the Oval Room, things may have been hopeless, but . . . with his sunny disposition. This one was written for a boy and a girl out of work and in front of [a] travel agency when they were looking wistfully at glamorous posters of the Taj Mahal, the pyramids, the Tower of Pisa, Paris . . . They haven't had a job in years, but 'Okay, we won't let that stump us. There's a man in the White House who says, "We will be to Paris pretty soon . . ."'"[21]

Verse
I never traveled further north
Than old Van Cortland Park
And never further south than the Aquarium
I've seen the charm of Jersey City
But first, let me remark
I saw it from the Empire State Solarium

But I've been putting nickels in the
Postal Savings Bank
And when those nickels pile up,
We can toddle off in swank
And I don't mean an ordinary Cook's tour;
I mean a "Cabin De-Luxe" Tour

Chorus
Someday we'll go places
New lands and new faces
The day we quit punching the clock.
The future looks pleasant
But, at present,
Let's take a walk around the block.

You're just the companion
I want at Grand Canyon,

For throwing old blades down the rock
The money we have'll
Go for travel
Meantime, let's walk around the block

Gangway! We'll begin
When our ship comes in
You'll sit on my lap
All over the map

To London in Maytime,
To Venice in playtime,
To Paris in time for a frock
To Boston in bean-time
Darling, meantime,
Let's take a walk around the block

Second chorus
In Winter at Christmas
We'll visit the isthmus
And see how they lock up a lock
And then in Caracas
On a jackass
We'll take a walk around the block

I give you my promise
We'll visit St. Thomas
And then at the Virgins we'll dock

She:
    The Virgins can wait, sir,
    It grows late, sir,
    Let's take a walk around the block

Both:
    Onward to Cathay
    Then to Mandalay
    Then Vladivostok
    Where Bolsheviks flock

We'll send the folks cables
Accumulate labels
Buy souvenirs till we're in hock
Right now we are flat in
Old Manhattan
Let's take a walk around the block.[22]

When he was interviewed, Yip usually spoke of his many songs connected to Broadway shows or Hollywood films, and of his light verse, especially those poems written later in his life. But one song kept appearing in his talks, a song that was never heard in the context of a revue or story. This was "Last Night When We Were Young," written in 1935 with music composed by Harold Arlen. As Yip told radio personality Jonathan Schwartz, "Harold had written this tune with no purpose in mind at all. He just needed to write it. And we were living together in Beverly Hills and he said nothing to me about it . . .

"I didn't know it at the time. But he went and played it for George [Gershwin], thinking that George would get a great kick out of it, pat him on the back. And George censored him. He said, 'Harold, why don't you stop trying to write beyond the public's comprehension?' He says, 'It's too sophisticated and too complicated.' Harold was just devastated. A few days later he played it for Jerome Kern, and Jerome Kern told him, he said, 'Well, it's a hell of a tune, Harold, you know, for your colleagues, for your peers. But don't think the public's going to [like it].' Then he went to Johnny Mercer with it. Johnny Mercer turned it down. Now, he never told me anything about this. Then they wanted a tune for Lawrence Tibbett at Fox and Harold came to me and said, 'Just got a call from Fox. They want a tune for Lawrence Tibbett.' He says, 'I think I got a tune that'll fit him.' And he played it for me. Well, I was awestruck by the tune. I had no title or anything. But that's what the tune inspired: 'Last Night When We Were Young' and the lyric came out."[23]

Yip gave greater detail of the song's trying path to success in another interview, one that differed a bit from the previously quoted one. In this version, Arlen simply asked him for a lyric to his tune. "But Lawrence Tibbett heard it one night at a party and he was doing a show for Fox and he asked Fox to buy it and they did, and they paid a handsome sum of money, and it was left on the cutting room floor. However, Arthur Freed, who led that beautiful group of song teamers in Metro, heard the song . . . a connoisseur. He bought it for Judy Garland. Judy Garland did it in a picture. It was cut out of the picture and left on the cutting room floor. Finally, Frank Sinatra heard it and he picked it up, made a record of it. He's been singing it ever since and luckily the tune has become a classic hit, thanks to him. Thanks to Harold who wrote this great tune, which he considers his best tune. I think it is too."[24]

Here are the lyrics that Yip wrote to Arlen's melody:

Last night when we were young
Love was a star, a song unsung
Life was so new, so real, so right
Ages ago, last night

Today, the world is old
You went away and time grew cold
Where is that star that seemed so bright
Ages ago, last night

To think that Spring had depended
On merely this, a look, a kiss
To think that something so splendid
Could slip away in one little day break

So now let's reminisce
And recollect the sighs and the kisses
The arms that clung
When we were young
Last night.[25]

Yip felt that his lyric for "Last Night When We Were Young" echoed "It's Only a Paper Moon." As he told one interviewer, "And I think that when you really compare 'Last Night When We Were Young' and 'Paper Moon' they're both the same theme, that the world . . . it's mythological, we're here on some kind of a little quick ride, you know, a quick roller coaster ride, it's all over and we thinking it's lasting. It isn't . . .

It's okay if you had the right kind of fun with it. You're on an excursion. If you meet the right people, you can have a hell of a lot . . . of fun . . .

"So 'Last Night When We Were Young,' to come back to that, I mean, that phrase itself, 'last night when we were young,' which means a whole lifetime in one evening, in one twenty-four hours. Love made the whole difference, that one day . . . One day was like living a whole lifetime. We were young last night because we had it . . . Today, in one twenty-four, in one little daybreak, love fled and the whole world grew old and we grew old. And it was a poetic way of saying it. But again, we come down to titles. I mean, a title that is enticing and that is meaningful and that is so attractive and enchanting . . . the juxtaposition of those two phrases . . . [has] almost a whole world philosophy in it. And when you get that, I don't know where it comes from. I wish I knew. I'd get a lot of them if I could. But I suppose the tune opened that up . . . The whole pathos of the . . . human situation, the human race, is in that phrase. Well, Harold gave it to me. I mean, I rode in on the coattails of his genius, there, didn't I?"[26]

As we have seen, after *Americana*, Yip wrote many songs for revues on Broadway. But the seriousness of "Brother, Can You Spare a Dime?" did not resurface in these pieces, nor in most of the other lyrics he would write in the future. Rather, he chose to use satire to put forward his political ideas. At the end of 1937, Yip wrote the lyrics for a show he also conceptualized, a hilariously funny antiwar musical called *Hooray for What!* It was his first story musical and had a book by Howard Lindsay and Russel Crouse with music by Harold Arlen. Yip's foray into the antiwar genre reflected the work of several dramatic writers of his generation, including Robert E. Sherwood, Maxwell Anderson, Laurence Stalling, John Haynes Holmes, Irwin Shaw, and Sidney Howard. The two major antiwar musicals of the era were the Gershwins' *Strike Up The Band* (1927, 1930) and Paul Green and Kurt Weill's 1936 *Johnny Johnson*. The 1927 version of *Strike Up the Band* had a caustic message on the ridiculousness of the causes of war and its militaristic effects on society. It was so severely criticized that it was revised and performed in 1930 in a much watered-down version.

Yip's contribution to the antiwar voice came a bit on the late side, during a period when war fever was growing. However, even with Adolph Hitler and Benito Mussolini firmly ensconced in Europe, their grabbing hands stretched out over the globe, and even with Japan's aggression in Asia, satire aimed at the League of Nations, the munitions makers, and international spies still tickled people's fancies. This was especially so after the Senate's Special Committee Investigating the Munitions Industry concluded in 1936 that industrialists seeking war profits had swayed former president Woodrow Wilson and congressional members into supporting US participation in World War I.

Hooray for What! relied on a Marx Brothers' type of humor and slapstick comedy, with spies at a hotel in Geneva during a League of Nations meeting jumping in and out of doors, closets, picture frames, and the like. The story attacked the development of poison gases, which were supposedly outlawed even before World War I. The plot, as Yip explained it, goes something like this:

"*Hooray for What!* was the first anti-war musical that I know of that was done in the United States, that was done on Broadway, or in musical comedy. [Actually, *Strike Up the Band* could make this claim.] It was a tirade against war done in a funny way with Ed Wynn, a funny man. It had more belly laughs than anything and yet we knocked the hell out of the idea of going to war. And the very title, *Hooray for What!*, what are we shouting hooray for? What do we win by going to war, you know? What does the victor come out with? Have we ever been victorious after a war—without a terrific calamity? I mean, the whole state of the world today is because of the last three wars, four wars, that we fought. No one is a victor. So what are we shouting 'hooray' for when we go to war? . . . The title itself tells you the whole satire and irony of the show.

"Well, it was about a funny inventor, Ed Wynn, who always invented *crazy* things . . . At that time we didn't have the atom bomb, but it was a gas that he invented, it was a death gas which he kept in a football. But he didn't want to release it to the world because it was so violent that anybody having it could conquer the world. It was . . . what the hydrogen bomb is. And . . . now, he was a very simple, charming, lovable human being . . . soft-hearted. . . . He had an apple orchard and he was trying to invent an insecticide that wouldn't kill the worms, he was so heartwarmingly human. And so while he's working on this insecticide, not to harm worms, because he felt, well, worms are animals, they have a life, they have a sex life, maybe they have a literary life . . . 'Take silk,' he says. 'We'd never have silk without little silk worms.' He says, 'We have lace,' he says . . . And this soft-hearted man, now, through his experiment, invents a gas that makes people leap-frog, makes cows turn purple, give red milk, and things like that. And so the ammunition companies that are making poison gas descend on him. They think they've got a great man who will give them . . . a gas that will be so terrible, whoever had it could conquer the world. Well, he won't give up that gas. He keeps it in a football, see? And that was the theme of the show. And somehow or other they get hold of it, some spies get a hold of it. And each country's spy sells it to another country. The German thinks he's the only one [who's] got it, and of course they double-crossed him and sold it to France, France sells it to Russia, Russia . . . So now everybody's got the gas and everybody thinks they're the only ones to get it. And that was the time of Hitler, Mussolini and Hirohito. The three of them got it.

"And we had a wonderful symbolic thing. We had three Macy's balloons blown up full stage. One was Hitler, one was Mussolini, one was Hirohito. And we had voices coming out of the loudspeaker, each one of them, you know, 'We have the gas, we have the thing, we have the . . .' But what they didn't know was that one of the spies copied the formula off backwards. Instead [of] $2NO$, it came out $N2O$, you see, so he got laughing gas instead [of poison], so when they let it loose on the soldiers, they all began to laugh, and when they began to laugh, they jumped out of the trenches and the Germans began kissing the Russians and the Russians kissing the Japanese and when they found that out, we let the gas out of these balloons and they were deflated and they came down, you see. That was the end of the show. That was *Hooray for What!*, a charming, beautiful show."[27]

Most of the songs in the show were not very political, and the one hit, "Down With Love," was a funny sort of a love song. The title song comes closest to the play's message of the blind follower, the patriot who shouts "Hooray" for anything with no understanding of what he or she is cheering for. The lyrics that Yip wrote to Arlen's tune went like this:

Hooray—Hooray—
Hooray for what—
We don't know what,
It's just hooray.
For there's no better way,
To enjoy such a beautiful day
Than to get up and get out in the open
And shout hooray.

Throw out your chest,
Throw up your hat.
Another strike—another war,
Can come from that.
If you can yell out loud in a crowd,
You're a great patriot.
Come along, shout hooray for what?

For it's always fair weather,
When good fellows get together,
With a hip-hip-hip and a rah-rah-rah.
And a yah-yah-yah,
And a martial tra-la-la.

Girl:
    The best reforms—the finest laws,
    Emanate from a common cause.
Man:
    But if you've got no common cause?
All:
    Get out and shout and move your jaws.
Man:
    From this will come a common cause.
All:
    Where on earth would Hitler be today
    How would Mussolini rule and sway?

Man:
> What would happen to La France,
> Or the mighty U.S.A.?

All:
> If it weren't for the fellow
> Who believes in Lux and Jello,
> And would give his life to bellow,

Man:
> Hip-hip!

All:
> Hooray!

Man:
> Hip-hip!

All:
> Hooray!

> Hooray for what?
> We don't know what.
> It's just hooray.
> If you can yell out loud in a crowd,
> You're a great patriot.
> Come along—come along—come along,
> Shout hooray—For what![28]

Hooray for What! received good reviews and ran for a year, so one can see that the antiwar spirit was alive somewhere in the country. However, for the first time, Yip began to feel the raised eye of patriotism, even from unlikely sources. As he told an interviewer in 1971, "It was a satire on war. It predicted the atom bomb—not in so many words but in general . . . We couldn't think in terms of atomic energy but we did think in terms of gas. A gas that was so demolishing that they couldn't even find a container for it and whoever owned the thing, whoever owned it, could rule the world. And then we went into all the humorous and absurd things . . . The gas turned out to be of course a phony at the end. And it made very many satirical points with a great deal of laughter. But to show how unattuned people were—and good people—to satire that ridiculed anything that was as patriotic as war

. . . War was a holy thing when we grew up. When the country declared war, my God, you waved the flag, you didn't think, you blindly went into it and said, 'For God and Country.' You even got God mixed up into it. Harold Arlen met [Oscar] Hammerstein at the Astor Hotel . . . while we were in rehearsal. And Hammerstein said to Harold, he said, 'Yip is such a good writer. Why does he always have to get mixed up with things like *Hooray for What!* and war?' He says, 'The stage is not a place for proselytizing, for propaganda. The stage should be used for entertainment.' [There is some question as to whether Yip misremembered this comment, and whether it might actually have been made around 1944, when he had written *Bloomer Girl*.] This was Oscar Hammerstein, a nice, human, decent, wonderful guy."[29]

But in terms of politics, *Hooray for What!* was the beginning of what would grow into a more sustained, more consistent effort for Yip to present controversial peace and social justice issues to the public.

6 | A Pause for Vernon Duke

Collaborations are not always easy. Sometimes, the writers involved will reveal to interviewers their problems with the partnership, and at other times, they will not. In the case of Yip Harburg and Vernon Duke, the relationship is unclear. Yip, perhaps to protect his self-image as a fun-loving, easygoing guy, never spoke much about it in his interviews, only to characterize Duke as a sophisticated, European-raised composer who helped him to elevate the level of his lyrical light verse. In his autobiography *Passport to Paris*, however, Duke was not so kind about Yip. Just the fact that he consistently referred to him as "Harburg," while calling others by their first names, tells us a great deal.[1]

To begin, Duke met Yip through the Gershwins. "It was at Iras's," Duke relates, "that I met, stocky, aggressive E. Y. ('Yip') Harburg."[2] Within moments, the three men had composed a song, "I'm Only Human After All." Soon Duke and Yip were writing tunes together for Paramount Pictures studio in Astoria, Queens, New York, and for theatrical productions on the Great White Way. In fact, it was because of "I'm Only Human After All" that Duke landed an assignment with the Theatre Guild in New York for the final contribution to its *Garrick Gaieties* series. In 1932, Yip and Duke began work on *Walk a Little Faster*, the revue that resulted in the writing of "April in Paris," one of the songs Yip liked talking about most. As we read how Duke described the song's inception, it immediately becomes clear that his and Yip's versions do *not* match at all.

"'April in Paris,' Duke wrote, "was written in April 1932, in New York, at Tony Somas's still-famous establishment, known to New Yorkers as the 'West Side Tony's,' as opposed to the plushier East Side bistro of that name. After auditioning some particularly untalented girls, we all repaired to Tony's; the 'we' consisting of Dorothy Parker, Evelyn Hoey, Robert Benchley, Monty Woolley, Johnny McCalin, [Courtney] Burr and myself.

"Evelyn . . . was to be entrusted with the singing chores in the new musical. After several Scotches, we all got pretty sentimental, the

Scotch reminding us of Miss Hoey's tartan skirt in her Paris number, and the mention of the number inevitably leading to Paris, how wonderful it was in the spring and how vile was Manhattan at that time of year. I can't think whether it was Benchley or Woolley who cried out: 'Oh, to be in Paris now that April's here!' The rest went off in true Class B musical-picture fashion. 'April in Paris . . .' said I, melodramatically. 'What a title! My kingdom for a piano!' No sooner were these words uttered than the ever-obliging Tony ventured the information that an old and wretched upright was at my disposal on the second floor. The piano was wretched, indeed, but it made appropriate sounds when persuaded and, using the title 'April in Paris' for what they call the 'front phrase' in the trade, I soon completed the reasonably immortal refrain. I then proceeded to 'ham it up,' telling all and sundry that I had just given birth to a masterpiece that was certain to 'make the show.' The lyrics were written a week later by Harburg."[3]

To produce *Walk a Little Faster*, Courtney Burr hired Boris Aronson for sets and costumes, Albertina Rasch for the choreography, S. J. Perelman for the sketches, and Monty Woolley to direct the dialogue. Of course, Yip was to do the lyrics. His and Duke's personalities did not always complement each other, however. As Duke wrote, "Harburg flew into a rage very easily. Upon demonstrating a song of ours called 'Speaking of Love,' he wound up with the last lines: 'Speaking of love, I'll be your *nin*compoop, just be my *in*compoop, speaking of love.' When Dorothy Parker, listening with her deceptively demure air, asked sweetly: 'Pray, dear Mr. Harburg, *what* is an *in*compoop?' Harburg let out an agonized yell, delivered a poignant address on the subject of Park Avenue Parasites and stormed out of the room. He was a busy man in the autumn of 1932 and could well afford to take such verbal duels in his stride."[4]

As was the custom at the time, the musical had its tryout in Boston. Duke described it this way: "The Boston *Walk a Little Faster* opening night was one of the roughest in history. Two or three of the more massive settings were not shown because of first-night handicaps backstage: two or three of the less agile stagehands unintentionally appeared with the actors, and some of the actors didn't appear at all, unable to find their way to the stage. To paraphrase the report of an eyewitness, it was a splendid performance, contributed both by the invisible actors and the visible stage crew, but the show easily rose above such trifles. The wonderful Boston audience—there is no better, as any showman will testify—ate it all up good-naturedly, overlooking such items as the crash of a drop and its removal from the scene *for good.*

"Again to the credit of Boston, it must be admitted that 'April in Paris' clicked during our tryout in that city, while it definitely 'laid a bomb' (in the current phrase) two weeks later in New York"[5] And part of that bomb for Yip was that only one New York critic, Bob Garland, mentioned "April in Paris," with the comment that it was "an unnecessary item."[6] As Duke explained it, part of the problem was that Evelyn Hoey, the main vocalist, had laryngitis and could hardly sing above a whisper. The Boris Aronson set that Yip spoke of so highly and the waltz choreography were, in Duke's opinion, not enough to make the audience take note.

After the show's second performance, Duke and his brother Alex sat "dejected and resentful of critics' indifference . . . in the Times Square Childs' restaurant . . . when in stormed Harburg, disheveled and obviously in a rage. 'Ah, so you liked your Boston notices, my fine friend,' he exclaimed, coming right to the point. 'I hope you're satisfied with the New York ones. I told you "April in Paris" might be all right for decadent Europeans, but not for this country—yet you wouldn't listen. Read this.' With a dramatic gesture he threw Bob Garland's notice on my table. My shy, soft-spoken brother came to my defense and upbraided Harburg for his untimely and unfriendly onslaught on his collaborator . . . The scene was not pretty and my lyricist left in a huff, claiming that 'April in Paris' should have been a saucy 'jingle' in the first place."[7]

Although *Walk a Little Faster* lost money, it was still a somewhat successful musical. Yip continued to work with Vernon Duke, but according to Duke, Yip often lost his temper and accused him of producing "decadent, 'unmanly,' affected music instead of the good, simple, American tunes expected by the people."[8] After fighting their way through the *Ziegfeld Follies of 1933–34,* the two parted company—but not in an unfriendly or hostile manner.

7 | From Hollywood to Oz and Back

The Great Depression had hit Broadway hard. By the 1933–1934 season, the very producers Yip Harburg had depended on for his livelihood were cutting back, giving up on revues and big extravaganzas, or they were aging, ill, or had died. These producers included Charles Dillingham of *New Faces*, Earl Carroll of *Vanities*, George White and his *Scandals*, and even the great juggernaut, Florenz Ziegfeld and his successors, the Shubert Corporation. For Yip and hundreds of other theater writers, performers, directors, and designers, the siren call of the movie musical lured them. Hollywood was one of the few places in the country where there was money to be made. So in late 1934, Yip moved out West, where he mostly settled in until the late 1940s brought him more frequently back to New York.

During this time, Yip became one more soul in a somewhat bicoastal commuter generation. It was during one of these trips back "home" that he wrote *Hooray for What!* As he told Bernard Rosenberg and Ernest Goldstein, "There was a huge migration to Hollywood in the thirties. When I first went west on the Santa Fe, George S. Kaufman and Harold Arlen were on the same train. Everybody was being shipped out. At that time movie musicals were bursting onto the American scene. A songwriter needed hits to get his degree in ASCAP [American Society of Composers, Authors, and Publishers]. For that, chances were much better in films. The New York critics looked down on them. Broadway was the snob literary Park Avenue and Hollywood skid row. But for a while, especially during the [Fred] Astaire/[Ginger] Rogers period, Hollywood was making some great pictures with a wealth of good songs. [Jerome] Kern, [Irving] Berlin, [B. G. "Buddy"] DeSylva, [Lew] Brown, and [Ray] Henderson were out West. So was the money.

"Socially we were a refugee colony of New Yorkers. We were doing well—life was luxurious. I had never lived in a house with a garden around me. Sunshine, sunshine every day, everywhere. Shorts, tennis, golf, swimming, kumquats. Refugees? Like hell.

"I shuttled to New York at least every two years to do a show. My heart, my big heart, was where the real tinsel blazed—Broadway. The cynosure, the center of all sophistication was still New York. The goal, the dream, was the Broadway show. Those of us who came back periodically to the stage were always honored, envied, and rewarded. In the movies the target was the mentality of a twelve-year old."[1]

It is quite evident that Yip was not impressed by the Hollywood film system but that he was willing to work within it to gain fame and fortune. What that meant was being contracted by a studio to write songs on demand. The studio assigned the project, estimated the number of weeks of work it would require, and then either accepted or rejected the writers' products. Although not so different from writing for revues, the environment was more exploitative and controlled. Yip accepted this unpleasant atmosphere so that he could move his songwriting career forward. As he later recalled, "No, I wasn't in the big money before I went to Hollywood. I'd just had one or two successful shows, and I was becoming known as a good lyric writer. It was Carl Laemmle [the founder of Universal Studios] who got me out there. He came here [New York], and he thought that I'd be a good bet for a studio. When you were offered $1,000 a week, at that time, that was quite unbelievable. Going out there, where there was no snow, no sleet, fig trees in your backyard, and tropical climate—this was a really joyous time in my life. It was something that you wished for, that you never believed could happen. So when you talk about working in pictures, you've got to think of this heaven that was offered you, and you weren't too critical of what you were doing, because the living was easy.

"At that time, when I came in, [Universal] was on the downgrade and they were trying to get a so-called transfusion, and I was the RH factor or something! That was about 1935. I'd done a show in '34, *Life Begins at 8:40*, with Ray Bolger and Bert Lahr. It was a nice hit show. He saw that and liked it, and he liked the other shows I'd done. So Carl Laemmle, and everybody about the studio, struck me as people who really didn't know anything, who were floundering, who just by hook or crook or luck or something once in a while were getting a picture that made money. I imagine that's the only way you can survive in an assembly line system. Wherever creative work is entailed, anybody who approaches the creative process on an assembly line basis must have some glandular, nervous structure for turning a thing out that is an assembly line product. The real art, the real fellow who writes from the inside, from his guts and from feelings and so on, can't possibly be that. He can't possibly do that. You cannot create on a mass production basis. You have got to live with your one thing that you're doing. You've got to have a certain amount of pregnancy, a certain amount of going through the recapitulation theory—from embryo to growth and birth—But these people don't have that. That's why they're able to do so many pictures a year, songs a year, whatever it is. They turn them out like gloves or fur coats, and their relationship to the result is the commodity relationship. Whereas the creator cannot have that relationship with his work. It's a deeper, profounder feeling. He has an emotional attachment to it. It can't be done on this quick line.

"I was at Universal until it got into trouble, I think for about a year and a half. Yes, Universal was a ghost city, it was a shadow of itself, just before I left. Of course, you couldn't tell—because of the block booking and because of these big companies owning their own distributing outlets, so that everything was pre-sold. Success therefore didn't mean anything, it didn't mean that your product was good or great or anything, it was automatic. The place thrived. It was a beehive of people working and so on. By the time I got there, it was all being cut down. It was a ghost city by then. Universal didn't own any theatres, which meant a quicker downfall.

"Then Warners called me to work with Harold Arlen on a [Al] Jolson show and a few others, some of the *Gold Digger* things. That was Hal Wallis, and they were a real mechanical group. I wasn't accustomed to that kind of work, of course, and neither was Harold. We both really had a pride in our work, and were sensitive, and we suffered under it quite a good deal. We couldn't quite get into the pace of things. We—as we say—'knocked out' some songs, but it was very frustrating, and I got very sick.

"Warners was still going strong, plugging away; everything was quick conferences in the front office. I remember one poor fellow, a refugee from Germany, who was also a sort of an artist. He was a grand musician from the other side, who had gone up with stars in his eyes, with a beautiful idea, to the front office. He finally got his admittance. And we met him coming back. He came back hang-dog, gloomy, melancholy. We said, 'What's the matter?' He said, 'That front office! No fantasy. No fantasy.'

"In the front office, there was Jack Warner, and Hal Wallis I knew, and Bob Lord. Bob Lord was a sort of an intellectual guy, one of the first intelligent guys to come along. I didn't meet Harry [Warner], just Jack. He was a flamboyant sort of a cockatoo, exactly that. I can only picture him on the massage table, being slapped around by two guys, with cologne and perfume, and while he was being slapped around, you were sitting there, and he was talking to you off the side of his mouth, from the table — telling you about his exploits, his trips, his pictures, his paintings. A good-time Charlie. Always talking about himself. Sort of a Don Juan, very romantic. That's the talk you got. Big man-about-town stuff.

"They never discussed creating things, they didn't talk to you. I mean, it was all cliché. After you'd go to an opening, a try-out, you'd get a few words: 'This is in the bag,' or 'This is a clever picture,' or their remarks, whatever it was. Oh, I don't know, everything was repetition of some phrase, everybody said practically the same thing, the same clichés, the same measurements and standards of scenes and things. It was vernacular, cut and dried. It might have been applied to the garment business or any other business. This needed more movement, this had to have more pace, this wasn't punchy enough, this wasn't funny enough — but never the soul of a thing at all.

"The director usually is in command of the thing. Of course, the writer too — but the writer only functions within the atmosphere of the director. At Warners we worked on several of the *Gold Diggers* and the Jolson show, *The Singing Kid*. [Busby] Berkeley directed the *Gold Diggers*. He directed the dancing and another director directed the book, Bill Thiele. At that time, it was the big spectacle, the formation, the big line of girls, all the new things that the camera and the eye had discovered — that's all. These were the outgrowth of *42nd Street*. Once that formula worked, they worked it to death, you know, until they really killed it. Warners was living on that formula. I didn't stay there very long.

"On the *Gold Diggers*, I did purely lyrics. I just worked with Harold Arlen, as a team. But I always came back [to New York] for a show every two years. My heart was right here, always, in New York. I'd always come back and do a show."[2]

Some of the films that Yip worked on from 1935 to 1939 included *Manhattan Moon*, *The Affair of Susan*, *The Singing Kid*, *Stage Struck*, *Gold Diggers of 1937*, *Merry Go Round of 1938*, and of course, *The Wizard of Oz*. This last had a most interesting background story. L. Frank Baum, a nineteenth-century progressive, created the story for his first full-length children's book. Published in 1900 as *The Wonderful Wizard of Oz*, it became an immediate hit and resulted in thirteen subsequent Oz stories. By 1902, there was a musical stage version, which had a respectable Broadway run plus multiple tours around the country. Audience members loved to share the adventures of Dorothy, a Kansas farm girl who got transported in a cyclone tunnel to the magical land of Oz. There, a scarecrow, a tin man, and a cowardly lion helped her reach the all-powerful Wizard of Oz, who might help her return home to Kansas and grant her three companions a brain, a heart, and courage, respectively.

Oz and its inhabitants were already a well-known part of American popular culture before the fall of 1937, when Louis B. Mayer of Metro-Goldwyn-Mayer (MGM) Studios bought the rights to the book from Samuel Goldwyn (of the Goldwyn Studio) for a whopping $75,000. The idea was to make a film that would compete with Walt Disney, whose *Snow White and the Seven Dwarfs* was creating quite a buzz. MGM, the largest Hollywood studio at that time, could well afford the fee and the subsequent $2,777,000 it spent on the production. Arthur Freed, an uncredited associate producer of the film and the person who selected the Baum book for a film adaptation, hired Yip and Harold Arlen to write the score, but the ultimate task for Yip included far more than creating lyrics.

When Yip spoke about *The Wizard of Oz*, he usually concentrated on a few specific items. First, he liked to tell how he and Arlen were chosen to join in the effort of changing this children's story into a film, and how that led them into writing an integrated musical, one in which the songs, dialogue, and dances were all part of the story. One of his recollections, designed to criticize the studios' contract system, began as a fantasy: "Once upon a time in 1937, two little girls with beautiful voices were kept captive in a castle by an ogre named Sam the Goldwyn. Their names were Judy [Garland] and Deanna [Durbin]. For several years they were kept silent—given high salaries but no songs. So they became a liability to Sam the G. Louis B. [Mayer], of the castle across the lane, who fancied himself a knight in shining armor, mounted his National City Bank Horse and rescued Judy from a fate worse than death—silence. A picture was designed for her based on the beautiful classic, *The Wizard of Oz*. The rest, as they say, is history."

Then Yip took on a more serious tone: "Everyone agreed that *Oz* would be great for Judy. Harold Arlen and I were in New York doing *Hooray for What!* starring Ed Wynn. In it was a song that hit the air waves called 'In the Shade of the New Apple Tree.' Arthur Freed, the [associate] producer of *Oz*, loved it; he thought it had just the charm and mood for *The Wizard of Oz*. Before us, many teams of writers had tried to get a musical version out of the delightful tale, without success. Finally Arthur agreed with me that we needed a new concept, to experiment, and let the lyrics and music wag the plot." MGM then contracted Yip and Arlen for fourteen weeks at $25,000, one-third of which was paid against royalties.

"So we put aside the six or seven existing scripts and started from scratch," Yip explained. "We let the songs tell the story, and wrote the scenes around the songs, saving as much of the existing scripts as we were able to cue into the songs. There was no rainbow mentioned in the original [Baum] story. We created 'Somewhere Over the Rainbow' to express the situation of a little girl who wanted to fly away from home, to go somewhere with more life and color than drab Kansas. The song gave birth to stunning visual effects and a new bit of plot.

"Whatever weakness existed in [Baum's] original story we replaced with new ideas. For example, my satiric sense rebelled when the Wizard gave the Tin Man a red pill for a heart and the scarecrow a white pill for a brain. It was pat—and meaningless. My humorous spirit said, 'Put a little bit into this. Why not show up some of the follies we live by?' When a guy goes to college, he doesn't emerge with any more wisdom than when he went in. All he's got is his diploma. So let's be realistic: give the scarecrow a diploma—and ipso facto, a brain. In like manner, the do-gooders of the world never achieve hearts, but testimonials. Ergo, a watch for the Tin Man—that ticks like a heart. Plus an inscription for good deeds done. And last of all, the coward who survives a war never achieves courage. But he does get a medal. And forever after, that medal terrifies the community . . . I demonstrated all the parts to Louis B. Mayer and others with all the passion of my schoolboy experience. Thank you, P.S. 64!"[3]

Yip gave more details of his feelings about writing an integrated musical in his interview with Max Wilk: "When Harold and I started writing the score for *The Wizard of Oz*, we weren't thinking in terms of classics. We were just doing work, earning a living and liking what we were doing, trying for a hit song or two. We never thought of posterity. We were very excited about the film; we loved it. For the first time we'd gotten something that we both felt had the feeling of being fun. It was a chance to express ourselves in terms we'd never been offered before. I loved the idea of having the freedom to do lyrics that were not just songs but *scenes*. That was our own idea, to take some of the book and do some of the scenes in complete verse, such as the scenes in Munchkin Land. It gave me wider scope. Not just thirty-two-bar songs, but what would amount to the acting out of entire scenes, dialogue in verse and set to Harold's modern music. All of that had to be thought out by us and then brought in and shown to the director so he could see what we were getting at. Things like the three Lullaby girls, and the three tough kids who represented the Lollipop Guild. And the Coroner, who came to avow that the Witch was dead, sincerely dead. All of that was thought up by us, it wasn't in the [Baum] book. Even a thing like 'Over the Rainbow'—there was no such thing as a rainbow mentioned in the book.

"When we brought in the song ['Over the Rainbow'], all we were thinking about was a little girl who was in trouble with her folks, in conflict with them, at an age when she wanted to run away, and knowing that somewhere, someplace, there was a colorful land that wasn't this arid flat plain of Kansas. She remembered a little verse from her childhood that mentioned a colorful place where bluebirds fly. The only thing she'd probably ever seen that was colorful was the rainbow. And that gave them the idea of doing the whole first part of the picture—when she's in Kansas—in sepia, black-and-white. And then when she got to Munchkin Land, the fairyland place, it became colorful. This whole new country was rainbow country.

"When you write music and lyrics, you have to think of all those things. You think of what's going to happen on screen or on stage—the action, what you can do pictorially—so that you really direct the lyric toward the pragmatic medium. If you can do that, it's working in showmanship terms, to work with your lyrics and music as a director would work, and as a book-writer would, and still have that song written in such a way that it could step out of the histrionic medium and plot—which it accelerates—and be made to flourish and blossom."[4]

The second thing that Yip liked to talk about was his participation in every aspect of the writing and visual conception of the film. The author Aljean Harmetz interviewed Yip for her wonderful study, *The Making of The Wizard of Oz*. He told her about the many problems with the original script, especially when it came to fitting in the music. "I knew how to change plot around to make the plot fit the songs. I liked a lot of things [Noel] Langley [the film's first screenwriter] had, threw the other stuff out. The whole Munchkin sequence was done in prose. I threw it out and lyricized it. That was daring . . . the whole 10 minutes in rhyme. Never done before or since. All rhymed up." Yip saw the purpose of the songs as simplifying the plot, "to take the clutter out of too much plot and too many characters . . . to telescope [it all] into one emotional idea. You had to throw out the unnecessary to make the songs work . . . All the songs in *Wizard* were plot, a kind of revolution in picture musicals."[5]

As Yip told Harmetz, the Munchkin sequence was not the only part of the film that he scripted. "I edited the whole thing and brought back Langley's story which was simpler and added my own. I clarified the whole story and made the songs do the magic."[6] Yet, when viewers watch the film, they see no credit for the work Yip did outside of lyric writing. The originality of his concept is most evident in the "We Welcome You to Munchkinland" sequence, of which he felt extremely proud. Dorothy, newly arrived in Oz, is presented to the little people by Glinda, the Good Witch of the North. The young girl explains about her accidental landing on the Wicked Witch of the East and is then greeted, in song, by such Munchkinland luminaries as the mayor, the coroner, and members of the Lullaby League and the Lollipop Guild. All celebrate together with the well-recognized "Ding-Dong! The Witch Is Dead":

Ding-dong! The witch is dead
Which old witch?
The wicked witch
Ding-dong, the wicked witch is dead

Wake up, you sleepy head
Rub your eyes,
Get out of bed
Wake up, the wicked witch is dead

She's gone where the goblins go,
Below, below, below, yo-ho
Let's open up and sing
And ring the bells out
Ding-dong, the merry-o
Sing it high,
Sing it low,
Let them know the wicked witch is dead.[7]

The third element that Yip liked to speak about was his influence on the casting of the Oz film and his observations of the actors. Although it was the studio's decision to assign Judy Garland the role of Dorothy, Yip liked her and admired her talent. But he also felt sorry for her, and, in a real sense, wrote "Over the Rainbow" with his take on her personal needs in mind. As he told Dick Cavett in 1978, "She was fifteen at the time and Mr. Goldwyn had her on contract. He didn't know what to do with her, so he dismissed her and MGM picked up her contract and they had to do a show for her . . . to get something that would fit Judy Garland and Arthur Freed thought of *Wizard of Oz* . . . I knew her on the set and she had a mother, a typical stage mother who was pushing her into destruction, and I could feel it right at the set and I almost knew the outcome. You see, when child players get into that position of being stars, she and Mickey Rooney, there was no play, there was no childhood. There was no real fun. It was sophisticated fun, artificial fun . . . It was a Hollywood kind of fun . . . And I think she missed that childhood all through her life. She never had real fun. She had acclaim, she had applause, but it's the kind of thing that is killing the people who get there, and who don't know how to use it.

"She was a most unusual quick study. She could sit at a piano with Harold Arlen and Harold would play the song for her and before he was through she knew it. She knew that song. She was fast, and . . . she never had to be directed. In fact, direction would have been death for her because she could do everything a lot better than any director could. Her innate feeling, her intuition, and, of course, she had a voice that simply . . . I think it was one of the rare voices of that half-century.

"And she could dance and she could clown. She could do anything. But her yearning for something which she never had, which I interpreted symbolically, poetically, as 'Over the Rainbow,' she never achieved."[8]

As for other casting, Yip's greatest input was in the selection of Bert Lahr, Ray Bolger, Buddy Ebsen, and then Jack Haley for the roles of the Cowardly Lion, the Scarecrow, and the Tin Man. The selection of Bert Lahr was obvious for Yip. He had worked with Lahr and Bolger previously in *Life Begins at 8:40* and knew their comic abilities. But with Lahr, he also immediately understood the beauty of taking a former burlesque performer and giving him something with meaning.

"You take a typical case—Bert Lahr," he later explained to Deena Rosenberg and Mel Gordon. "He starts in burlesque. Burlesque is the lowest element that you can possibly conceive of . . . Billy Watson's Beef Trust, as some of them were called, was built around some gal coming out and doing a striptease, but between the striptease[es], you had to make those people who are less than common denominator laugh out loud belly laughs. Now, that was the kind of training that Bert Lahr got . . . They would be doing one joke for about five weeks until it was a terrific laugh and there was enough circuit for them to get around and to make a living and finally come back to New York to the big burlesque houses. By the time they got here, that joke was developed. They milked it. They got audience reaction from it, east to west, from coast to coast . . . Then vaudeville came in. These people finally became the headliners in vaudeville . . . Then they'd give them a little better kind of (writer) . . . and finally vaudeville shows sprang up all over the United States.

"I took him [Bert Lahr] out of the burlesque field and gave him intelligent lyrics, lyrics that had meaning. And the juxtaposition of Bert Lahr saying those lyrics was terrific because he was essentially a comic. His whole visage was that of a clown."[9] In fact, Yip claimed that he had "tailored" the role of the Cowardly Lion for Lahr. "You see, when you have a fellow like Bert Lahr, you're unlimited in your inspiration and your imagination and ideas for fun, because you've got a master who can take your lyrics and wing them into laughter."[10] As he told Harmetz, "I suggested Lahr. I knew what the picture needed was some real broad comedy. I knew I could write for him. I knew his style. I could visualize the Cowardly Lion song, 'If I Were King' and what it would be like in his hands.

"I was in on casting . . . [Ray] Bolger looked like the scarecrow. It was a natural. I was torn between whether to have [Jack] Haley as Scarecrow and Bolger as Tin Man because I thought Haley more of a weakie [with] more pathos. Bolger has no pathos. His voice and delivery has none of Haley's pathos. I was won over because Bolger was a much better dancer and in the Tin Man's suit I knew I couldn't get a dance. I would have preferred Buddy Ebsen for either part to Haley or Bolger."[11] In fact, Buddy Ebsen worked on the Tin Man role for two weeks until he was hospitalized from a dangerous allergic reaction to toxic aluminum dust used in the Tin Man's makeup.

Yip's greatest casting disappointment was in not having the great comic actor W. C. Fields play the Wizard. In fact, he had written the part with Fields's "satiric and cynical" take in mind. "W. C. Fields wanted $75,000 to do that little part," Yip recalled years later. "They offered him $50,000. He wouldn't take it . . . an example to me [of] a man giv[ing] up immortality for a lousy few dollars he didn't need. I would have done that part for nothing . . . When we got [Frank] Morgan, the style changed, the humbug, frightened little man himself surviving through humbugging."[12]

The fourth, and perhaps what Yip considered the key element of the Oz experience, was its message. He liked to share his vision of how the story and characters reflected basic human needs, and how the characters were linked with each other and also with the most important us political figure of the time, Franklin D. Roosevelt. As Yip told Studs Terkel, "I cannot work on anything that doesn't have some meaningful basis as a foundation, even in *Wizard of Oz*. I mean, if you examine that, the reason I was attracted to it is because [of] the great basic truths, or the great basic seekings . . . *The Wizard of Oz* on the surface seems to be a childish fantasy, but it is far from that. It is the very basis of all our hopes and lives and things we live for . . . the three basic things in life are knowledge, love, and courage. And here we have a little—and also roots—a little girl who runs away from home and now misses her roots and wants to get back home. So that's number one, your basic. So you're rooting for her. Number two, she meets a Tin Man who has no heart and would like to have a heart. Again, the basic: love. And how is he going to get a heart? How do we all get hearts? [We] want love. Children do. They want love in its very deep, elemental sense. A grown up can do a lot of substituting for wanting love. He thinks he wants money, things of that sort. And the Lion wants courage. Here he is, king of the forest, but he has no courage. How many guys do we see going around with big shoulders and epaulets and things of that sort, who lack courage, who are big cowards? And then again, there is the Straw Man, who wants the very basic . . . He wants brains. Now, how are they all going to get it? This is the thing that intrigues not only a child, but a grown up. And the basic thing of *The Wizard of Oz* that keeps it going, and I think makes it . . . It is the most played picture of all time, all over the world, and the most livable. Because these three basic, elemental things are done with humor, with fun and I try, I try to do everything I write in that vein, and it has to have a basis."[13]

"Over the Rainbow" was central to Yip's concept for the Oz film, but from the start, it proved to be a challenge for both him and Harold Arlen. As he told interviewer Paul Lazarus in 1980, "I worked very well with Harold, excepting when we got to the ballad, but you always have trouble writing a ballad—how to say 'I love you' in another way after it's been said how many thousands of times, but this particular ballad was a ballad for a little girl who was at odds with her schoolteacher and her mother and she was in trouble, and like all little girls, wanted to get away from where she was at. And where was she at? Kansas. A dry, arid, colorless place. She had never seen anything colorful in her life except the rainbow. Well, where would a little girl like that, not knowing the world, want to go? Over that rainbow. On the other side of the rainbow. So I had that idea in mind of a little girl wanting something, a place somewhere that was around that rainbow. And I told Harold about it and he went to work on a tune.

"I can't tell you the misery that a composer goes through when the whole score is written, but he hasn't got that big theme song that Louis B. Mayer is waiting for. The contract is for 14 weeks and we're on our 14th week now and we don't get paid after the 14th week. And he surely sweated it out and he couldn't get a tune for that until one night he called me. It was about 12 o'clock at night and he said 'please, please, come right over, I've got the tune.' Well, I walked over [to his house]. It was Beverly Hills at that time, in 1937—we weren't afraid of being mugged. And he played me this tune and he played it this way: [Yip plays "Somewhere Over the Rainbow" slowly and heavily on the piano.] I said 'Harold, that's for Nelson Eddy. It was a symphony. It's not for a little girl yearning to be over a rainbow,' and his spirits fell and we both more or less respected each other and I went home, very sad and he did too and for two weeks after, without money from Metro, he was still working on that tune and finally he called me over and he said 'Yipper, I feel this tune—this is a great tune, now you must write it.' When a composer like Harold says that you've got to, as Willy Loman's wife [in Arthur Miller's play, *Death of a Salesman*] says, 'Pay attention.' I said, 'All right, I'll try to write it, but at least the middle, the release, can you bring it down, can you make it, if not a little girl, at least adolescent?' He couldn't get a middle until finally one day—they had a little dog, Pan, a silly little dog who ran away and Harold had a little whistle for her and it went like this: [Yip plays middle music for the song.] I said, 'Harold, this is the crazy life we lead—this is the way songs are written.'"[14]

In another interview, Yip gave more insight into the writing of the song and how his old friend Ira Gershwin gave some additional sup-

Yip with composer and friend Harold Arlen, 1935.
Courtesy of the Yip Harburg Foundation

port for the team. "And at that time, after two or three weeks went by and this was the last song; [we] had to have it in, and Harold got real worried and anxiety-ridden, so did I. And we said—and this is something we always did with each other—when Ira or George were working on a thing and they met an impasse, they'd always call me or they'd call Harold. And I was in as arbiter on many decisions . . . So I called in Ira. I said, 'Ira, Harold's got a tune here . . . and here's the situation.' I told him I was too involved emotionally [to] analyze the thing, to put my finger on [the problem], to communicate to Harold, but Ira, being a third person, and more clear-headed and less involved . . . said, 'Harold, will you play that tune with a little more rhythm?' And Harold sat down, said, 'What do you mean? This way?' And he played [hums first ten notes of the chorus with rhythm]. And then the thing cleared itself up for me, and Ira . . . said, 'It's just the way Harold's playin'.' But we were both too intense to have figured that thing out. Well, after he got that, I said, 'All right.' I immediately saw and I said, 'Gee, you're right, Ira. That's fine.'

"And then the process of getting a title was very hard for the tune. I knew I wanted something with 'rainbow' in it . . . And I said, 'Well, the only colorful thing in her life would have been, she should see a rainbow.' And if I were that little girl, I would imagine [her thinking] that 'There's a colorful place to run to. I wish I were somewhere away from here, some colorful place, maybe over that rainbow, beyond the rainbow.' I didn't have 'over.' I had the other side . . . I had 'other side of the rainbow' and it didn't fit. So we finally got down to 'over the rainbow.' So it was pure logic and pure putting myself in the girl's position, also trying to put myself in the position of a child's mind."[15]

Yip explained to Aljean Harmetz another problem he confronted lyrically. "'Over the Rainbow is Where I Want To Be' was my title, the title I gave Harold. A title has to ring a bell, has to blow a couple of Roman candles off. But he gave me a tune with those first two notes [an octave apart]. I tried, 'I'll go over the rainbow,' 'Someday over the rainbow,' or 'the other side of the rainbow.' I had difficulty coming to the idea of 'Somewhere.' For a while I thought I would just leave those first two notes out. It was a long time before I came to 'Somewhere Over the Rainbow.'"[16]

In 1975, at a time when Yip took on more of a teaching role in his lectures, he explained the precise art of constructing a message within a lyric: "I have a job to do. I am a blacksmith or a carpenter, excepting that I do it instead of with nails, I do it with words. And that's my job ... So there's your premise ... Dorothy, like every child, is in a situation with her teacher who wants to take the dog away, the dog barked or bit or something. And Dorothy at this point in life, again, can't understand older folks, can't understand teachers, can't understand mother and father, [or] school. She's in rebellion, as all children are at a certain age. And she wants to run away from home and does run away from home on the cyclone ... flown over the rainbow into a completely new world and she's dreaming this thing and in her dreams of course [are] all the people that she identifies with.

"Now, before she's throw[n] over the rainbow and wants to run away, when things are so bad she'd like to get away from here ... this calls for, instead of four pages of dialogue on why she wants to run away which would all be pretty routine dialogue, 'I want to get away from here, I don't like my mother, I don't like my father. My teacher's a so-and-so, the hell with all these grown-ups.' What would a child think? ... The writer has to put himself into the character he's writing for. And I put myself in the shoes of this little girl and into her heart and in her soul and she was not a mean little girl. She didn't know much about love, where is love, why don't people love me. And if I had never seen anything but aridity around me, no flowers, dried, arid neighborhood, and the only thing colorful in my life that I'd ever seen was a rainbow, that rainbow would make a terrific impact on my whole life, on my whole existence. And probably before she sang that song, night after night after seeing a rainbow, 'My God, there must be something prettier than Kansas. There must be something better than all this dryness and misery around. Must be something colorful over that rainbow.' That would be the thought and that would be the first thing she would think of, that [Yip sings]

Somewhere over the rainbow
Skies are blue

And the dreams that you dare to dream
Really do come true.

A child contemplating. 'Somewhere over that rainbow, way up high.'
Now, here's another line.

There's a land that I heard of
Once in a lullaby.

I didn't want to write a song with a child saying, to another child, 'Over
the rainbow, that's the place to be. There's a beautiful land. We'll get
over there some time and all your troubles will be solved, once you get
over that rainbow.' That would be wrong. So I really worked very hard
at hooking up something that she had heard in a lullaby, you see?

Way up high
There's a land that I heard of
Once in a lullaby.

In other words, the lullabys and the songs that a mother sings to a child
are so important for what impact you make on a child . . . And therefore this is a hangover of something that she heard in a lullaby. And it's
not a panacea for all your troubles, over the rainbow. And so then we
go on with the metaphor:

Someday I'll wish upon a star
And wake up where the clouds are far
Behind me.

Now, what metaphor would a child use?

Where troubles melt like lemon drops
Away above the chimney tops
That's where you'll find me.

Somewhere over the rainbow
Bluebirds fly.
Birds fly over that rainbow
Why then, oh why can't I?

If any little bird can fly
Beyond the rainbow
Why oh why can't I?[17]

"Isn't that not only a child's idea . . . but a grown-up's too? Aren't we all always reaching for something? [A] rainbow is only a symbolic thing. It's a poetic expression of a colorful thing that nature has made for us in our lives and the poet uses that rainbow as the symbol for, really, what the human being's always trying to evolve toward. Every human being is trying to reach for something a little beyond his grasp, or, as [the poet, Robert] Browning says, our grasp must . . . be beyond our reach or what's a heaven for? As soon as you reach the thing you want to do, it fades into nothing. Perfection is never to be had on this earth. Certainty is never to be had on this earth. If we know how to live with uncertainty but with ideals *toward* certainty, that is the fun of life.

"And this is what I mean by, when you are writing a song these are the thoughts that go into it. It is everybody talking about happiness, happiness, happiness. I don't know what happiness is and I don't think anybody knows what happiness is, nor did the founding fathers of our constitution tell you that they are making a land and a constitution that will give you happiness. They say, 'Life, liberty, and the *pursuit* of happiness.' Pursuit is the secret word in the meaning of life. It's the pursuit of something that the spirit inside you tells you that some-where, as exemplified by the rainbow, that it isn't just this little bit of arid earth that we're on, but that there is a liaison, a bridge, a galactal [*sic*] bridge between our little planet, our little earth that we're on and the heaven of your imagination. Because this is where heaven is—it's in here. It's not in the books that you read, or the Aries and the Aquarius and everything else. It's within you. And 'Over the Rainbow' has its effect that it has, not only because it's a beautiful [song] that is almost majestic and symphonic, which Harold Arlen wrote . . . But all these things that I'm telling you about, that went through me as I wrote those simple children's words, that there was a whole philosophy and a whole background behind it, and that unless we think that way we cannot be good artists."[18]

It is most difficult to imagine what *The Wizard of Oz* would have been like without Judy Garland singing "Over the Rainbow"; yet the song was originally cut from the final version of the film. As Yip described it in later years, "Like every motion picture, the show, after it was finished had to have a secret preview to see how it was going. And the director was a man by the name of Victor Fleming and they previewed it secretly in a little town called Whittier which has always been a disaster area. [Here, Yip is making a political statement about Whittier as the birthplace of former president Richard Nixon.] And after the preview Mr. Fleming, Victor Fleming, walked into the office and he was a very, very pretentious-looking gentleman with a big chest and stentorian voice, and above all he was Anglo-Saxon, and that made an awful impact in the movie business. And he said, 'I'm sorry to say,' he says, 'that the whole first part of that show is awful slow because of that number, you know, the rainbow, over the rainbow, I don't know . . .' He said, 'We gotta take it out.' Well, at that point when a man like that comes in who doesn't talk but makes pronunciamentos, you've got to listen. And Mervyn LeRoy, who was the producer of the picture at this point, suddenly regressed to little Mervyn Levine again and the song was out. The song was out of the picture. Then they went and screened it at Azuza and other smog-ridden towns like that and the song was out of the show.

"Well, Harold and I just went crazy. Harold Arlen and I, we knew that this was the ballad of the show, good God. This is the number we were depending on. And we decided to take action. We went to the front office, we went to the back office, we pleaded, we cried, we tore our hair, Harold ran to *shul*. There wasn't a god around who could help us until finally Arthur Freed, who was associate producer and who was a lyric writer before . . . realized the value of the song, went to Louis B. Mayer, pleaded with him, told him about it, and Louis B. Mayer, he was a kind of a . . . strong-arm man when it came to humanity, but when it came to song writers, he was quite sentimental. They're always sentimental with song writers because they always thought that maybe if they die you'll write a song about them. . . . Well, L. B. Mayer was very nice with Arthur Freed and said, 'Aw, well,' he said, 'let the boys have the damn song. Put it back in the picture. It can't hurt.' So the song went back in the picture and of course you know what happened."[19]

As a side note, it is interesting to know that another song, "The Jitterbug," which was also cut during previews, was never returned to the film. It was a song performed while Dorothy and her three companions were on their way to the Wicked Witch's castle and were attacked by little pink and blue mosquitoes that Yip had created. The musical number had cost $80,000 to produce over a five-week period, but neither Arthur Freed nor the writers could save it. Yip felt that its removal added to the lack of song during the film's final sequences, thereby lessening the movie's impact. Clips of the number can be seen on modern DVD versions of the film.[20] But let's return to "Over the Rainbow."

One interviewer asked Yip what he thought made "Over the Rainbow" such a success. He responded, "Well, hindsight always furnishes you with a lot of material for analysis. First, we had the luck to have a good picture. Many great tunes and fine songs have been lost and have faded way in the framework of shows that didn't stand up. Harold and I have had some beautiful songs in shows that just didn't make it. And then we had a book based on a classic. *Wizard of Oz* was known to so many people. And then, of course, there was Judy Garland. She found an identity with all the young children. One of the great voices of the century, one of the great entertainers. She had an emotional quality that very, very few voices ever had. The whole world seemed to have an empathy with her, not only because of the way she sang that song but because her own life was the epitome of it. This girl who was so loved, and who had everything in the world that she'd reached out for, was the unhappiest. She could own everything that she reached for, and yet couldn't touch the thing, somehow, that her soul wanted. I think people must have felt the condition of her spirit. Her whole life, almost like a Dostoevsky novel, seemed to fit this beautiful little child's song that had color and gaiety and beauty and hope . . . and yet she was so hopeless. That must have had a lot to do with the song bringing into everybody's life almost the sadness of being a human being."[21]

For Yip, the Scarecrow, the Tin Man and the Cowardly Lion had strong universal characteristics as well. "Here are three characters," he explained in 1965, "a tin man who hasn't got a heart, a scarecrow who hasn't got a brain, a cowardly lion who has no courage. Three of the essential things in life. Without them, we perish. Everybody is looking for wisdom, knowledge. Everybody is looking for love, the heart. Everybody is looking for courage to face life courageously, not hysterically. And with these three basic things that the show starts off with, these people seeking them, and little Dorothy is looking for a home, which is another basic. Without the soil, there is no soul. And then comes the search for these magnificent basic things. And they think a wizard will get it for them. It'll come from the outside. The wizard is a humbug and how true that is for everybody, that we're all looking for somebody to give us these essential, the elementary and basic things in living. And so the picture, I think, gives children who really think more clearly than grownups about the real moralities of life, the real values in life, gives them something to cling to and to feel instinctively that this is good, that there is goodness there. And on top of that, when you make it enchanting by giving it melody and twinkle and rhyme, you've got the set up. And this is the basis of all good art."[22]

But Yip also saw in these characters the spirit of the Franklin D. Roosevelt Administration and its tremendous efforts to alleviate human suffering during the Great Depression. "His sunny leadership was reflected in so fanciful a medium as *The Wizard of Oz*," Yip later remarked. "'Let us have freedom from want,' he pleaded, 'and time for learning and the arts.' And so the Scarecrow, long[ing] for knowledge sang ['If I Only Had a Brain']:

I could while away the hours
Conferrin' with the flowers
Consultin' with the rain
And my head I'd be scratchin'
While my thoughts were busy hatchin'
If I only had a brain.

I would not be just a nuffin'
My head all full o' stuffin'
My heart all full of pain
And perhaps I'd deserve you
And be even worthy erv you
If I only had a brain.

FDR's Good Neighbor Policy was translated onto the screen with the Tin Man's tune ['If I Only Had a Heart']:

> When a man's an empty kettle
> He should be on his mettle
> And yet I'm torn apart.
> Just because I'm presumin'
> That I could be kinda human
> If I only had a heart.

And the Cowardly Lion. He too heard the message: 'The only thing we have to fear is fear itself.' And he sang ['If I Only Had the Nerve']:

> Life is sad, believe me missy
> When you're born to be a sissy
> Without the vim and verve
> But I could show my prowess
> Be a lion, not a mow-ess
> If I only had the nerve.

The whole period of writing was for me a reflection of the glow that this one man's humanity cast over the nation, and the glow was mirrored in a song that an unknown little girl of fifteen named Judy Garland sang ['Over the Rainbow'].

"By now you've begun to see that the minstrel worth his lute is somewhat of a lyrical historian. I try to write songs that are rhymed chronicles of a crazy but exciting world spinning aimlessly around a small unimportant galaxy. On this trip, along with your humble minstrel, were the following passengers: Hitler, Mussolini, Stalin, Hirohito, Joe McCarthy, the Shubert Brothers—How did they get in on such a galactic ride?—and Metro-Goldwyn-Mayer."[23]

The Wizard of Oz left a huge legacy, even though in spite of a substantial publicity campaign and the pre-opening popularity of "Over the Rainbow," the film was not as great a financial success after its opening on August 17, 1939, as the studio and creators had hoped. Perhaps the fact that World War II officially began in Europe just two weeks after the movie's premiere had an impact on public enthusiasm for anything and everything. Although thousands of people viewed it in

1939, *The Wizard of Oz* was not a big money maker until it was released for television viewing in 1956. From then on, its reputation soared. So did its desirability in vinyl record form, then VHS and DVD formats, innumerable versions of "Over the Rainbow," and demands for dolls, Christmas ornaments, greeting cards, clocks, computer games . . . you name it.

The film has been seen by audiences the world over. Gleeful citizens have sung "Ding-Dong! The Witch Is Dead" after successful union strikes and the deposing of corrupt business and government leaders. The image of the nasty school teacher, Miss Gulch, on her bicycle morphing into the Wicked Witch of the West on her broomstick has been parodied in many films, including Spanish film director Pedro Almodóvar's *Women on the Verge of a Nervous Breakdown*. Audiences always immediately acknowledge the reference with cheers and laughter. In 2011, even London's West End entered the field with a musical version of the film using the original Harburg and Arlen songs supplemented by new additions by Andrew Lloyd Webber. The Scarecrow, Tin Man, and Cowardly Lion are mainstays in the world's popular culture, political cartoons, and comedic spoofs—in Yip's conceptualization more so than in L. Frank Baum's. And who doesn't immediately recognize any reference to a pair of ruby slippers? But mostly, "Over the Rainbow," which received the 1940 Academy Award for Best Song, is sung throughout the world.

As Yip told Max Wilk about the success of "Over the Rainbow" (but which applies to several of his other songs as well), "When you write music and lyrics, you have to think of all those things. You think of what's going to happen on screen or on stage—the action, what you can do pictorially—so that you really direct the lyric toward the pragmatic medium. If you can do that, it's working in showmanship terms, to work with your lyrics and music as a director would work, and as a book-writer would, and still have that song written in such a way that it could step out of the histrionic medium and plot—which it accelerates—and be made to flourish and blossom. In other words, if the song can be taken out of the picture and still have a life of its own, be a popular hit, then you have accomplished the real premise of songwriting. This is a pretty hard thing to do."[24]

As "nerve-racking" and "brain-racking" as it was, Yip continued to write lyrics, many which are still popular today.[25] Between the last half of 1939 to May 1943, he worked on no less than eleven projects, including songs for the 1939 film *At the Circus*, the 1940 Broadway show *Hold on to Your Hats*, and the film version of the show *Cabin in the Sky*, all of which he spoke about in later interviews. *At the Circus* was particular fun because Yip had the opportunity to work with the extremely comedic and socially conscious Marx Brothers. As he related in 1959, "The Marx Brothers were, of course, a real outstanding bit of Americana. I think they were a zany, wonderful, great Alice-in-Wonderland group of people, that did things that took you really out of the world and made you laugh. Groucho still retains that great sense of comedy. I knew Groucho. He's a very bright man, an intelligent man, an intellectual man, a man with deep feelings for good things who puts on a big act. Of course, the act now has overpowered the man, so that he has become a victim of the act, you see. But he has facets.

"Now, his brother Harpo is quite an artistic fellow. He has depth. He has a relationship to humanity. For example, during a certain period, the Roosevelt period, when people in Hollywood were fighting for decent causes and the New Deal and what it meant, socialization and unemployment insurance and things of that sort, and we were quite a voice, politically—Harpo was on the bandwagon. He understood and contributed, and he did nobly. Even Groucho, in his way, did too. I mean, these were people who had more than just a sense of self. They had a sense of society, brotherhood, contribution. And that's why they were important artists. They weren't just slap-bang comics, they were much more than that. They belonged to part of our history, and they said things in a laughing, bubbling, American way which was truly a part of our culture. They gave millions and millions of people a great time."[26]

Writing for the film, Yip also recalled, "was an assignment . . . I knew that . . . Groucho was a devotee of Gilbert and Sullivan. Every week we would have dinner at Groucho's house . . . about twelve or fourteen of us, screenwriters and so on, and he'd put on one of Gilbert and Sullivan's records and sing along with it. So I knew he loved words and fast rhyming things . . . I had this job to do for Metro[-Goldwyn-Mayer] and here was a barker in the circus. I thought of some Gilbertian way of doing a circus thing for him and 'Lydia' came out. Of course, it had his type of humor, an impertinence . . . risqué."[27]

"Lydia, the Tattooed Lady" brought Yip into the realm of censorship. Looking at some of his lyrics provides us with an understanding of the problem.

Lydia, oh, Lydia
Say, have you met Lydia?
Oh, Lydia, the tattooed lady
She has eyes that folks adore so
And a torso even more so

Lydia, oh, Lydia
That "encyclopidia"
Oh, Lydia, the queen of tattoo
On her back is the Battle of Waterloo
Beside it the wreck of the Hesperus too
And proudly above waves the red, white and blue
You can learn a lot from Lydia
La, la, la, la, la, la
La, la, la, la, la, la
She can give you a view of the world in tattoo
If you step up and tell her where
For a dime you can see Kankakee or Paree
Or Washington crossing the Delaware

Oh, Lydia, oh, Lydia
Say, have you met Lydia?
Oh, Lydia, the tattooed lady
When her muscles start relaxin'
Up the hill comes Andrew Jackson

Lydia, oh, Lydia
That "encyclopidia"
Oh, Lydia the champ of them all

For two bits she will do a mazurka in jazz
With a view of Niag'ra that no artist has
And on a clear day you can see Alcatraz
You can learn a lot from Lydia.[28]

Although Yip enjoyed singing "Lydia" and telling the story of his first, but in no way last, encounter with censorship, his was not Hollywood's first experience with censors. Indeed, to avoid constant assaults from state, local, and individual studio censorship rules, on January 11, 1922, a group of film company producers and distributors, under the guidance of former postmaster general Will Hays, created the Motion Picture Producers and Distributors of America, which established a set of guidelines for industry self-censorship. Under these guidelines, censors demanded that the lyrics of "Lydia, the Tattooed Lady" be altered so as not to present sex in an improper manner nor portray vulgar postures and gestures, which were fairly explicit in the lyrics and in Groucho's performance. But added to the pressure of following the guidelines was Hays's 1934 creation of the Production Code Administration (PCA) to mollify the Catholic Church's insistence on monitoring morality (and immorality) in films. Every film from then on had to receive the PCA seal of approval. Hays named Joseph I. Breen to head the PCA, and Breen was a meticulous holder of that seal.[29]

In explaining the censorship of the song, Yip liked to sing up to the final verse and then stop. "Hold it, hold it," he called out in one interview, "Because at this point we were censored. The Breen Office said, 'Can't be in the picture.' Groucho Marx, he was desperate. He banged at Louis B. Mayer's door, he went to the front office and the back office and said, 'Count me out of the picture!' Louis B. Mayer calls [me] and says, 'What can we do? Can't you clean up the song a bit?' I went home, got an inspiration. I legitimized the song . . . Third chorus did it."[30] The deciding words included these:

Oh, Lydia, the champ of them all
She once swept an Admiral clear off his feet
The ships on her hips made his heart skip a beat
And now the old boy's in command of the fleet
For he went and married Lydia.[31]

Lydia's marriage to the admiral made the song morally acceptable to the censors.

Not so much fun was working with the superstar Al Jolson on the 1940 show *Hold on to Your Hats*. Yip had worked with Jolson on one film, his 1936 *The Singing Kid*, and recognized his great talent. As Yip related in 1959, "You get to know a man pretty well, as a professional. Of course, in his day he was top dog, and he had a voice that really had something. At one time, his singing, which was derivative from ha-zonish type of singing—you know, the cantors—it did pack a wallop, it stirred. It had projection. For the times, he was a great performer. This was one of his last films, and he'd gotten a little corny by that time. He'd gotten a little old-fashioned. Also, he wasn't a big enough person to have grown. He was a small potatoes person, I'd say, inside. He was terribly scared all the time. He was a hypochondriac. He was always on the phone, with doctors and pills, and worried that he was falling apart, and frightened. Always what goes with that picture is a man of great aggressiveness and exuberance, and also when it came to treating people he worked with, he was a real punk. He was as childish as a man could be. There was no consideration for anybody but himself. He was an egomaniac, a megalomaniac, everything else—everything was 'I, I, Me.' On the show we were working on, *Hold on to Your Hats*, he was so disgustingly selfish and parsimonious. Oh God yes.

"I will never forget, I was at the Essex House, and we were working on the show, and Hitler was in the air then. His Luftwaffe and blitz-krieg. We were living on a bed of hot nails—everybody that had any feeling at all. I was awakened one morning with the news cry that Hitler's men had just taken Amsterdam. The Luftwaffe had come down, and they were on to Paris. I got a frantic call from Jolson. He says, 'Yip, kid, do you know what happened? Boy, do you realize what happened?' He says, 'My stocks are down a million!' That was Jolson."[32]

So what did Yip get out of this experience that it remained so firmly in his mind? The answer is that it was the first time since *Americana* in 1932 that he had worked with composer Burton Lane. As he explained to Max Wilk, "Show business is a strange thing. Right after we did the score to *The Wizard of Oz*, Harold and I went through a period where we didn't get too much work . . . Then Harold went off to write with Johnny Mercer on some other films—he felt he needed a change, and so did I—so I teamed up with Burt Lane on the score of *Hold on to Your Hats*, which Al Jolson starred in on the stage. Burt and I wrote what I've always thought was a very fine score. The show had a respectable run, but Al got itchy to leave for Florida—he missed his horse-racing—and he closed up the show. Al was that kind of guy."[33]

Although the songs that Yip and Lane wrote for the play did not become great hits and popular standards, the lines for one, "There's a Great Day Coming, Mañana," did carry some of Yip's by now well-known political satire, with many references to current events. The lyrics to the second chorus reflect some of Yip's political playfulness:

> There's a great day coming, mañana
> We'll be wealthy and ready to share
> Here's your ace in the hole
> Guys from off o' the dole
> Will be paid to play polo, mañana
> There'll be hallelujah, mañana
> There'll be brotherly love in the air
> Florida will love Cal
> Ruby's gonna love Al
> Martin Dies'll kiss Stalin, mañana
>
> There's a great day coming, mañana
> We'll be Aryans walking on air
> We'll be Nordic and fair
> With blue eyes and blond hair
> We'll be living on ersatz, mañana
> There'll be beer and pretzels, mañana
> With bicarbonate soda to spare
> There'll be glasses to clink
> And tequila to drink
> Everyone'll be stinkin', mañana
> Mister Hitler and Mister Goering and Mussolini
> Are beating drums
> For that great day coming, mañana
> But mañana never comes.[34]

As luck and his career would have it, Yip and Harold Arlen would return to work with each other time and time again, as would Yip and Burton Lane. To end this part of Yip's career, at least those parts he liked most to share with others in his later years, we need to look at one song that he and Arlen wrote for the film version of the Vernon Duke/John Latouche Broadway musical *Cabin in the Sky*, produced in 1943. *Cabin* told the story of a black couple, Petunia and Joe, who live in a small segregated Southern town. Joe, a gambler, is tempted by his vice and by a beautiful woman; Petunia wants only to love Joe and to have him "saved" by her church. In total, Yip and Arlen added three new songs for the film: the most popular, and in later years most controversial, was a love song titled "Happiness Is a Thing Called Joe." This became Yip and Arlen's second song to be nominated for an Academy Award. Its lyrics reflected Petunia's great heart and grinding poverty.

It seem like happiness is jes' a thing called Joe
He's got a smile that makes the lilac wanna grow
He's got a way that makes the angels heave a sigh
When they know little Joe's
Passing by
Sometime the cabin's gloomy an' the table bare
Then he'll kiss me an' it's Christmas ev'rywhere
Troubles fly away an' life is easy go
Does he love me good,
That's all I need to know
Seem like happiness is jes'
A thing called Joe
Little Joe,
Mm, mm, mm,
Little Joe.[35]

As Yip related in the late 1970s, *"Cabin in the Sky* was a Broadway show written by Vernon Duke and [John] LaTouche and it was a nice show, but when we got it, Harold and I felt it was a southern background and there wasn't one southern song in it. Vernon Duke had written a beautiful score. He couldn't write bad music but he was a . . . well, he was a concert composer, you know? Very . . . like 'April in

Paris,' my God, you know, you couldn't have a more beautiful tune, and his domain was writing these smart, charming, sophisticated songs and when he brought the show to me, [he] wanted me to do it with him on Broadway. I felt he was wrong for the music and I turned it down and he got mad at me and never talked to me again for a long time, and that's when I hooked up with Harold Arlen and by some . . . serendipity, while I was working at MGM, they bought the product to make a picture of it, and [Arthur] Freed . . . came to me and said, 'This show needs some song[s] that apply to the south, southern songs, and it hasn't got 'em.' And I said, 'I know it. That's why I turned it down.' He said, 'Would you do it?' I said, 'All right. As long as you bought the property, let's do it.' And I got Harold because I knew that this was Harold's meat . . .

"Well, . . . it had a charming score. We had some grand songs in it. [Eddie] Rochester [Anderson] was in it, we had a darling [song] called 'Life's Full of Consequence'—'that old devil consequence,' which I enjoyed more than the rest of the show, the rest of the score. And then there was Ethel Waters and all she had in life was a man named Joe, and lived in a cabin that was always bare and so on, so I got my little social licks into that song too. You see, even though it was a love song, all she had was happiness, just a thing called Joe. By the way, that was the first time that the word 'happiness' was applied in that way, that happiness is a thing. Again, we come back to the power of, you know, song . . .

"Anyhow, the 'happiness is a thing' became a popular phrase for advertising a lot of things . . . Now, Harold had that tune. He had it for a long time and he was not proud of it . . . Here he had a tune that he had never wanted written up. He thought it was too . . . too ordinary. And I always loved that tune and I always begged him to write it, but when we got to *Cabin in the Sky*, I said, 'Will you dig that tune out of the trunk?' And he did. And when I said, 'Happiness is a thing called Joe,' put that to him, for the first time he began liking the tune and he let me use it. And he was going to throw it away . . . And, well, I tried to get lines in it like 'Sometime the cabin gloomy and the table bare / Soon he kiss me and it's Christmas ev'rywhere.' Again, poetic images that were not clichés.

"Another thing I tried to do with that song which . . . most laymen never know about, it would take a real connoisseur of light verse to realize what I had done with the song, you see, the rhyming and lyrics when you're writing a song, where the rhyme falls makes it either hard or easy to remember, and there are certain tricks that the skilled lyric writer has to make a song memorable, provided it doesn't become mechanical and the hinges don't stick out. In other words, to rhyme as many places as you can without the average ear spotting it, feeling it's mechanical . . . Now I'll break this down for you. What I mean is this: You take the stress syllable:

> It seem like happiness is jes' a thing called Joe
> He got a smile that make the lilac wanna grow
> He got a way that make the angels—

Notice all the internal rhymes?

> When they know little Joe passing. . . .
> Sometime the cabin gloomy an' the table bare.

That 'and' is rhyming with 'ca–' whether you know it or not. That was very difficult to do, but once you accomplish it, it makes the song live, makes it easy to remember, and if the ideas are good, the whole thing begins to sparkle and take on four new lives instead of one. I'm only giving you a couple of tricks, how you break your head from those kind of things. But I can go into many more phases of that thing.

"Well, I could go on and on for a lot of things like that, but that takes great . . . a lot of patience, a lot of craftsmanship, a lot of know-how, and a lot of roots, you know, a lot of reading, a lot of literature. In other words, you're making poetic images plus technically ingenious, almost crossword puzzles, scrambled, they come out finally acrostics . . . You juggle them around."[36]

As we have seen, everything had political potential to Yip, but in 1943 his writing took on a consistently more political bent, one that emphasized his great commitment to human rights activism. In the end, as we will see later, even "Happiness Is a Thing Called Joe" came to be seen as part of Yip's "political agenda."

8 | A Pause for Harold Arlen

Yip Harburg's collaboration with Harold Arlen was one of the happiest and most productive of his lyric-writing career. Together, the two created approximately 150 songs, and although they took breaks from working with each other, they remained friends and always seemed to drift back to form their indomitable team. Yip, the word master, was an easy talker; Arlen, the music master, not so much. Therefore, in seeking to elucidate the nature of their partnership, it's necessary to use Yip's voice as well as Arlen's. In fact, Yip's is often more prevalent, but as Arlen chimes in, we see that Yip was also quite a storyteller, recrafting memories to match the message he wanted to put forward or the audience he wanted to entertain. As a result, as the years passed, some of his versions of what happened during their collaboration differed from Arlen's.

Harold Arlen, as the son of a Jewish cantor, had a life steeped in music. He received piano lessons as a young boy, showing an early musical talent . . . and he proved to have a nice singing voice as well. Being from a musical family, it's not surprising that his career headed in that direction. When Arlen left Buffalo for New York City, he used his experience as a jazz band musician back home to obtain a job playing at the Cotton Club in Harlem and writing tunes that reflected his Jewish roots and appreciation for African rhythms. As Yip explained it, "Harold's singing . . . derives from his father who was one of the great cantors in Buffalo and in Syracuse. And when Harold was a young sprout he sang in his father's choir and of course his great melodies are mostly improvised. They have a traditional sound but the cantor has to improvise most of his melodies and I think Harold comes to that directly inherited genetically but on top of that I think Harold adds something to it. He has everything that this great American democracy—at that time a great melting pot—has given him. And in it is almost a complete, wonderful contradiction, the whole suffering of the Hebrew children as they were being chased from one country to another, as well as the great humor of Shalom Aleichem."[1]

Yip noted in another interview that Arlen's music was "so special and so individual." He explained, "Well, first of all Harold doesn't use . . . anything that's recognizable as a cliché or the old tunes . . . he really uses the archaic theme and then develops it in his own individual way with great adroitness and beauty . . . Arlen background music really is Semitic plus Congo. It's the Negro music, the American Negro and the American rhythm and the American less sentimental, but a good deal of it is affected by, yeah, the Southern blues, jazz, plus the melodic Hebrew. And it's a terrific combination."[2]

Yip was attracted to Arlen's "ability to feel sorrow, to feel emotion and to feel laughter. But to do it not in terms of cliché, but in his own special contribution." As Yip compared him to George Gershwin, for example, Arlen was "deeper, more sorrowful, more introspective . . . which I kind of liked. But when he got out of that mood he could also fly and use whimsy and laughter in his own way. And I found that I could write both themes that had some profundity and meaning and that gave me, really, a teardrop feeling. And when he wrote his gay songs, even his gay songs had a little sadness in them."[3]

By the time that Yip and Arlen began work on *The Wizard of Oz*, they had become known as a successful team, especially because of *Life Begins at 8:40* and *Hooray for What!* Each enjoyed working with the other. As Arlen recalled, tunes such as "Fun to Be Fooled," "You're a Builder Upper," and "Let's Take a Walk Around the Block" from *Life Begins at 8:40* were "pretty smart stuff. And to be asked to do it, and to take it on, took *guts*. So I proved that I could come out of the Cotton Club. That's not a big deal . . . but it was an interesting road to travel . . . Then Yipper got an idea for a Broadway musical show—a satiric story about war, and how stupid it was. He called it *Hooray for What!*

"Now just see how strange things are in this business. We had some good songs in that show—'Down with Love' and 'God's Country' . . . But there was one sweet little ballad that was called 'In the Shade of the New Apple Tree' and *that* song got us *Wizard of Oz* . . . And I can tell you, there were plenty of other major songwriters who were damned unhappy and shocked when they heard that we'd gotten it, because they'd all been sitting around, *waiting* for that job."[4]

There was no question that Arlen loved working in Hollywood. "It was a great period! Maybe it was the accident of all of us working there because of the Depression. Practically every talent you can name. So many. Jerry Kern, Harry Warren, the Gershwins, Dorothy Fields and Jimmy McHugh. Oscar Hammerstein—even [Irving] Berlin, although he didn't stick around. All of us, writing pictures so well. We were all on the weekly radio *Hit Parade*. If we weren't first, we were second; if we weren't second, we were fourth. A sensational period. Lovely for me. I went to the studio when I damned well pleased, or when they called me. Got my check every week. And we were pouring it out!

"Oh sure, we all wrote picture scores that were bad. But people were having flops on Broadway, too, weren't they? It was a great life. Most of us played golf or tennis, or swam, and did our writing at the same time. I wrote at home. I could write at midnight, or at five in the afternoon, at nine—it made no difference. As long as I came in with something that the so-called producers liked . . . And, believe me, when it came to matters of quality, their guess was as good as mine."[5]

For Arlen, collaborating with a lyricist was very natural. "You wonder later," he told Max Wilk, "in mystery, how it all happens. It seems so natural. It seems like they were all born together, the music and the lyrics. They're not apart, you can't separate them . . . I guess I've always been very lucky in my collaborators. And lucky because I've always had something in my music that 'lights them up,' gets them enthusiastic. I don't know where it comes from. Every time I face a job, part of myself says, 'Jesus, how will I do it?' And then some other part of myself says, 'Go ahead—you have to.' Brother, you have to keep reminding yourself that you're a writer, to stand off and tell yourself, '*Go. Do it*.' A song becomes memorable *despite* its author. Oh, sure, you know if what you've written is good, or melodic, or well made, or all three. But nobody can sit down to write a hit. Think about how accidental it all was! I became a songwriter by accident!"[6]

Yip described their collaboration this way: "There was always a great knowledge between us of the psychological delicacy in criticizing each other and we were very careful not to hurt each other . . . we had certain means of communication, like birds, you know, of knowing when the other fellow was hurt and how to go about saying, 'Well, Yip that doesn't sing well,' or 'This needs a vowel sound,' or 'I don't feel this idea,' or I would say, 'Harold, I don't think this follows . . . I don't think I can express this thing in this way.' And we were able to change. He was able to change and I put great value on . . . whether he had my literary level, or not, or whether I had his musical level or not. I respected finally . . . for him to make the final decision musically, me to make the final decision lyrically. And lots of times we compromised when he didn't like a lyric or when I didn't like a tune . . . to respect each other's opinions."[7]

Yip also felt that "to work with Arlen is to experience the highest pleasures and the deepest pains of creativity. I thought I was a masochist but he beat me to it. He is more demanding of himself than ever my wife thought I was. More note paper would go into that paper basket, tune after tune, great tunes, that he wasn't satisfied with. Of course, the final result was a sense of achievement that was lasting and rewarding. One thing about working with Harold Arlen was to know that even if you didn't understand his music the first time you heard it, you didn't have to worry as a lyricist because you knew that your ear couldn't possibly attain the fine sensitivity that his was and that in a week or so after you slept on that song, it would get into your guts, into your dreams. And so that Johnny Mercer once came over to him after struggling with Harold Arlen's complicated tunes and rhythms. He was a little drunk, a little happy, at a party, he says, 'Your music gives me the heebie-jeebies.' And this is right after he had written 'Blues in the Night.'"[8]

There were times, later in life, when Arlen contradicted Yip's recollections of their songwriting experiences. He amusingly told his biographer, Edward Jablonski, and an interviewer that Yip was a major storyteller who fabricated some of the details of their collaboration. For example, Arlen remembered the writing of "Over the Rainbow" in a different way. After completing the "lemon-drop songs," a term Arlen used to describe all of the songs except for the ballad, he and Yip had to face the deadline that MGM had imposed on them. "We had finished most of the songs," Arlen told an interviewer, "all of the songs but the one for Judy in Kansas . . . and I knew what I wanted. Arthur Freed, the associate producer, couldn't understand what I was worried about. Most people don't understand what you're worried about because they think you do this and out it comes. But when you have to labor, most writers don't like that. It's nice to be gentle about gettin' at the piano and, you know, foolin' around a little while and coming up with an idea. But when it doesn't come, it becomes one of those things that bug ya. And most of us don't like to be bugged, not too long. And I said to Mrs. Arlen, I said, 'Let's go to Grauman's Chinese.' I said, 'You drive the car. I don't feel too well right now.' I wasn't thinking of work. I wasn't conscious of thinking of work. I just wanted to relax. And as we drove by Schwab's Drug Store on Sunset, I said, 'Pull over, please.' And she knew what I meant, and we stopped and I really don't know why, bless the muses, and I took out my little piece of manuscript and put down what you know now as 'Over the Rainbow.' Of course, it needed Mr. Harburg's lyric."[9]

Arlen reported that he did not call Yip at midnight, but rather the next day. During that time, according to his biographer, he also "contrived a simple, contrasting bridge, which he based on the idea of a child's piano exercise." When Yip told an audience at the 92nd Street Y (Young Men's and Young Women's Hebrew Association, or YM-YWHA) in Manhattan that this middle section of the song was inspired by Arlen's dog whistle, Arlen, who was in the audience, chimed in, "Not true." All those sitting around him chuckled as Yip continued with his story.[10]

The other major expansion on the truth that Arlen recalled of this period had to do with the writing of "Happiness Is a Thing Called Joe" for the film *Cabin in the Sky*. According to Yip, Arlen had brought the previously unused tune out of a trunk, a tune that Yip had always loved and Arlen hated. According to Jablonski, however, "Arlen's version, revealed to a friend long after, was different. Harburg arrived one day for work, excited over a poem he had clipped from a popular women's magazine (he forgot which). A contributor had written a verse about happiness being a thing called . . . Arlen forgot that name, too. A slight change in name would result in 'Happiness Is a Thing Called Joe.' Arlen liked it, but he had qualms. They could not lift an idea from a large-circulation publication and not expect some sort of repercussion and legal retaliation. Harburg was persuasive, assuring the uneasy Arlen that their song would not be an arrant plagiarism, but a variation on the theme. Besides, Harburg further assured Arlen, if the original author raised an issue, they would share the royalties (which would have been considerable) . . . Despite the Harburg flair for a good story, it is more likely that the melody was crafted to Harburg's final lyric—this was not a trunk tune."[11]

Memory is always an interesting and funny business. But none of these discrepancies affected Yip and Arlen's long-term friendship or future collaboration.

9 | Human Rights Activism Takes Center Stage

After the writing of "Brother, Can You Spare a Dime?" Yip Harburg became known for his commitment to human rights. For close to twenty years, he was able to flex his political muscles, especially because his ideas matched US rhetoric as fascism spread in Europe, imperialism in Asia, and military altercations worldwide. Yet, Yip's views made his so-called employers feel uncomfortable. As he told Max Wilk, "I had trouble all the time at Metro[-Goldwyn-Mayer], with executives. They'd call me in and say, 'Now look, we want a show here that has no messages. Messages are for Western Union. We like your stuff, but you're inclined to be too much on the barricades. Let's get down to the entertainment.' Sam Katz, Arthur Freed . . . they were always worried about me. But I always felt my power. They had to have me. If they wanted funny songs, there weren't too many around that could do them. If they wanted songs with some kind of class and quality—well, there weren't too many guys around like Larry Hart and the Gershwins. There were just a few of us, maybe five or six. I figured, hell, if they wanted me, they'd have to endure my politics.

"My wife thinks it was because I was liked—and she maintains I have a certain spell-binding charm, with men especially. Now that I look back on those days, I think she may be right. They were all frightened of my ideas, but they all liked me. All of them, even Louis Mayer. Maybe it was some sort of chemistry. I was never a wheeler-dealer, never a businessman *per se*, and they always thought I was a pretty poetic sort of guy and not a conspirator. They couldn't connect me with conspiratorial things, somehow. They always thought of me as living in a fairyland world of leprechauns and rainbows . . . therefore, I couldn't *really* throw a bomb. And I'd also always laugh at their fears. I'd joke with them, I'd kid them. I'd quote George Bernard Shaw. But in the end it wasn't so sunny—I was blacklisted."[1]

Perhaps Edelaine Harburg was right in her assessment that Yip's charm convinced others that they could overlook his politics in order to work with him. Or perhaps it was as Yip said, a matter of needing his keen wit and sensitivity . . . and his proven gift for writing lyrics. As Edward Jablonski wrote of Harold Arlen, "His relationship with the kinetic Harburg was curious. They did not agree on political matters, and Arlen at times admonished Harburg over the 'propaganda' in some of his lyrics. Yet he never refused to set them to music."[2] In spite of his more apolitical bent, Arlen was quick to say that music "doesn't argue, discuss, or quarrel . . . it just breathes the air of freedom."[3]

As Yip himself expressed it, "Harold was the gentlest person I've ever worked with. He had such feeling for me as a writer in how he criticized the work—even when I stepped on his cerebral toes every now and then because he thought I was too involved in politics all the time and that it was polluting the stage. The stage was not a pulpit, not a place for 'propaganda,' which he called it. I called it education; he called it propaganda.

"Harold had a feeling for my striving to be poetic in everything I did and he forgave me the political exuberance which I exuded. [But] one of the reasons there was a little split when he started to work with Johnny Mercer was because he thought I was what Bert Lahr called 'too foyvent' [fervent].

"[In time, Arlen came to see that my politics] was never destroying the entertainment value or the poetic value for the propaganda value. And besides, I never tried to propagandize. I tried to reason; I tried to educate. But he was very gentle with me. Most people were . . ."[4]

It's important at this point to consider how Yip Harburg defined human rights. It was evident from his earliest writing that he felt that all people were entitled to basic needs: housing, food, clothing, jobs, decent incomes, and the like. But it was also evident that he saw these basic needs as required for humanity to reach higher goals: freedom, equality, and peace in the broadest sense. Racism, religious bias, sexism, violence (whether local or global), greed, exploitation, self-centeredness were all factors that divided the world into the haves and the have-nots. As part of his own personal mission, Yip participated in human rights endeavors, which could mean campaigning for a particular political candidate; donating his own money, or raising money for causes he believed in; and, most important, using his talent for writing and his reputation in the film and theater worlds to work for the betterment of humankind. His preferred way to address any issue was through humor. Whether it was the urgency of the World War II years, his sense of confidence in his public persona, his seemingly steady (and comfortable) income in the early 1940s, or a combination of these, it appears that this was the historical moment that pushed him forward.

Yip's activism spanned from coast to coast. In April 1941, for example, he took time to write an appeal to Mayor Fiorello La Guardia of New York City, protesting possible budget cuts to his alma mater, Townsend Harris High School. In effect, Yip was defending the right of poor children to a top-notch public education. "The men it has turned out have added in great measure to the coffers of New York City," he noted, "because of their unique training in this unusual school . . . I, for one, doubt whether my contribution in the form of citizenship and taxes to the City and State of New York could have been as great were it not for the start I got at Townsend Harris."[5] Later that year, he and Burton Lane turned over proceeds of a song they wrote, "Share a Little," to the Los Angeles Community Welfare Federation. In fact, they had created the tune for the Community Chest effort, thereby lending their support to helping the poor receive basic needs.[6]

During the next year, 1942, Yip gave approval for the USO to use several of his songs for entertaining American troops—a nice gesture of support to the war effort, for although Yip loathed war, he understood the human rights crimes being committed worldwide and the need to stop them. In supporting the military effort, however, he maintained his use of wit and humor. This was evident in the lyrics he wrote to Lane's music for "The Son of a Gun Who Picks on Uncle Sam," which pointed out all sorts of national tensions that were thrown aside when the nation as a whole perceived itself under attack:

Verse
I hate war and war hates me,
And all you sailors hate the sea
The soldiers all hate reveille
Of that I am convinced
But no matter what or whom we hate

We're mighty glad to liquidate
When someone knocks the ship of state
I don't get it!
Well for inst.

Chorus
The army hates the bloomin' sight of the navy
And how the navy hates the bloomin' marines
But the army and the navy and marines'll take a slam
At the son of a gun who picks on Uncle Sam
Oh capital may take a wallop at labor
The C.I.O. may slug the A.F. Of L.
But the A.F. Of L. and the C.I.O.
Are ready to take a wham
At the son of a gun who picks on Uncle Sam

Though our melting pot may boil red hot
With a thousand diff'rent types
Though we lefts and rights may have our fights
We all stand pat on the no good rat
Who belittles the Stars and Stripes.

Oh, Florida may love to roast California
Republicans may roast the old Democrats
But a hundred and thirty million strong
Are ready to roast the ham
Of the one who picks on Uncle Sam
Of the son of a gun who picks on Uncle Sam.[7]

A particularly tricky part of international politics during World War II was determining how to handle the Soviet Union's participation on the Allied side. On the one hand, Russia was a friend, a nation to be supported and to sympathize with as it lost land and millions of lives to the Nazi onslaught. President Franklin D. Roosevelt himself had shown that giving a hand to the Soviets could help the United States as well. As early as 1933, he formally recognized the Soviet Union, after which trade, loans, and technical assistance steadily increased during the darkest days of the Great Depression. But on the other hand, the

Soviet Union had a communist government, one that had taken hold in 1917 after the Bolshevik Revolution. And communism was the natural enemy of capitalism.

An ideological cold war had begun between the Soviet Union and the US soon after World War I had ended in 1918, and this had a great effect not only on international relations, but on domestic policy. A Red Scare in the 1920s resulted in blacklists, government persecutions, and deportations of a number of citizens and residents who had shown sympathy not only to the reconstructed Russia, but to liberal causes such as labor organizing, women's suffrage, and peace. These hostile feelings were never resolved, so that even during World War II when people supported the Soviet war effort, there was an undercurrent of distrust and suspicion. Yip and others who were blacklisted several years after the war ended were often victimized simply because they had displayed compassion and promoted understanding of the Soviet system during the war years.

Yip was not the only celebrity who wished to help the beleaguered Russians. Take, for instance, the Tribute to Russia Day held at the Hollywood Bowl on June 22, 1943, in which Yip participated. The event, sponsored by Russian War Relief, Inc., Southern California Division, was designed to raise money and awareness of the tremendous loss of life, property, and freedom the Russian people were experiencing at that moment. The national committee of this organization included none other than First Lady Eleanor Roosevelt and Wendell Willkie. Among the list of Los Angeles sponsors were Harry Braverman, Joan Crawford, and Samuel Goldwyn. The mayor of Los Angeles, Fletcher Bowron, wrote a proclamation for the souvenir program, proclaiming June 2 "a day of tribute to Russia," and child actor Margaret O'Brien of MGM studios wrote a letter for the publication about her pen pals there. Actors Olivia de Havilland and Edward G. Robinson were on the evening's program.

Yip and composer Jerome Kern contributed a song, "And Russia Is Her Name," for the Tribute to Russia Day, and then used it in the 1944 MGM film *Song of Russia*.[8] The film, a love story between a prominent US symphony conductor (played by Robert Taylor) and a Russian concert pianist (played by Susan Peters) just before the German invasion, was quite sympathetic and immensely popular. The lyrics were most romantic in spirit and also interchangeable among countries. In later years, Yip recycled the piece as "And Israel Is Her Name."

> When I was very young I gave my heart away,
> Her cheeks were all the cherry trees
> That bloom in May;
> Her eyes were stars that lit the darkness
> With a silver flame,
> And she is still my love,
> And Russia is her name.
> She stood beside my plow, she kissed away my tears.
> And warmed my empty hands through all the empty years;
> And when she smiled, the heartbreak vanished,
> And the daybreak came,
> And she is still my own,
> And Russia is her name.
> I heard her sing,
> I heard her sing to me,
> It was the song of all the world
> In Spring to me.
> Then all the earth was green,
> Then all the fields were fair,
> And there was bread and wine and song
> For all to share,
> And there was love,
> A love that set my hungry heart aflame,
> And now that love is mine,
> And Russia is her name.[9]

For Yip, "And Russia Is Her Name" was a special ballad. As he noted, "That was a time that Russia was our ally. And we were making beautiful pictures and she was saving our boys on her front."[10] But in a short while, as we will see, the song contributed to Yip's loss of freedom to write for film and television.

Much of Yip's political work at this time centered around his commitment to the Roosevelt Administration. During 1943 and 1944, when the president's supporters were campaigning for his unprecedented fourth run for office, Yip was an outspoken organizer of the Hollywood Democratic Committee. Not only did the group work to raise money and awareness, and to campaign for FDR, but it also worked for state-wide candidates in both the primaries and the nationwide election. In 1942, Yip actively aided Culbert Olson in his unsuccessful bid for the governorship of California against Earl Warren, the Republican who went on to become chief justice of the United States. One of Yip's primary contributions was a song (with music by Arthur Schwartz) called "Don't Look Now, Mr. Warren," which listed many of Warren's weaknesses. Yip and Schwartz recycled it in the fall of 1944 against Thomas E. Dewey, who was running for president against Roosevelt. As these excerpts illustrate, the lyrics are quite pointed but full of the light-verse humor Yip valued:

> Don't look now Mr. Dewey
> But your record is fooey
> The soldier vote you jumbled
> On Russia you fumbled
> On Lend Lease you grumbled
> On World Peace you mumbled
> The Dumb'lls you've "assembled"
> Will be stumble-bumbled
> So Dewey . . . don't look now.
>
> Don't look now Mr. Dewey
> But the boys at your tables
> Don't wear union labels
> Roosevelt gave Labor . . . its labor gains
> But you give Labor . . . its labor pains
> The Icy isolationists will all be put to rest
> The blighters on the Dewey side
> Will be committing suicide by popular request
> November Seventh . . .[11]

The song was performed by Ethel Merman at the Liberal Party campaign rally for Roosevelt, Harry S Truman, and Robert Wagner at

Madison Square Garden in New York City on October 31, 1944. Other performers included Victor Borge, Bill Robinson, Frank Sinatra, and the ILGWU (International Ladies' Garment Workers' Union) Chorus.

Also during this time, Yip approached the folk songwriter Earl Robinson about collaborating. Robinson, creator of "The Ballad of Joe Hill," was active in crafting songs for political causes, and for Yip, this was the type of partner he needed to reach more people during the election year. Their first song together, "Free and Equal Blues," was first performed in November 1944, on a pre-election broadcast. Introduced by the hugely popular actor Humphrey Bogart, it was performed by Earl Robinson and Clarence Muse. The song told the story of the segregated blood supply that the armed services created during World War II—"white" donor blood for white soldiers; "black" donor blood for black soldiers—and was particularly meaningful as news of German, Italian, and Japanese raced-based atrocities became more widespread. The first four verses give an idea of the message of the song:

> I went down to that St. James Infirmary,
> And I saw some plasma there,
> And I ups and asks that doctorman
> "Is the donor dark or fair?"
> The doctor laughed a great big laugh,
> And puffed it right in my face,
> He says, "A molecule is a molecule, son,
> And the damn thing has no race."
> And that was news,
> Yes, that was news,
> That was very, very, very special news,
> 'Cause ever since that day
> I got those Free and Equal Blues.
>
> You mean you heard that Doc declare
> The plasma in that test tube there
> Could be white man, black man, yellow man, red?
> That's what he said.
> The Doc put down his doctor book,
> Gives me a very scientific look,

Speaks out plain and clear and rational,
"Metabolism is international."
And that was news,
Yes that was news,
That was very, very, very special news,
'Cause ever since that day
I got those Free and Equal Blues.

So he rigged up his microscope—
The doc I'm talkin' about—
With some Berlin blue-blood,
And by gosh it was the same
As Chungking, Kuibyshef, Chattanooga, Timbucktoo blood.
Why, them Aryans, they thought they were noble
They didn't even know the corpuscle was global,
Tryin' to disunite us with their racial supremacy,
Flyin' in the face of old man chemistry,
Takin' all the facts and tryin' to twist 'em,
But you can't overthrow the circulatory system!
And that was news,
Yes, that was news,
That was very, very, very special news,
'Cause ever since that day
I got those Free and Equal Blues.

So I stayed at that St. James Infirmary,
Wasn't going to leave that place,
This was too interesting.
I said to the Doc, "Gimme some more of that scientific talk-talk,"
And he did.
He said, "Melt yourself down into a crucible, son,
Pour yourself out into a test tube,
And whaddaya got?
3500 cubic feet of gas,
Same for the upper and the lower class.
(Well, we'll let that pass)."[12]

In the autumn of 1944, Yip and Robinson also wrote "Get Out and Vote," a song that first appeared in an animated film, *Hell-Bent for Election*, backed by the United Auto Workers Union:

Here's the way to win the war, win the war, win the war
Here's the way to win the war,
We gotta get out and vote.

To clinch that happy ending
On the Tokio, the Berlin, and the home front
The fellow with the bullet is depending
On the fellow with the ballot on the home front.

With management and labor
We'll keep our production humming
So go and tell your neighbor
That the New World Special is a coming.[13]

Yip felt passionately about his political work. For him, every aspect of it was tied to his commitment to human rights. While busy with the 1944 primary and national elections, for example, he found the need to reprimand David O. Selznick, an influential film producer who would not, apparently, take an active role in defeating the Republican candidates in California. Yip wrote to Selznick in May:

When you came to me two years ago asking for a song to be
written for China, I did not have to be cajoled or pleaded with. I
not only wrote the song gladly, but I also donated money gladly
. . . I responded to you because you came with a humanitarian
light in your eye, and with an important fire in your heart. I
did not ask you whether the Chinese that we are saving were
Republicans or Democrats. I did not make my contribution
dependant upon an illogical political line of demarcation. I made
it only on one consideration that they were people, people who
had to be saved from fascism. When I now came to you with the
same humanitarian plea to save your own State and your Country
from the incipient stages of fascism . . . by [the state legislators']
records in Congress, you let an illogical political obsolete party

line paralyze you into inactivity, thus giving up the good fight and forfeiting your very democracy by default . . . What if Himmler or Goering were running on the Republican ticket in the 12th and 13th Districts of California? Is there any logic in being a bad Republican first and a good citizen second?[14]

Amid all of this 1943–1944 political work, Yip and Arlen worked on the score for the musical *Bloomer Girl*. In essence, the show reflected some of Yip's most pronounced concerns. Set in the fictional upstate New York town of Cicero Falls in 1861, the book tells the story of Evalina Applegate, the daughter of a highly successful hoopskirt manufacturer. Evalina is also the niece of Dolly Bloomer, a feminist newspaper publisher who eschews hoops for the more comfortable but infamous bloomer costume. Evalina's father wishes her to marry Jeff Calhoun, a southern cotton plantation and slave owner, but Evalina, an abolitionist at heart, despises the idea. Jeff woos Evalina, and because of her influence on him, when war breaks out, he aids the North. Add to this the subplot of Pompey, Calhoun's runaway slave who is being protected by Dolly, and you have the makings for a musical with serious intentions.

Bloomer Girl surely encompassed Yip's desire to educate people about racism, misogyny, and war in the context of slavery, the early woman's rights movement, and the Civil War. He hoped that his audiences would be able to link the then current Jim Crow laws and practices, Rosie the Riveter assertiveness, and war stories with an earlier historical period—in other words, to give people food for thought within a lighthearted, funny, romantic musical. As he told Max Wilk, "There were so many new issues coming up with Roosevelt in those years, and we were trying to deal with the inherent fear of change—to show that whenever a new idea or a new change in society arises, there'll always be a majority that will fight you, that will call you a dirty radical or a Red. Or a Christian. I love [George] Bernard Shaw's *Androcles and the Lion*, because Shaw took such delight in showing how, when Christianity arose, the Romans considered the Christians such radicals, so dangerous, that they had to be thrown to the lions."[15]

The original idea for *Bloomer Girl* came from Lilith and Daniel

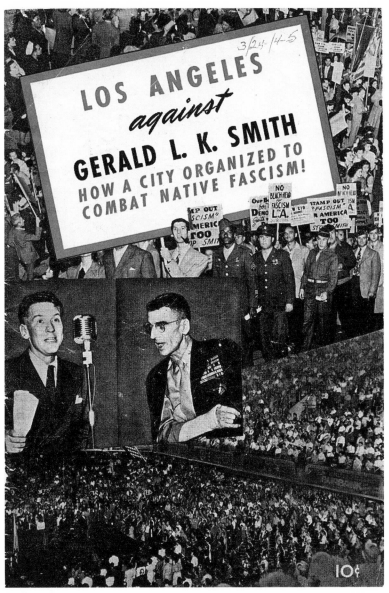

Cover of a pamphlet published by Mobilization for Democracy, 1945.
Yip was part of the effort to oppose Gerald L. K. Smith's attempts
to gain a foothold in Los Angeles.
Courtesy of the Yip Harburg Foundation

James. As Yip remembered, "I was working for Metro, he [Harold] was working for Paramount at that time. We were split up. And the Jameses, she was a costume designer and she'd come across a costume, the bloomer, and when she went back into research she found that the bloomer was a creation of a woman named Dolly Bloomer who was [part of the] first women's suffrage, women's rights movement; she was powerful and she was a contemporary of Susan B. Anthony and a group of wonderful people that decided that the way to release women . . . [was through dress reform]. The symbol was the hoop skirt they were wearing and the hoop skirt was an abominable torture chamber, really, for women. Most of them weighed fifty, seventy-five pounds. You know, they had all sorts of whale bone and everything else, and for the sake of Puritanism or whatever the style, they were all victims of that . . . that thing. And she thought, and very wisely so, she was ahead of Madison Avenue, Dolly Bloomer, in knowing that if she would just talk women's rights to women, it'd be in one ear, out the other. But she said, 'Get rid of those heavy hoop skirts. Wear bloomers like men. Let's get pants. Let's get their equal.' That they understood, their symbol, see? And through the bloomer she started the women's rights movement for the vote, for suffrage, for freedom to go to college, for freedom to be professionals and anything they wanted—doctors, lawyers. That was the first movement. That intrigued me. And that's all they [Lilith and Daniel James] had. Really that and some outline of a bad story.

"I said, 'Look, we'll give you some percentage of this. Let us take the idea and work it up.' And we got Fred Saidy, my collaborator, Sig Herzig, myself, we worked up the plot of the thing. They went ahead with the dialogue, Fred Saidy [and Sig Herzig] I mean. And I went ahead with the lyrics and music, and Harold . . . Harold was intrigued with the idea . . . Harold was never concerned with the sociological background of a thing. He kind of left that up to me and he sort of laughed that off. He thought that was an idiosyncrasy of mine, you know . . . But he was intrigued with the period, with the skirts, with the charm of the music of the time . . ."[16]

Fred Saidy, Sig Herzig, and Yip created a tale that was not particularly historically accurate, but it had a good sense of the politics that consumed upstate New York and the nation from 1848 to 1861. Of course, at the time it was written, much of women's history and the story of the antislavery movement were not that well known by the average person and certainly not taught in the schools. But beyond thinking about the past, Yip also wanted to write something with lasting value. As he said in 1977, "Now the songs I wrote tried to have, besides good rhyming, great music, well-expressed, and all the technicalities there, I wanted that other dimension which is the social comment because that gives the song a greater depth, greater meaning, and leaves you with something . . . To make social comment you must make it poetically. You must make it universally. You must make it so it isn't for a moment, it isn't for a time, but for timelessness."[17]

Let's take a look at each of the overriding themes, as they appear in the musical and as compared to reality. First is the early woman's rights movement. On July 19 and 20, 1848, this nation experienced its first Woman's Rights Convention, which was held in Seneca Falls, New York. The five organizers—Elizabeth Cady Stanton, Lucretia Mott, Martha Wright, Mary Ann McClintock, and Jane Hunt—were all active in the antislavery and temperance campaigns. Seneca Falls human rights activists resided side by side with the growing industrial nature of upstate New York that sprouted along the Erie Canal system. Factories and a new railway line brought with them immigrant and poor laborers as well as the early nineteenth-century evangelical revivalist awakening, giving the area its nickname, the "Burned-Over District." One of the numbers Yip presented to his audiences was "Sunday in Cicero Falls," a tongue-in-cheek portrayal of such a town as Seneca Falls in 1861 that hints of Christian morality, temperance, and a sexual awakening more in tune with the twentieth century than the nineteenth. A sample of the lyrics includes these lines:

Sunday in Cicero Falls
Sunday in Cicero Falls
In this lovely merry land
Main Street looks like fairyland
When the Angelus calls
Ginghams are bright
Collars are white

Sunday in Cicero Falls
Sunday in Cicero Falls
Hearts never blunder where
Girls wear such underwear
Sunday in Cicero Falls
Sunday in Cicero Falls

Sunday in Cicero Falls
Sunday in Cicero Falls
With all this underpinning there
Who would think of sinning there
When the Angelus calls
Morals are right
Corsets are tight
Sunday in Cicero Falls
Sunday in Cicero Falls

The sinners join up with the virtuous fringe
They pass the saloon with that righteousness cringe
And Bartender Murphy remarks with a twinge
"Virtue is its own 'revinge.'"

Old Banker Hodge with a nose for investment
Is making his weekly appeal to the test-ment
He's giving his conscience its weekly repairing
His morals are getting Sabbatical airing
He's taking his soul out of camphor balls
Sunday in Cicero Falls
Sunday in Cicero Falls.[18]

The 1848 Seneca Falls Woman's Rights Convention resulted in the creation of a document called the "Declaration of Sentiments," which was fashioned after our nation's Declaration of Independence. In this case, however, the authors listed grievances against the male-dominated political and social system that resulted in discrimination against women, and then announced the resolution to work for women's rights in all areas of life. Once the movement got underway, there were conventions in state after state; lobbying on the local, state, and federal levels to change laws; and efforts to achieve equality for women within their personal relationships with men. Religion, education, employment, marriage, domestic violence, and child custody were just a few of the areas addressed.

The one issue that attracted momentary attention, and was soon discarded because of the criticism it also attracted, was dress reform. This involved the wearing of the bloomer outfit, a fashion introduced by Elizabeth Smith Miller, Elizabeth Cady Stanton's cousin, and made popular by Amelia Bloomer through her newspaper *The Lily*. The bloomer costume consisted of loose, Turkish-style trousers gathered at the ankles and covered by a dress that usually reached somewhere between the knee and mid-calf. In the end, however, even such strong-minded women as Stanton decided that wearing the outfit, no matter how sensible and comfortable it was, harmed the movement's work on other more demanding issues.

For Yip, the bloomer costume became a symbol for this serious movement about which little was known in 1943. He used his ficti- tious Dolly Bloomer, her costume, her outspoken manner, and her great effect upon her niece, Evalina, to bring out the issues and emo- tions that would resonate with contemporary audiences. For example, in the lively number "Grandma Was a Lady" (later renamed "It Was Good Enough for Grandma"), Yip illustrated the changing expecta- tions from one generation of women to the next:

Verse
Grandma was a lady, she sewed and cleaned and cooked
She scrubbed her pots and raised her tots
The dear old girl was hooked
She stitched her little stitches
Her life was applesauce
The thing that wore the britches was boss.
Yes the thing that wore the britches was boss
She had no voice in gov'ment
And bondage was her fate
She only knew what love meant
From eight to half past eight

And that's a hell of a fate!
It was:

Chorus
Good enough for Grandma that good old gal
With her frills and her feathers and fuss
It was good enough for Grandma
Good enough for Grandma
But it ain't good enough for us.

Verse
When Granny was a lassie, that tyrant known as man
Thought woman's place was just the space
Around a frying pan
He made the world his oyster
Now it ain't worth a cuss
This oyster he can't foister on us.
Our brains against his muscle
Our tea against his rum
Look behind the bustle
For the shape of things to come
Join up with fife and drum!
It was:

Chorus
Good enough for Grandma that good old gal
With her frills and her feathers and fuss
It was good enough for Grandma
Good enough for Grandma
But it ain't good enough for us.

Verse
We won the revolution in seventeen seventy six
Who says it's nix for us to mix
Our sex with politics
We've bigger seas to swim in
And bigger words to slice
Oh sisters are we women or mice?

Oh sisters are we women or mice?
Look twice before you step on
The fair sex of the earth
Beware our secret weapon
We could stop giving birth.
Take that for what it's worth!
It was:

Chorus
Good enough for Grandma that good old gal
With her frills and her feathers and fuss
It was good enough for Grandma
Good enough for Grandma
But it ain't good enough for us.[19]

Yip also identified one of the most important links in the struggle for human rights in the nineteenth century and, in a sense, predicted its importance in the twentieth: the connection between women's rights and civil rights. In *Bloomer Girl* he presented the antislavery and woman's rights movements as interconnected as they truly were. In 1840, for instance, Elizabeth Cady Stanton and Lucretia Mott met and became friends at the World Anti-Slavery Convention held in London. It was there they first spoke of organizing a woman's rights meeting. In another case, Mary Ann McClintock and her husband, Thomas, became founding members of the Western New York Anti-Slavery Society. Martha Wright, who lived in neighboring Auburn, actively supported the work of Harriet Tubman, who eventually established a home there. Hiding and helping runaway slaves to reach Canada, raising money for the cause, and working against the 1850 Fugitive Slave Act were all part of the everyday life of activists in the Seneca Falls area.

Yip explained his understanding of this historical connection in several interviews in which he also discussed the dynamic song of the runaway slave Pompey, "The Eagle and Me." In the story, the song is prompted by the "master's" arrogant question to his errant slave, "What made you do this to me?" In his musical answer, Pompey (and Yip) express the essential human need for freedom—the right of all people to

Margaret Douglass as Dolly Bloomer; Dooley Wilson as the runaway slave, Pompey; and Joan McCracken as Daisy in *Bloomer Girl*, 1944. Courtesy of Eileen Darby Images, Inc.

own their lives. This message is given deeper meaning when the young women working on the woman's rights newspaper join Pompey in the chorus.

Verse
What makes the gopher leave his hole
Tremblin' with fear and fright
Maybe the gopher's got a soul
Wantin' to see the light
That's it oh yes oh yes that's it
The scripture has it writ
Betcha life that's it
Nobody like hole
Nobody like chain
Don't the good Lord all around you make it plain?

Chorus
River it like to flow
Eagle it like to fly
Eagle it like to feel its wings against the sky
Possum it like to run
Ivy it like to climb
Bird in the tree and bumble bee want freedom
In Autumn or Summer time.
Ever since that day
When the world was an onion
'Twas natural for the spirit to soar and play
The way the Lord wanted it
Free as the sun is free
That's how it's gotta be
Whatever is right for bumblebee
And river and eagle is right for me.
We gotta be free
The eagle and me.[20]

In 1978, Yip told Studs Terkel, "You know, everything is related. When you think of the Whole Man, you're a whole man. In *Bloomer*

Girl, . . . [w]e showed that the women's movement was part of an indivisible fight for equality. Equality cannot be divided."[21] In another interview, Yip traced his thoughts to his own history as a Jew. "Well of course the song comes out of the show, naturally. I mean, you've got a scene, you've got a plot point to make and at this point in *Bloomer Girl* where you have the important point to make of a Negro slave who runs away from his plantation and ends up in the underground sanctuary of the women who were . . . with Dolly Bloomer at the time fighting for women's rights . . . And the women at the time who were very farsighted in their thinking, very progressive, knew that when you fight for freedom, when you fight, it isn't just for women's rights. It's for all rights, that freedom is indivisible, that the fight for freedom is the same as the fight against slavery, that it's all one fight and that slavery which is a much more obvious fight than women, of course, is the front line of that fight, that if you lose that fight you lose this fight, if you win that fight, if you can free the slaves, you free the next minority.

"And the Jews have known this for a long time. The Jews were more aware of it than any other tribe in the world because they were the first ones to suffer fascism under Pharaoh, which is thousands of years ago. The first freedom rider was Moses who came along and the whole Passover Seder and ceremony is devoted entirely to freedom, to a fight for freedom, to how you get out of slavery, so that the Jews being a minority have always known that if there's any other minority being enslaved anywhere in the world that it's their fight. If that fight is lost down south, the fight for the freedom of the Jews is lost and the women knew that. If the fight for . . . Semitism is lost, the fight for slavery's lost and the fight for women is lost.

"So in the show we showed that hook up in a remarkable way, a rather very ingenious way. The girl is a northern girl who is the daughter of a hoopskirt manufacturer and so we brought in the economic determinism there too, whose whole factory and economic status depended on hoopskirts. Now, Dolly Bloomer came in to fight the hoopskirts by saying, well, let women be liberated from the fifty-pound hoopskirts and wear bloomers the same as men, [but this is] why [the manufacturer] loses business . . . his daughter, now, becomes enamored of a southerner who has a slave and the slave runs away and she teaches [her suitor] this lesson then. No matter how much he thinks he's done for that slave, no matter how much he thinks he's helped and been his brother, he still hasn't given that slave freedom. He may have given him . . . medical care, but the slave is a man. He hasn't given him his manhood. And when the slave confronts his master with this point . . . and the master says, 'My God, Pompey, how could you do this to me?' . . . 'Such infidelity. Didn't I treat you good? I give you education and . . . food, always liked you, never whipped you . . .'And the guy says, 'Boss, . . . There's a disease,' he says, 'that can't be cured by . . . well-meaning, patronizing thing.' And he says, 'And that's freedom.' And he proceeds to teach this young man through a song . . . Well, when you do it with a beautiful Arlen tune, why, a lecture like that might go in one ear and out the other but it doesn't when you say [Yip sings]

> River it like to flow
> Eagle it like to fly
> Eagle it like to feel its wings against the sky

You see, the power of music and the power of words and that those two powers are interrelated and connected artistically, you're teaching, you're doing for humanity what teachers do for children, what we all must do for each other."[22]

When asked by an interviewer how he came up with the line, "Ever since that day when the world was an onion," perhaps one of the lines most commented on in all of Broadway's lyrics, Yip responded, "I remembered it from a geology class. I remember the instructor saying [the earth] had layers of layers like an onion. And I never forgot that image of the world."[23] None other than the great Broadway composer/lyricist Stephen Sondheim praised this particular image. In his 2010 book *Finishing the Hat*, Sondheim referred to Yip as "one of the most brilliant technicians of the Golden Age," Irving Berlin and Cole Porter being the other two. "One of my favorite lyric lines," Sondheim continued, "comes from a song of his, as does one of my favorite couplets . . . both for the same reason: they each conjure up an ethos. The line is from the song, 'The Eagle and Me':

Ever since the day
When the world was an onion . . .

The couplet is from 'Sunday in Cicero Falls':

Even the rabbits
Inhibit their habits
On Sunday in Cicero Falls.

Lyrics don't come any better than that."[24]

Toward the end of *Bloomer Girl*, the townspeople of Cicero Falls turn out to see a presentation of *Uncle Tom's Cabin* during which a slave auction is staged. Pompey, the runaway slave, is brought on stage while his "master" is in the audience. The auctioneer sings "Man for Sale," a plaintive and heart-rending song:

Man for sale
Nice big man for sale
Look at them hands look
Look at them strong cotton pickin' hands
Look at them rock-bustin' hands
Log-rollin' steamboat-loadin' hands
He good as forty mules
Look at them shoulders
Good shoulders
They can hold up the sky

He's yours for the price of a rabbit's foot
And he don't eat much and he don't dream much[25]

By a twist of fate, just as Pompey's master tries to reclaim him, news of the outbreak of the Civil War is announced. This brings us to the third element of Yip's human rights concerns—peace. One of *Bloomer Girl*'s central expressions against war came through Agnes de Mille's choreography. De Mille had originally worked with Yip and Arlen on *Hooray for What!* but her "Hero Ballet" was not included in the final production. She subsequently gained critical acclaim for her dream sequence in Rodgers and Hammerstein's *Oklahoma!* which opened in 1943. Yip brought her in on *Bloomer Girl* soon after. For this musical, she created the "Civil War Ballet," which reflected the torment for women who had to send their men and boys off to war only to see them return home wounded or in coffins. Yip felt that de Mille's choreography did not match with his otherwise humorous tone; Arlen, however, liked it. The ballet was constantly changed, but it still was a very serious art piece that illustrated the tragic consequences of war on women's emotional lives. In the end, audience reaction to the ballet was so positive that Yip admitted he was wrong. It remained a vital part of the final *Bloomer Girl* production.[26]

Still, Yip was determined to end the musical on an optimistic, romantic high note. Besides having the federal government purchase bloomer outfits from Evalina's father's factory for a special 241st Volunteer Zouave Regiment, he also wanted a song. As he later recalled, "We needed an anti-war song there and I thought [about] . . . the battlefield, the terror of war's not confined to the battlefield alone. The poor lads that we send over there to be sacrificed, well they're soon liberated from a world that rests on this crazy premise for its existence, and I thought that the suffering of the wives and the women and the sweethearts that goes on forever, forever, is certainly the most unbearable part of war, because they're waiting for the boys to come home."[27] The song Yip used was "When the Boys Come Home," which originally started the musical as Evalina's sisters waited for their traveling salesmen husbands to return home from business trips. At the end of the show, the song holds a completely different meaning — one most emotional and poignant for World War II audiences:

Verse
Stitch stitch pray and sleep
Men must work and women must weep
'Twas ever thus since time began
Woman oh woman must wait for man
Stitch stitch tie the strings
This is the sorry scheme of things
And only one song keeps hearts abeat
And only one thought makes waiting sweet

Chorus
When the boys come home
The clouds will trip lightly away, away
The clouds will trip lightly away
When the boys come home
We'll all be as merry as May, as May
We'll all be as merry as May
There'll be drums and trumpets, tea and crumpets
Out on the village green
A silver moon for that reunion scene
Oh, what joy when the boys come home
The clouds will trip lightly away, away
The clouds will trip lightly away
There'll be drums and trumpets, tea and crumpets
Out on the village green
A silver moon for that reunion scene
Oh what joy when the boys come home
The glorious sound of the tramping feet
Will echo down the winding street
That leads to a land where lovers meet
And may it prove so sweet, so sweet
That they will never more roam
When the boys come home.[28]

As Yip's son Ernie later recalled about the appearance of the song near the beginning of the show, "I was in the audience, and I assure you that every single heart and head in that audience interpreted the last two lines to mean, 'When the war ends and the soldiers come home.' So the big 'joke' was that it was actually salesmen that were coming home. Typical Yip—because this was about as clever an antiwar message that one could possibly pull off during the great patriotic fervor of the times."[29]

As with all of Yip's musicals, there had to be a good solid ballad that would wow audiences and produce income. In the case of *Bloomer Girl*, this honor went to "Right as the Rain," a beautiful Harburg/Arlen song. As Yip recalled, "I needed a love song in *Bloomer Girl*, so I wrote

'Right as the Rain.' I didn't want to say, 'Oh, I love you forever. You are the spring and the blossoms.' I said it more poetically: 'Right as the rain, that falls from above . . .' It's a good, mature evaluation of a love situation, not an attempt to compare feelings associated with love to a clichéd notion of romance . . . It didn't say it's a miracle, sent by God, only something between us two . . . It's a feeling on a plane of person to person, not riddled with myths or miracles."[30]

Right as the rain
That falls from above
So real so right is our love
It came like the Spring
That breaks through the snow
I can't say what it may bring
I only know, I only know
It's right to believe
Whatever gave your eyes this glow
Whatever gave my heart this song
Can't be wrong
It's right as the rain
That falls from above
And fills the world with the bloom of our love.
As rain must fall, as day must dawn
This love, this love must go on.[31]

Bloomer Girl opened on October 5, 1944, and was a huge success, running until April 27, 1946. Songs such as "Evalina," "The Eagle and Me," "When the Boys Come Home" and "Right as the Rain" were recorded and sung for the eager ears of radio and live audiences. It's also interesting to note one final thing about *Bloomer Girl*. In 1977, Yip wrote some new material for the musical. There is no evidence that Arlen ever set the lyrics to music or that they were ever performed. This particular lyric is important for what it says about Yip and his continuing belief that human equality is the key element in an equation for world peace. The song was written for Dolly Bloomer to sing at a rally during which she is being heckled by a group of men.

'Till the flag we wave
Waves for all of us,
The strong, the meek,
Mighty and small of us,
This home of ours
Will never be
The home of the brave,
Or the free.

'Till the land we love,
Loves every one of us,
The black, the white,
Daughter and son of us,
This land of ours
Will never be
The shining gem,
From sea to sea.

We will never be free,
We will never be strong,
We will never have peace,
'Till we all belong,
'Till we all belong,
'Till we all embrace,
'Till we all belong
To the human race.[32]

As World War II wound down, Yip turned his eyes to the formation of the United Nations. For him, as for so many other people, this
new reenvisioning of the League of Nations held some hope for world
peace. The United Nations promised to be more inclusive than the
former league, and with US leadership, Yip and others felt sure that the
world would take on a democratic and humanistic aspect. The fact that
Franklin D. Roosevelt was a key voice in the creation of the UN Charter
signaled to Yip that the institution would focus on human rights.

To write a new song in honor of the founding of the UN, Yip turned
once again to Earl Robinson. Together, they crafted "The Same Boat,

Brother," a rousing, uplifting number. It became part of radio producer Norman Corwin's tribute to the UN presented live on CBS on June 17, 1945 (a mere two months after FDR's death), for which Yip provided several of his World War II era songs and wrote part of the script. The song was repeated on November 15 in Hollywood for "A Folk Musical Based on Front Line Songs of the United Nations." "The Same Boat, Brother" expressed Yip's hope for a new, interconnected, peaceful world.

Verse
The Lord looked down from his holy place,
Said, "Lordy me, what a sea of space,
What a spot to launch the human race."
So he built him a boat for a mixed up crew,
With eyes of black and brown and blue,
And that's how come that you and I
Got just one world with just one sky.

Chorus
We're in the same boat, brother,
Yes, it's the same boat, brother,
And if you shake one end you're gonna rock the other
It's the same boat, brother.

Verse
Oh the boat rolled on through storm and grief,
Past many a rock and many a reef.
What kept them going was a great belief
That they had to learn to navigate,
'Cause the human race was special freight.
If we didn't want to be in Jonah's shoes,
We better be mates on this here cruise.

Chorus
'Cause it's the same boat, brother,
Yes, it's the same boat, brother,
And if you shake one end you're gonna rock the other,
It's the same boat, brother.

Verse
Well, the boiler blew somewhere in Spain,
The keel was smashed in the far Ukraine,
And the steam poured out from Oregon to Maine.
Oh, it took some time for the crew to learn
What's bad for the bow ain't good for the stern.
If a hatch takes fire in China Bay,
Pearl Harbor's decks gonna blaze away.

Chorus
We're in the same boat, brother.
Yes, it's the same boat, brother,
And we must live with each other
In the same boat,
The very same boat, brother.[33]

But the end of World War II on August 15, 1945, did not bring an end to the world's troubles nor to Yip's concerns. That year's use of the atomic bomb on Japan on August 6 and 9 established the United States as the only nation to have this lethal, terrifying weapon, but within a short time, a nuclear arms race between the United States and the Soviet Union added fire to the Cold War and tensions within the UN. Albert Einstein worked with the Emergency Committee of Atomic Scientists, which aimed to control the bomb and its further development. On June 29, 1946, Einstein wrote a letter thanking Yip for a contribution he had made to this effort.[34] But Yip's political work did not stop there. As the years went by, he continued to express his concerns about equality, freedom, and peace in his lyrics, his activism, and eventually, his poetry.

10 | A Pause for Agnes de Mille

During the staging of *Bloomer Girl*, choreographer Agnes de Mille created the "Civil War Ballet," a serious performance piece designed to illustrate women's reactions to war and its effects on them. Once the dance was performed, Yip Harburg, in particular, had a strong reaction against its seriousness in a musical that he had meant to be lighthearted, romantic, and humorous although carrying serious messages. The disagreement between Yip and de Mille became quite intense. As her memoir *And Promenade Home* illustrates, artists can come to near blows during the intense process of creativity; yet they can also compromise and admit when they are wrong.

As de Mille wrote, "I was offered a show about the Civil War by Harold Arlen and E. Y. Harburg and I thought I saw an opportunity to do a ballet which would embody the almost universal feeling of sacrifice of those at home. The score contained one rhapsodic outburst, a colloquial Hymn to Freedom, 'The Eagle and Me,' and eight or ten of the loveliest songs I'd ever heard . . . I quickly agreed to do the show, thankful that I would have a chance at last to put on the stage what was in my heart. But would they accept a serious ballet about women's emotions in war? I asked. About why people were willing to go out and die? About why we were willing to let them? Yes, yes, they said. Of course they would. They hoped this would be a show with significance, seriousness and poignancy . . . I gathered that, in this group, the ideas of freedom, patriotism and brotherhood might be considered and even mentioned, albeit, indirectly. I signed for *Bloomer Girl*."[1]

De Mille was inspired by her assignment. Within four days she had drafted out her twelve-minute ballet and had her dancers well on their way to performance level. Among them were artists who would become well known—James Mitchell, Nora Kaye, and Alicia Alonso among them. After five days, de Mille showed the work to her "bosses with self-satisfaction and the complete pride and belief of the whole group. I have never felt so smug in my life, delighted to find such tragic strengths within me. Hitherto I had been only wistful or comic.

"At the end of the showing there was not a sound. The silence did not, however, betoken awe. The men were all just as disappointed as they could possibly be. Harburg found voice first and, stepping over the bodies of three prone, sweating girls, addressed me. 'No. No. No. This is all wrong. Where is the wit? Where is the humor?' I was naturally taken aback and a little short in my answers.

"'Humor? In war?'

"'But this is tragic. Where is the courage? This isn't real de Mille. This isn't what we bought.'

"'How the hell do you know what real de Mille is? I think this is the realest thing I ever did. It is not *Oklahoma!* if that is what you mean. If you wished to buy *Oklahoma!* you're a little late.'"[2]

As the dancers sat around wide-eyed and tired, the others began throwing ideas around. Some, especially Yip, wanted the women to be shown waiting for their husbands in a hopeful and humorous way. Harold Arlen wanted the dance to end with a celebration of peace with all of the men arriving home unhurt. De Mille thought that this was all wrong, especially because she wanted to touch audiences about the current war. Somewhat stunned, she finally forced her own voice into the conversation: "'I took this show in order to do a ballet about women in war—and we don't find the war funny. A frivolous ending would not be true to what everyone in the whole world is feeling.'"[3]

De Mille started revising the work. Her first attempt included a happy ending with neither death nor injuries. The dancers thought it dishonest. She sat down to think again, but could not come up with a new version. "It is one matter to think up a new variation when you find you have not said what you intended. It is another to have said exactly what you intended and then, under duress, try to force a fresh version," she recalled.[4] That fresh version came when she thought about her husband, Walter Foy Prude, who she had married on June 14, 1943, and who was then fighting in the war.

The next day, after the dancers had rehearsed the new changes, de Mille once again showed her ballet to the creative team and the producer, John C. Wilson. And once again, she received a strong reaction, especially from Yip, who was most concerned about how the audience would receive it. As de Mille told it, Yip responded,

A tense moment during *Bloomer Girl* rehearsals, 1944. From left: Agnes de Mille, Fred Saidy, Yip, Miles White, Lemuel Ayers, and Sig Herzig. Courtesy of Eileen Darby Images, Inc.

"'Look . . . Women will faint. They'll weep. They'll leave the theater.'

"'You don't know women,' I countered. 'They'd rather have their grief talked about and shared than made light of.'

"'Well, it doesn't go in. Not this version. That's final.'"[5]

De Mille felt that because the other dances in the show were jubilant and humorous, the show's other creators understood that she meant this particular number to be serious. In addition, by now, the entire Broadway community seemed to be talking about the conflict, and de Mille herself became nervous, dazed, tired, and bad-tempered. She truly believed that the ballet was the best work she had done to date. So she became subversive:

"Whenever one of the bosses was in the theater, I showed the version they liked, but at home, at night, I tried to rework the whole matter on paper. And in the mornings, with dancers posted at the doors to give warning, I secretly rehearsed a fourth version. I had composed four ballets in four weeks. I don't know how the dancers stood it. But by this time they were as mad and as determined as I was. Every time I gave way on a point they despised me. Every time I stood fast, their approbation shone in their eyes and they silently changed shirts and shoes and waited at attention for the next set of orders."[6]

Arlen was the one person let in on de Mille's secret plan. He believed the ballet was "close to being great" and worked with the choreographer to "fix what's wrong." "I hope to God," de Mille remembered him saying, "it stops the show opening night and shuts their clamoring mouths."[7]

Things came to a head when *Bloomer Girl* arrived in Philadelphia for a preview run. It was there that John Wilson informed de Mille that the ballet was out, to be replaced by a not-yet-determined song. De Mille requested that her dancers be allowed to perform the number on opening night, just so they could experience an audience's reception to their hard work. So that night, de Mille's secret, fourth version of the ballet was performed. As she related, "White-faced, the dancers performed with a tension that tightened the exchange between stage and audience to the point of agony. Their gestures that night were absolute, their faces like lamps, and in the hush when Lidija Franklin faced [James] Mitchell, looked into her returned soldier's eyes and then covered her own because of what she saw, no one breathed. In the stillness around me several women bowed their heads.

"I stood at the back . . . At the end, there was no sound, but as Mitchell and Franklin returned for the hallelujah parade, there was cheering.

"As the people filed out past me, one woman, recognizing me, stood for a moment with her eyes covered and then quietly handed me her son's Navy wings."[8]

Yip, too, was very moved. At the post-opening party, he put his arms around de Mille and exclaimed, "Goddamit! I've begun to like the dreary thing. To think that a lousy bit of movement can make people weep, and me among them! A lousy bit of movement!" Wilson, too, admitted that they had all been wrong. Only Arlen shouted "Hurrah!" and kissed de Mille in glee.[9]

And so ended one of the most famous artistic differences in Broadway history.

11 | Yip's Case Study of *Finian's Rainbow*

After *Bloomer Girl* opened, there was a lull in Yip Harburg's musical career as compared with the previous years. Besides his political work, he wrote songs for the 1944 films *Hollywood Canteen* and *Can't Help Singing*, the 1945 stage revue *Blue Holiday*, and the 1946 film *Centennial Summer*. But most important was his 1946 collaboration with co-librettist Fred Saidy and composer Burton Lane on *Finian's Rainbow*. The musical opened on Broadway on January 10, 1947, and ran for 725 performances, closing on October 2, 1948. It won the first Tony Awards ever given for choreography (Michael Kidd) and acting (David Wayne), and six Donaldson Awards (established in honor of W. H. Donaldson, the founder of *Billboard*), including Best Musical and Best Book (Yip and Saidy). It is noteworthy that at the time, *Finian's Rainbow* was one of those rare new musicals not based on a book or film.

Finian's Rainbow is a fun musical with serious human rights messages about people's desire for wealth—whether it be gold, property, material goods, or even power—and the idiocy of racist ideologies and practices. The first theme, that of the quest for wealth, involves the story of Finian McLonergan, an Irishman with an ingenious idea about how to get the riches he has desired but never had. He decides to steal the leprechauns' crock of gold, and with his daughter Sharon in tow, to flee to the US state of "Missitucky" and plant the crock near Fort Knox, where it will certainly reproduce itself. An extra bonus is the three wishes that come with the crock. Once settled in Rainbow Valley, Missitucky, where Finian obtains a small plot of land, he and Sharon become embroiled in the town's affairs. Sharon falls in love with sharecropper and would-be organizer Woody Mahoney, and, with Finian's help, immediately starts planning her life with him. In the meantime, Og, a leprechaun, pursues Finian in order to recapture the crock before its magic disappears and Og becomes mortal.

The second theme in this complex, yet amazingly easy-to-follow plot involves racist senator Billboard Rawkins, who wants to obtain Finian's land because government geologists report there is gold on it.

Rawkins is inadvertently turned into a black man when Sharon, unknowingly standing over the ground where the crock is buried, wishes that he could understand what it's like to be black in the racist South of 1947. To add to this, the report that gold has been discovered in Rainbow Valley leads the businessmen of the great mail-order company "Shears-Robust" to offer unlimited credit to the sharecroppers, who use the money for tools to farm tobacco and for useless luxuries. With many twists and turns, funny dialogue, and hummable tunes, *Finian's Rainbow* ends happily except that Finian himself moves on in search of his next rainbow, leaving Sharon behind.

Yip told Max Wilk that he "really loved" *Finian's Rainbow*. "I was so wrapped up in it. The whole thing had come to me as two separate ideas which somehow worked together. I'd wanted to do a show about a fellow who turns black, down South; and I'd always loved the idea about a leprechaun with a pot of gold. And when Saidy and I had written it all—bang, it was there. It was right. No rewrites. Just the way I'd always wanted it to be."[1] (Actually, there was constant rewriting during the creation and production process.)

To an audience at Northwood Institute in Dallas, Texas, Yip went into more detail: "It was written in Roosevelt's time. For the first time, the black man was being given some recognition. So it occurred to me to do a show about [Senator Theodore] Bilbo and [Representative John] Rankin [of Mississippi]. The only way I could assuage my outrage against their bigotry was to have one of them turn black and live under his own [Jim Crow] laws and see how he felt about it. I was making a point to every white person: 'Look—we use the word reincarnation. You might come back as a black, and here's how you'll be treated if you do. How do you like it?' I said to myself, 'Gee, this is a great idea; how can I make it into a musical?' Well, it was a little grim. So I put it in my notebook for future reference and forgot about it.

"Two years later, I was reading James Stephens's *The Crock of Gold*, a beautiful book with all the lovely Irish names and the leprechaun ... I love Irish literature—James Stephens, Sean O'Casey. I felt easy working with Irish ideas ... Of course, I was still fed up with our economic system and the whole idiocy of taking gold from California and planting it in Fort Knox. Suddenly, the three streams of thought about

Ad for the Philadelphia tryout of *Finian's Rainbow*, 1946.
Courtesy of the Yip Harburg Foundation

Bilbo and Rankin, the Irish stories, and about Fort Knox clicked in my mind. I said to myself, 'Wouldn't it be wonderful if a pixie Irishman, Finian, poverty-stricken, working his hands to the bone year after year to feed his daughter, told himself, "I'll never get anywhere diggin' this soil for spuds and potatoes. Every American is rich and you know why? Because they plant gold in Fort Knox. If I had a little gold I'd plant it there and get rich too."' Makes sense. Well, how can he get the gold? Only from the leprechauns, who have a crock of gold. So he'll have to lay a trap for a leprechaun.

"Things began to work out in my mind. I next remembered an old Irish joke about an Irishman who manages to catch a leprechaun and borrow his crock of gold to get the three wishes that come with it. He and his wife ride to Dublin to consider how to use the wishes wisely. They agree to sleep on the matter when Bridget, the wife, sees a beautiful waffle iron in a shop window. 'Oh, Casey, I wish I had that waffle iron.' And there it was beside her. Her husband, furious, shouts, 'You used up one-third of our wishes! I wish the goddam waffle iron would get right up your ass and stay there!' And sure enough it does. Of course, it took the third wish to get it out. I never got over the implications of that story. You could relate it to the gold, for example: I wanted to show how gold turns to dross, and all that's left is the rainbow that leads to the crock of gold. That's all man has left: the rainbow.

"So I thought in my play, Bilbo or Rankin can be wished black. Then his transformation won't be through villainy but through whimsy. How do I build up to this, how does Rankin become the target? After the Irishman plants the crock of gold, two geologists find it and let the word out. Rankin hears and wants that ground. A greedy capitalist, he says, 'I don't have to pay anything for it. Blacks live there and there's a covenant that it's for whites only, so we can throw the bunch of them out.' Thus I show that racial prejudice is generated partly because of economic greed . . .

"Here's a show that was written in 1946. 1946. There had been no such song as 'We Shall Overcome.' There was no Martin Luther King. There was just a downright lack of civil rights for a minority of people whose skins were black . . . Why should there be a thing like racism? It's so idiotic. Volumes and books and lectures and God knows what were written about it; nothing seemed to help. We thought of one way—how could we prick the bubble of this idiocy? How could we reduce this thing to absurdity? Now you see how one thing usually leads to another—in order to show this folly, I used a dramatic form that will help us laugh this prejudice out of existence—the musical play."[2]

The composer for *Finian's Rainbow*, Burton Lane, was not unknown to Yip. Ira Gershwin had introduced them back in 1929, and the two ended up working together on *Americana* (although Lane's songs were not used in the final production) and *Hold on to Your Hats*. Lane, born in New York City in 1912, was much younger than Yip and had always looked up to him. As for Yip, "Burt had a gaiety and a bounce, and he bubbled. He was really very much akin to George Gershwin in his lighter vein. He struck a very responsive chord in me because his music gave me the chance to do the kind of light, airy, humorous-satiric things that I've always loved to do. He has zest, life—he has verve. He has upbeat in all of his music.

"Another thing about Burt is that he's very, very concerned about getting the right thing for you, and he's very critical of himself. Burt will never fight you for a tune. He's always changing, and he's always saying, 'Is this right, or isn't it?' He always wants to try and get something better. But that's true of any good writer, isn't it? The writer who isn't a hack is always afraid of what he's written. Never gets incensed, always feels that criticism is valid. Never knowing, and never sure. It's the hack who's always sure of what he's written."[3]

Although Yip and his collaborators had worked out the *Finian's Rainbow* libretto and score in Hollywood, when it came time to start the production process, there was no money available for them. As Yip explained to one interviewer, "We had a hard job getting it on Broadway, I'll tell you that. We finally had to go—Burt, Fred Saidy and myself—and have auditions to raise money and we practically raised the money ourselves for the show. Nobody would touch it. We knew the reason. The problem in the show was the black man's problem, the white man's problem, the racist problem, the gold problem, the Fort Knox problem. Our system was reduced a little bit to absurdity. To think that we plant gold in Fort Knox and that upon what happens to that gold there a whole nation either eats or doesn't eat, or a stock market goes up and down. And this is a fantasy that's beyond the fantasy of Finian."[4]

"It was off the beaten track and nobody really wanted to do it," Yip added in another interview. "We sent it around to all producers and they turned it back. Well, in a way I couldn't blame them. It was rather shocking to think that in a musical a man was going to turn black in front of your eyes and that you were going to have laughter out of it . . . And so they all turned it down until we got one fellow by the name of [Lee] Sabinson who . . . had done *Home of the Brave* and he loved this. He said, 'I'd like to do it but I'm broke.' He said, 'I have no money.' I said, 'Well, then, of course we have a slight problem.' But we said since nobody wants to do it, we do have the score written and the play written, I said, we'll go to New York—and we had about fifteen auditions. You know what these auditions are. Anybody with a hundred bucks is invited and the lyricist sings his heart out and the librettist . . . puts different hats on and imitates everybody. The composer sits at the piano and at the end of the day . . . the hat is passed around and people drop a hundred, two hundred, five hundred dollars . . . There were some hearty souls who put ten thousand in and put five thousand dollars in. We did have a hundred fifty thousand dollars at the end of all the auditions. We needed twenty thousand dollars and I was brave enough to supply that. I sold some of my wife's stock and we got the show on."[5] (In an interview done ten years later, Yip claimed that he put in "the last twenty thousand dollars" from "MGM money" that he had.)[6]

Yip also spoke of other problems the production had before getting started: "We couldn't get a director. The first director we tackled said he had to go back to Carolina every Christmas and he wouldn't be able to show his face if he did the show. [Yip later revealed this to be Joshua Logan, who was actually born in Texas.] And the dance directors, one of whom was Jerome Robbins, wouldn't take it. They said, 'Well, we don't feel we have much chance with a show of this kind.' All down the line we couldn't get any of the people—producer, dance director, and so on. So we got all unknowns. We got Michael Kidd who had never done any choreography before except his own. We watched him in a little thing called *Stage Hand*, we liked him, he was to get the opportunity.

"David Wayne, who was unknown, was doing bit parts. Said he couldn't sing. I said, 'Well, try "Flowers That Bloom in the Spring, Tra-la"' which he did and did very nobly. And he [had] just the cracked voice enough [for the leprechaun] . . . And there was Ella Logan whom we had in mind when we wrote the show. Lovely Scotch brogue, Scotch-Irish brogue . . . She was a nighclub entertainer. She had not done anything on stage. And we got Bretaign Windust [director] who had never done anything excepting a few straight plays, never done a musical. In fact the whole thing was an amateur night thing. It was a first crack. There were no real musical comedy professionals in the thing . . . It was a first for everybody. And it was even a first for me as a money investor."[7]

In his later years, Yip took great pride in talking about *Finian's Rainbow* and using it as a teaching tool. He would deconstruct it as a musical, explaining its creative process, its various parts, its songs, and its meaning in terms of politics and human rights. In presentations given at the University of Vermont, Northwood Institute, and the 92nd Street Y, Yip used the show as a case study in musical theater:

"We're going to talk [about] musical comedy," he told Vermont students, "and musical comedy is certainly, as you know, one of the great art [forms] that America has contributed to the world . . . I think we are known more all over the world for the treasury of songs . . . and the ability . . . to mix them into dance and the joy of musicals . . . And so that is an important contribution. And the reason it's an important contribution is because it is the one art form that employs almost every art form that is known to us. In other words, when you get a play, a simple play, a drama, you have a plot . . . but in a musical . . . song becomes an important part of the play . . . you have to stop dialogue and start song in order to enhance the play in order to give character to the play.

"Then, an important part of the musical is dancing. Or choreography. Now, songwriting implies a lyric and music. Dance means choreography. Now, you have many more scenes in a musical than you usually have in a straight play which means designs, scenic designs. Then you have to think about choral arrangements because there is singing, so you have to have a man who does choral arrangements. Then you have to have . . . the fellow who does the arrangement of the orchestra, right? So you've got the arranger for the show. Then you have to have a conductor who has to know every note of that music, who has to know every song that's being sung, how it's going to be sung, when the chorus comes in, and his job is one of the most important. A conductor can spoil a show or can make a show come to life, he can make it vital or he can lift an actor up to the rafters or he can just throw an actor down into the dumps, depending upon his tempo and the vitality . . . and his magnetism when he's up there in front of that stage. You have no idea how important that conductor is to the show. Then you have, especially in a musical . . . a costume [designer] . . .

"[An] important thing is the lighting. A lighting man, the wrong lighting man, can kill a show . . . a song is something that is facial registration. It's something that is the height of emotion and . . . the lighting [must be] right, completely right . . . you will find probably three or three hundred and fifty light cues that a man must be careful of. We've got one art form, two art forms, three, four, five, six, seven, eight, nine—all combined in a musical show.

"Now, the man who writes the book, the librettist, must worry about each of these things. To know how to write a book that will give each one of these people a chance to show their wares. Now, that's like writing a jigsaw puzzle and a crossword puzzle within an acrostic and make it come out . . . Now, you also have to have a play. Without the play and without the action, none of this can happen. So when you think of a musical, and you think of a musical libretto, you've got to think of locale, character and people that can sing and do all these things to make that musical, that charming, beautiful . . . artistic and musical enjoyment [that it is]. Now, a musical libretto . . . must still have all the dramaturgy and all the architecture that a straight drama must have. Now what must the play have to encompass all these things? A play itself . . . must have a premise and that premise must be a good one. If you're going to have an uninteresting premise of a play, you might as well not write it . . . in other words, it's got to intrigue you right away. You've got to hook that audience immediately with an idea. If you don't hook 'em in the first four minutes, you're dead. That play is over. So you always have to look for a theme that is intriguing and that will intrigue the audience.

"Now, after the premise there must be a sense of suspense . . . If you have a play without suspense, that audience is gonna fall asleep, not gonna follow you, right? They gotta follow something, some idea down to its completion. And that suspense, if it's just a suspense, will mean nothing unless the suspense has surprise. You've got to surprise an audience every ten or fifteen minutes in a show if you want that show to be good.

"After surprise . . . is the plot. And the plot must not have platitudes. It should be original, it should be something that hasn't been done before, something that isn't warmed over, something that is new.

"And finally when . . . you've gotten the surprise and you've brought people up to a climax which is somewhere in the middle of the show . . . you've got to . . . go down to the end of the show and the end of the show is called resolution. And the resolution must have satisfaction, gratification. If it doesn't have that, people will just go [out] and say, 'Aw, I saw a show.' But don't go back. [It] must be satisfying.

"These are the things that a man must think about when he starts writing a show. These are the things that an audience should think about when they're looking at a show. Has it got all these qualities? If it hasn't got these qualities, we might as well not write it. All right. Now, so you see, writing a musical show is not an easy thing. It's a very difficult job . . . to give it all these elements and yet to make it zing and live after the show is done."[8]

To his audience at the 92nd Street Y, Yip spoke in more detail about Fred Saidy and their work together on *Finian's Rainbow*: "Now in *Finian*, Fred Saidy and I gave ourselves another challenge, as if that weren't enough: to see if we could mix all these numerous elements of a musical comedy with fantasy, politics, social problems and economic myths. Was it possible? Were we equipped for it? *Finian's Rainbow* is a fanciful tale of our own imagining about a nimble-witted Irishman, Finian McLonergan. Now, he was an amalgam of Fred's father and mine—Fred's a Lebanese Catholic, mine Russian Jewish. Both looked at the world with an ironic, twinkling eye. So, of course, we were equipped. Also, we were well-mated in our literary backgrounds. Fred's hero [was] George Bernard Shaw, and mine was Hans Christian Andersen. With two such models covering all generations, how could we miss?

"As for the political aspect, the year was 1947. Roosevelt was beyond the sunset and [Richard] Nixon and Joe McCarthy on the horizon. Reactionary [Theodore] Bilbo was in the Senate and [John] Rankin in Congress . . . It was not a good vintage year for social satire. A writer had to be cautious. He was immediately labeled subversive if his thinking was a notch above their Southern-fried, finger-lickin' chicken thinkin'. But Mr. [George Bernard] Shaw taught us that truth can have many disguises. One of the best was laughter. And Hans Christian Andersen taught us, if you don't want to be jailed for the truth, tell it as you would to a child. And my favorite songsmiths, Gilbert and Sullivan, taught us that no one is ever going to be offended if you sing it.

"So we thought we would take a chance through song, because the libretto really is nothing but a vehicle for song . . . [and with Burton Lane] . . . here's what we tried to make the songs do. And this is the task we set ourselves. Can we for the first time in a musical comedy ridicule the folly of racism? Dare we integrate black and white people on the musical comedy stage, which we did for the first time? Is gold man's best friend? . . . Is it necessary for man to create necessity? Is it necessary to begat and begat indiscriminately until we out-begat ourselves? Is it necessary for the idle rich to manipulate our society so that consumption consumes the consumer? Is it necessary to wait for a messiah to make today the great come-and-get-it day? And is it ordained by nature or by divine providence that love and sex be reserved for that one and only? All these things, all these things we thought we would tackle in *Finian*."[9]

In Vermont, Yip told students, "Now, the main thing of the musical, of course, are the lyrics and the music because that's what makes it different from the straight show. Now, lyrics and music become a whole new . . . entity and a life of its own. How do you write music and lyrics? The lyric must be an integrated part of the dialogue. In other words, you do not know where the dialogue ends and where the song begins. Because if you do, it'll be like a fig leaf suddenly coming out of an apple tree and a good musical, a good musical is so imperceptibly woven from dialogue into music that you hardly know where the dialogue ends and the music begins.

"For example, let's . . . start from Finian, a little Irishman who has an idea that he's tired of being poor, a very good idea because it's something that almost everybody identifies themselves with. That's what makes it important. Nobody wants to be poor. And everybody gets tired of it. But living in Ireland, living on spuds, [with] no place to go to make money, [he] never will get out of his emptiness of life in that situation. [He says,] 'By God, in America everybody's rich! Everybody has a radio and an automobile. Why can't I have it?' And he analyzes America. He says, 'In 1849 they dug gold up in the ground of California. A hundred years later they plant it in another hole in Fort Knox. Now you've got to be pretty silly to do a thing like that,' he says, 'unless there was something about the soil of Fort Knox,' he says, 'that's magic, that makes you rich, if you plant a little gold in Fort Knox.' That's not a bad theory. It's not wrong in a country where, let's say, a president will tell you he can cure inflation if you wear a button. [The audience laughs to Yip's reference to then-president Gerald Ford's 'Whip Inflation Now' campaign.] Not far-fetched. We do that. We somehow get by. He says, 'Well, why can't I bury a little gold in Fort Knox? But—how do I get the gold? Well, there's no gold in Ireland. The only ones who have gold are the leprechauns.'

"So he lies in wait for a couple of years until he sees a leprechaun coming by, grabs his pot . . . gets his daughter and inveigles her to come to America so that he can plant a little gold. Now that idea is your premise. There's your premise. A premise with a promise. A funny [premise]. We want to see what happens to this little fella. Will it be true? You're immediately hooked at the beginning because the idea is also a suspense; [we'd] like to see him [plant] that crock of gold. Will it happen? It's not a platitudinous plot. I've never seen that plot worked out before that way. I've never heard of a thing like that. It's different. It isn't a boy, saying, 'I'm in love with a girl but she's gonna make him jealous and I'll go to a lunch party and make him jealous,' . . . or whatever . . . That's all there is to most of the musicals . . .

"So already that plot has all its elements . . . Now, here's another thing about writing for shows. We could have gone . . . and [said], let's go to Ireland and show Finian, show his poverty and his daughter and show that leprechaun and show how he gets the pot of gold, show how he comes to America. Now all that would be exposition and it wouldn't be very interesting because it would just be exposition, exposition, exposition. So what do we do? We don't stop now. We telescope the whole thing by starting right in America where he lands with his daughter.

"Now, another thing you gotta look out for in writing a musical. When he lands with his daughter, what do we do? Does he tell his daughter, 'Darling, I've got a beautiful idea. We're gonna plant a little crock of gold, we'll all get rich because all Americans get rich.' That would be very, very dull. So what does the good dramatist do? He puts this girl in opposition to the father. They fight. She didn't want to come here. He inveigled her here. He wanted her to come. She accuses him of being wily and out of this quarrel, out of this, we get all the exposition in dramatic form instead of just a dull recitation of what's happening. In other words, what is drama? Drama is conflict, and conflict must appear in practically every scene that you do. If it's just talk, it's gonna be empty dialogue, and dull. If you were walking down the street and heard two people talking and one is telling something, an idea, to another, in a nice quiet voice, you just walk by. But if you heard them quarreling and you heard one mad at the other, you'd stop. Right? So, now . . . the daughter . . . is outraged. 'How dare you bring me down to America in the sweet, green month of April, across an ocean and down a continent, and for what?'

"'For what?' he says. 'For a beautiful new land, a beautiful new land, where bees give certified [honey] and the cows . . . give certified milk and the spiders spin their webs of nylon.' Now you've got an interesting character. You've got them quarreling. You've got them at each other's throats, and in the meanwhile you can get in some very nice little things about America and satire and so forth.

"[And she says], 'Father, how could you do a thing like this?'

"He says, 'A thing like this? I did it all for you.'

"And finally the quarrel reaches a point where it would be a continuation with words. Well, this is the time that the songwriter knows—or the lyric writer knows—the librettist knows—that the only way to heighten the emotion or end the problem is with a song, because a song is a final outburst of an emotional scene. Music is pure emotion. Words, you can be outraged, you can talk . . . But they will never give you . . . the complete outlet that music will give. So when they reach this impasse, there's no more to say, she's stubborn, he's stubborn, he finally tries one of his wily mischievous things. He hears a lark. [The pianist at the lecture plays a few notes.] Immediately that's interesting. You've broken the quarrel, you've broken the intensity of the dialogue, right? Suddenly a note, music. And Finian, a little mischievous man, [says], 'A skylark.' And she says, 'Ay, the same skylark music we have back in Ireland.'

"'I told you,' he says, 'America has everything.'

"Now she looks at him but she's a little wilier than he is and she says . . . 'I can't get him back. No argument will make him come back from America. This fantastic little idea he has, this crackpot idea of burying a crock of gold, I will get him back through nostalgia.' Now you see the song, in comes a song here."[10]

Yip interrupted his talk at this point to sing a few lines of "How Are Things in Glocca Morra?" and then interrupting them with his explanation:

"I hear a bird
A Glocca Morra bird
It well may be it's bringin' me a cheerin' word.

[Now he's sold] his daughter . . . on his crackpot ideas.

I hear a breeze
A river Shannon breeze
[It well may be it's followed me]
Across the seas
Then tell me please.

Now, she has one eye cocked on him while she's singing the song.

How are things in Glocca Morra?
Is that little brook still leapin' there?

'. . . that boy who came to visit me. How do you feel about it? Are you guilty?'

So I ask each weepin' willow

This man was awash in tears, he's back in Glocca Morra.[11]

"Now, when you sing that song on the outside, it's just a song. It's a lovely, beautiful ballad . . . All right. It's not a song. It is an adroit piece of dramaturgy. This is what real songwriting is. And this is what you've got to think about and mathematically figure out all the way through a show as you go through it. And as we go through *Finian*, even though we do it hurriedly, we will find cause and effect. You'll find a very disciplined, scientific reason for every song that's done, for every piece of dialogue . . . This is what makes songwriting . . . important to the theatre."[12]

At a lecture at Northwood Institute in 1978, Yip went into more detail on the creation of the song: "Now, I have a composer. He doesn't think the way I do. He thinks in music chords, the primitive, you know, the old heart beat . . . Burt says, 'What kind of song do you want?' I want a nostalgic song. I want it to bring out this old man. It's gotta be about Ireland. It's gotta have an Irish flavor. But we don't want another 'Come back to Erie, my bonnie, my bonnie.' We don't want it. We want your own development. Give it an Irish flavor, but for God's sake, don't make it sound like all the Irish songs . . . And now he goes to work, and don't think that's easy. He wrote about fifteen tunes and each one of them sounded too Irish and we don't want that. You want to contribute something of your own to it too. He says, 'Give me a title, give me an idea.' And I say, 'No, Burt. I don't want to give you a title because if I give you a title, then you'll start being boxed in by that title. I want you to get that tune, your own inspiration. All I will give you . . . keep the word "Glocca Morra" in.' But he came up with about six or seven tunes and finally he says, 'Well, I can't do it.' I said, 'All right, there's a glen in Glocca Morra.' I know I want 'Glocca Morra' in it, because just as Finian McLonergan is a lovely word, just as Billboard Rawkins means something, I want the place they come from, the thing they're after, which is a better life, to mean something to an audience.

Albert Sharpe as Finian and Ella Logan as Sharon soon after their arrival in Rainbow Valley in *Finian's Rainbow*, January 10, 1947. Courtesy of Eileen Darby Images, Inc.

"So I want to write about a place called Glocca Morra. There is no such place on the map, but it sounds Irish . . . [Burton] says, 'What does it mean?' [I said,] 'To me it means, *glocca* is [a] Teutonic word for *glück*, which finally got into English as *luck*. *Morra*, which is [a] Teutonic word for *morgen*, which got into English as *tomorrow*. Glocca Morra—Lucky Tomorrow.' I've got a title now whether you knew it or not. Subliminally. . . . There's something lovely about Glocca Morra, that also everybody is looking for every minute of the day. Now this is using poetry, song writing, subtly, theatrically. All right. Now he finally comes up with 'There's a glen in Glocca Morra . . . [Yip hums tune].' I said, 'Burt . . . that's the way the Irish do it.' . . . It took him a couple of weeks to work out that [thing] and [it] made a difference . . ."[13]

Yip was correct to use the word *subliminal* in reference to the song. In James Stephens's *The Crock of Gold*, there is a village named Gort na Cloca Mora and a Celtic god named Angus Óg.[14] But as First Lady Eleanor Roosevelt commented on March 31, 1948, in her syndicated column "My Day," "When I first looked at the program [of *Finian's Rainbow*], I thought perhaps the story of the play was based on James Stephens's book . . . but there is no real resemblance except the fact that leprechauns and the crock of gold at the end of the rainbow seem to appear in all Irish stories."[15]

"Now we come, let us say, to our second song," Yip told his Vermont audience. "[Sharon] lands in Rainbow Valley and lo and behold she meets a boy, Woody, who is a sharecropper and [there are] blacks and some whites sharing a little bit of land and eking out a living. And the boy, of course, has ambitions, maybe to make this the first kibbutz back in Mississippi. [Yip, of course, meant his fictional state of Missitucky.] And meets the girl and suddenly the girl begins to like him, doesn't want to go back to Glocca Morra. So here we get our love story working. A love story is very important for a musical because without a love story you don't have ballads and you don't have love songs, so we integrate into the *Finian* plot this love song . . . The girl falls in love with the boy but we want to get a song in here—it can't be an all-out love song because if you're a little more mature in life than the old musical comedies where you say, 'You meet someone across a crowded room and suddenly you fall in love . . .' I don't believe in that kind of business. I don't believe that love happens that way. I believe that love is an honest evolvement and a development. Two people know each other.

"Now this is where songwriting also has to be true to [it]self and true to the world. I mean, you can't write those old, romantic love songs where love is put on a pedestal of idealism, that nothing happens, there is no development. The girl, although she likes this guy, they may be chemically attracted, wants to know a little bit about him, wants to tell him about herself and the kind of man she likes. And so what does she do? When she introduces her father, he [the boy] says, 'What's your name?' And she says, 'Sharon McLonergan.' And she says, 'What's yours?' And he says, 'Woody Mahoney.' And the father says, 'That's fake.' And he [the boy] says, 'Where do you come from?' She says, 'Well, where we come from we have an old legend, that you'll never grow old and you'll never grow poor if you look to the rainbow beyond the next moor.' He says, 'That's a lovely legend. Now who thought that up?' And she says, 'Me father.'"[16] Sharon then sings the song "Look to the Rainbow":

Verse
On the day I was born
Said my father, said he
I've an elegant legacy
Waitin' for ye
Tis a rhyme for your lips
And a song for your heart
To sing it whenever
The world falls apart

Chorus
Look, look, look to the rainbow
Follow it over the hill and stream
Look, look, look to the rainbow
Follow the fellow who follows a dream

Verse
Twas a sumptuous gift
To bequeath to a child

Oh, the lure of that song
Kept her feet runnin' wild
For you never grow old
And you never stand still
With whip-poor-wills singin'
Beyond the next hill

Chorus
Look, look, look to the rainbow
Follow it over the hill and stream
Look, look, look to the rainbow
Follow the fellow who follows a dream

Verse
So I bundled me heart
And I roamed the world free
To the east with the lark
To the west with the sea
And I searched all the earth
And I scanned all the skies
But I found it at last
In my own true love's eyes

Chorus
Look, look, look to the rainbow
Follow it over the hill and stream
Look, look, look to the rainbow
Follow the fellow who follows a dream

Follow the fellow,
Follow the fellow,
Follow the fellow,
Who follows a dream.[17]

Yip then explained Sharon's lyrical message to Woody. "'Young man, that's the kind of a fellow I want. Are you that kind of a guy? Got a dream? D'ya follow it? Like my dad there. I'm quarreling with him but I love his sense of adventure, I love his pixie quality, I know he's screwy as hell but he's got somethin' that makes life worthwhile. And that's the kind of a guy I'm looking for.' All right. Now we know a little bit more about Sharon. The song did it. We didn't have to use dialogue, we didn't have to use exposition. A song is a synthesis, it's a telescoping in an emotional way of a whole scene, what would take five pages of dialogue—boy and girl bantering, immature dialogue, overwrought sentiments and sentimentality—that song did it very clearly with heightened emotion again. And you know that these two people [are] in love but you know that he has to prove himself. Now you know . . . how endearing her father is to her, and now [through the song and a dance] also there's a cementing of friendship between the black people in this sharecropping group and the white people in the sharecropping [group]—and an Irishman, a complete foreigner who comes from way outer space."[18]

Besides having the Rainbow Valley black and white sharecroppers living and working side by side, Yip, Saidy, and Lane offered other scenes to illustrate the contrasting face of racism and xenophobia. As Yip explained at the 92nd Street Y, "Well, we have got to get on to our antagonist now . . . Senator Rawkins . . . to see what things are happening with him. We open up on his plantation estate which is rotting away and his big hang-up is pigmentation . . . The senator learns through two mineralogists who are inspecting the land for a government project that they have discovered a rich vein of gold under [nearby] property. The concentration is so huge it broke the needle of the meter. The senator is wild with rage that he was outbid by an immigrant [Finian] for that treasured parcel, and he must get moving before the news about the gold leaks out. So we let the audience know that Rawkins is not going to give up the prized land easily, that he is already working on a scheme with Fred Saidy that will be so ingenious and Machiavellian that it will surprise us all. In the meanwhile, sit on the edge of your seats and brush your nails."[19]

"Now," as he told the Vermonters, ". . . when you do a show, what kind of a show do you want to do? Do you want to do a show that when you leave the theatre, the show leaves you? Or do you want to use the stage as a podium for education, for uplifting, for giving people something to think about? . . . Drama is probably the most important part of the education system. In fact, you can teach more through play and through entertainment than you can through lecturing and sermonizing . . . Shows have been terribly important all through the ages. Or do you want to just write a show for a little laugh, a little slipping on a banana peel . . . ? Or do you want to use the show as a means of pushing your planet maybe a tenth of a centimeter ahead? I mean, so that when they go out they think about it. The children who saw *Finian's Rainbow* never lived after that one day without thinking of 'but for the grace of God, there go I' because when the Senator turns black and has to live under his own laws, if you'll remember, and can't get into [a] beer saloon, can't get into a church, that scene is impressed upon a child . . . It doesn't spoil the laughter, the entertainment is there, the fun is there, the songs are there. But you've got another dimension. It's the dimension that Bernard Shaw added to all of his plays that makes him alive forever. Now you can do it with any art form. You could do it with musicals, you could do it with straight drama, you could do it with painting, you could do it with songwriting. Do your songs have meaning? Do the things that you say live after and produce something in the minds of the people that you touch? Is it more than just a laugh or an emotion?

"And *Finian* did the following things. Not just a show. It was a complete education in things to come. 1) Is it necessary to have racism? We showed in *Finian* how things bounce back on you. This man who turns black after making all the laws against the black finally has to live by his own laws. And what happens to the Senator? They're all funny, they're all laughable and they're all entertaining, but they're all very lasting as far as effect goes on an audience. 2) We have another theme in *Finian*. Gold. Is gold necessary as an economic factor in our civilization? In other words, if the Arabs who now own all the money in the world were to buy up all the gold in Fort Knox, so you'd have no gold there, would America be a richer country in its values and in its humanitarian concern? And if they left us only our wheat, our lands, our machinery, our wizardry, and all the things that we could produce and distribute, without the necessity of everybody having a certain amount of gold, could we still do that? Would we be a poorer country without the gold idea? Well, let's see.

"In *Finian*, when Finian plants the gold crock in the soil and everybody discovers gold in the land, they want to dig it up. Finian and Woody [do] not let them dig it up. The word gets around . . . Sears-Roebuck, or Shears-Robust [in the musical], who represent ITT and General Motors hears that the people of Rainbow Valley have gold. My God, in comes the credit, in comes 'We'll give you anything. Just sign. You've got collateral.'"[20]

At this point in his talk, Yip introduced "That Great Come-and-Get-It Day" in which Woody, Sharon, and the sharecroppers plan what they will purchase with their newly granted credit:

Woody:
    On that great come and get it day
    Won't it be fun when worry is done
    And money is hay?
    That's the time things'll come your way
    On that great, great come and get it day

    I'll get my gal that calico gown
    I'll get my mule that acre of groun'
    Cause word has come from Gabriel's horn
    The earth beneath your plow
    Is a buddin' and now it's your'n
Sharon:
    Glory time's comin' for to stay
    On that great, great come and get it day
All:
    Come and get it
Preacher:
    Sez here!
    Sez it in the good book, it sez
    A mighty mornin' is nigh
All:
    Universal Fourth of July!
Woody:
    Gonna get your freedom and pie
All:

Freedom, freedom, freedom, freedom pie
What a day for banjos ringin'
What a day for people in overalls
Can't you hear all the angels singin'?
Man:
Come and get your gravy and two meat balls!
Chorus:
Come and get it
Sez it in the good book
Hallelujah
Chorus:
Bells will ring in every steeple
Woman:
Come and get your test on the movie screen
All:
Come you free and you equal people
Man:
Come and get your beer and your Benzedrine
All:
Sez here, come and get it, come!
Preacher:
There's gonna be a world shaken
Bread breakin' day!
Chorus:
Great day!
First Woman:
Does that mean I can get a washing machine?
Preacher:
Glory to you!
Second Woman:
Can I get a waffle iron?
Woody:
With your initials!
Boy:
Can I get a juke box?
Preacher:

Sez here
First Man:
   How about a helicopter?
Preacher:
   Helicopter?
All:
   Hallelujah!
   On that great come and get it day
   Won't it be fun when worry is done
   And money is hay
   That's the time things'll come your way
   On that great great come and get it day
Sharon:
   My gown will be a calico gown
   My feet will dance all over the town
Woody:
   Cause word has come from Gabriel's horn
   The earth beneath your plow is a buddin'
   And now it's your'n
Chorus:
   Yes now it's your'n
All:
   Glory times
   Comin' for to stay
   On that great, great
   Come and get it,
   And keep it,
   And share it,
   Great, great
   Come and get it day![21]

Yip continued: "So in come the beautiful clothes and in comes the beautiful machinery, harvesters, tractors, things that they never had before and suddenly they begin planting and bringing up tobacco leaves as they never have before. They sell and become rich . . . Why have they become rich? They became rich because Shears-Robust gave

The chorus from "That Great Come-and-Get-It Day"
in *Finian's Rainbow*, January 10, 1947.
Courtesy of Eileen Darby Images, Inc.

them a thing called credit. It gave them tools of production, and with these tools the people went to work and made themselves rich. They produced and they distributed. Now, at the end of the show their crock of gold is turned to dross and the people are rich. Well, doesn't this open your mind up to some kind of thinking about our own gold system? Is maybe the idea of brotherhood that Buddha and Christ and Moses and all the other religions have promulgated through the years, is brotherhood maybe credit without collateral? And there is the theme of *Finian*, that brotherhood is credit without collateral.

"Another point we tried to make in *Finian*, all through this little crock of gold, is 'On That Great Come-and-Get-It Day.' [*sic*] . . . I call that the Messiah song. Do we have to wait for a messiah to come, second coming or third coming, to give us that beautiful day when mankind can have the things they need for living, for brotherhood, for peace, for not starving? . . . for thousands of years people have been seeing the great day, that there's a great day comin'. We call it the great come-and-get-it day. Is it necessary to postpone that day for some time in the future as we have been now for over five, six thousand years. But is it here now—if we want to take it, actually, and bring it about? With science, with logic, with humanity, with the right kind of legislation . . .

"Fun is absolutely imperative. The entertainment comes first, above everything else. The medium is the important thing, just to be able to say these important things flavorsomely, refreshingly, and the people laugh while you're doing it. In other words, gild the philosophic pill. In other words, to know your art, to know how to do these things. Not to sermonize, not to preach, not to be on the pulpit, not to be bitter . . . if you make [your enemy] laugh and you laugh at him and you reduce all his things to ridiculosity, he's afraid of you. You've got courage. Humor is courage. So that even though we tackle these big themes in *Finian*, we do it with [fun].

"Now, [regarding] the theme . . . [of necessity] . . . Is necessity necessary? Or is it man made? Now, we all know that there is enough oil and enough soil and enough everything in this world, with the physical know how, our assembly lines and our computers, to give us abundance if we wanted to take the cellophane bag [off] all the machines in the country. But we do everything we can to make laws against abundance. We have to create necessity. The reason we have to create necessity is because of the law of supply and demand. If there's too much supply, you don't make profit. Therefore, cut your supply. If you cut your supply you will have profit. So that a system oriented toward the profit system cannot possibly be without all the skullduggery, the trouble that we're in now . . . At one point in our history scarcity was natural. We had no machines, we had nothing. But now necessity is an artificial, man-made thing and it's done to keep profit going. So is necessity necessary? That's the third thing that we take up."[22]

Yip's musicalization of this idea can be seen in a sample of the lyrics for "Necessity":

Verse
What is the curse
That makes the universe so all bewilderin'?
What is the hoax
That just provokes the folks they call God's childerin?
What is the jinx
That gives a body and his brother and ev'ry one aroun'
The run aroun'?

Chorus
Necessity, necessity
That most unnecessary thing
Necessity
What throws a monkey wrench in
A fellow's good intention?
That nasty old invention
Necessity

My feet wanna dance in the sun
My head wants to rest in the shade
The Lord says, "Go out and have fun"
But the landlord says
"Your rent ain't paid."

Necessity, it's plain to see
What a lovely old world

This silly old world could be
But man, it's all in a mess
Account of necessity.[23]

And Yip continued: "The fourth. When the idle poor become the idle rich, what happens? What does affluence do to our society? Well, [in the musical, they] come out in mink underwear and gold-braided combs and things of that sort. In other words, we're going from things they sorely needed and wanted and couldn't get to fine things they have absolutely no use for. This is what our society is now. In other words, we reach a point, when the idle poor become the idle rich, where consumption consumes the consumer . . ."[24]

Audiences always particularly love the song "When the Idle Poor Become the Idle Rich":

Sharon:
    When the idle poor become the idle rich
    You'll never know just who is who
    Or who is which
    Won't it be rich
    When ev'ryone's poor relative
    Becomes a "Rockefellative"
    And palms no longer itch
    What a switch!
Women:
    When we all have ermine and plastic teeth
    How will we determine who's who underneath?
Men:
    And when all your neighbors are upper class
    You won't know your Joneses from your As-tors
Sharon:
    Let's toast the day
    The day we drink that drinkie up
    But with the little pinkie up
    The day on which
    The idle poor become the idle rich
Chorus:

Du du du doot de du, de du, de du du
Du du du doot de du, de du, de doot

Sharon:

When a rich man doesn't want to work
He's a bon vivant
Yes, he's a bon vivant
But when a poor man doesn't want to work,
He's a loafer, he's a lounger
He's a lazy good for nothing
He's a jerk

When a rich man loses on a horse
Isn't he the sport?
Oh, isn't he the sport?
But when a poor man loses on a horse
He's a gambler, he's a spender
He's a lowlife, he's a reason
For divorce

When a rich man chases after dames
He's a man about town
A man about town
But when a poor man chases after dames
He's a bounder, he's a rounder
He's a rotter, and a lot of
Dirty names

Chorus:

Du du du doot de du, de du, de du du
Du du du doot de du, de du, de doot,
You'll never know just who is which
When the idle poor become the idle rich,

When the idle poor become the idle rich
You'll never know just who is who
Or who is which

Sharon:

No one can see the Irish or the Slav in you

For when you're on Park Avenue
Cornelius and Mike
Look alike
Women:
When poor Tweedle Dum is rich Tweedle Dee
This discrimination will no longer be
Man:
When we're in the dough and off of the nut
You won't know your banker from your but-ler
Sharon:
Let's make the switch
With just a few annuities
We'll hide those incongruities
In cloaks
From Abercrombie Fitch
Chorus:
When the idle poor become the idle rich
When the idle poor become the idle rich.[25]

As Yip explained at Northwood Institute, "People of the soil, bringing up tobacco as a crop, now suddenly go in for obvious baubles and silly things that they don't need . . . [and] must look at themselves a little bit and say, 'What are we doing to our values?' And yet in the show we show we do not know how to handle money. Even the poor people, we want to be good to them, give them the opportunity and they do become rich, what are they going to do with the riches? Are you going to do something valuable? Are you going to become better human beings? Are you going to waste? Right now, this world, this country, is in a situation of affluence for a great deal of the people, and waste. Waste, waste, waste. And I think shows like *Finian*, songs like ("Idle Poor") . . . yes, you laugh, but you must go away carrying some other thought about how we are conducting ourselves and what we are doing with our lives and that's what makes this song funny, and that's why you were laughing. If it were just empty laughing, you wouldn't be laughing that much . . ."[26]

Yip brought out yet another point to his Vermont audience: "Do we have to begat and begat and begat promiscuously so that we finally begat ourselves out of existence? In other words, the population explosion. I don't have to explain this. You've read about it. You know what it is. If we don't control our population and the things that nature has given us the wisdom to control, how far can we go? So we've got the begat. Now as you know, we treat the begat, the population, not with any kind of seriousness at all. It's done with just [fun]. 'The white begat, the red begat, the folks who shoulda stood in bed begat. Why, even the Britishers begat, in tweeds begat . . . The Lapps and Lithuanians begat, Pennsylvanians begat, honorary Aryans begat, fat filibusterers begat, income tax adjusterers begat . . . Sons of habitues begat . . . Sometimes a bachelor, he begat.'[27] Well, it's all fun and it's all laughter. But behind the fun and behind the laughter is the problem we are having today with all this begat business. Big problems. Now, whether you know it or not, while you're sitting there and laughing your heads off, giving . . . the quartet, applause, something subliminal is happening . . . to the audience. They are taking away thoughts that they may not analyze outright, but . . . will somewhere along the line . . . become pregnant.

"Now we come to one little Freudian bit here to which we're a little bit ahead of the times on, and that is . . . our attitude toward love and sex. Is marriage, is love, is sex all the traditional things that have been piled up on us by our Puritan ancestors? How does it conform with Freud and Jung and Fromm, all these people?"[28] In *Finian's Rainbow*, Yip used Og, the leprechaun who chases Finian from Ireland to reclaim his crock of gold, to bring sex (as opposed to love and romance) into the plot. As Og becomes more mortal (as all leprechauns will without that crock of gold), every woman he sees excites him. It doesn't matter if it's Sharon or Susan or some other young lass. In Vermont, Yip offered a sample of the lyrics of "When I'm Not Near the Girl I Love," and at the 92nd Street Y, he explained something about his use of language in Og's other song, "Something Sort of Grandish":

"When I'm not near the girl I love, I love the girl I'm near . . .
Ev'ry femme that flutters by me
Is a flame that must be fanned

When I can't fondle the hand I'm fond of
I fondle the hand at hand.
My heart's in a pickle
It's constantly fickle
And not too partickle, I fear.
When I'm not near the girl I love,
I love the girl I'm near.[29]

All fun, right? And when the leprechaun sings it, it's adorable, funny, you applaud. But behind it is a nice big theme, is a little bit Freudian, Freudian honesty."[30]

"Og is getting half mortal but he doesn't know [how] to express it completely as a full-fledged human being. So he expresses himself in ish-es. Now the suffix 'ish' is a rather indecisive suffix. If you want to meet somebody at the Algonquin at twelve o'clock, but not quite, you say, 'Well, meet me at twelve-ish.' Or one-ish. In other words, you're not quite sure, and in this case he is not quite sure about himself and his love and his . . . so everything now is in the 'ish' form. That makes him a true leprechaun."[31] So Og sings,

Something sweet
Something sort of grandish
Sweeps my soul
When thou art near

My heart feels
So sugar candish
My head feels
So ginger beer

Something so dare-ish
So I don't-care-ish
Stirs me from limb to limb
It's so terrifish, magnifish, delish
To have such an amorish, glamorish dish

We could be
Oh, so bride and groomish

Skies could be
So blueish blue

Life could be
So love-in-bloomish
If my-ishes
Could come true.[32]

In Vermont, Yip continued to elucidate the characters: "So when we talk about *Finian* we're talking about a political, economic, social, psychological group of things that are all combined in a way to give you fun, to give you pleasure, to make an audience laugh and sing and dance and at the same time to carry away some very nice [messages].

"You gotta like Susan," he added, "because she's [a] deaf-mute . . . and can't talk. Now this is another interesting thing about *Finian*. How do we get dancing into a show without suddenly stopping the show and starting to dance? That would hurt the whole dramatic quality. Well, Susan can't speak so she dances her thoughts. What a wonderful way, anytime we want to know what Susan's saying, she does a little dance and they interpret her dance. A little trick which comes in very handy. So you've got to like Susan."[33]

Yip often returned his discussions to the issue of depicting racial bigotry on stage, and noted how he expressed his ideas in a satirical way. "And as we have to have one villain . . . because if we don't, we'll have no conflict . . . and here we have Billboard Rawkins. Now, Billboard is a nice name. He likes to get his face on billboards . . . of course every show is a reflection of the time . . . Every writer is always, always pushed into one thing or another by the canvas of history. At that time we had two senators who were terribly bigoted . . . Bilbo and Rankin—who were against every law that was being made that would help the depressional people. They were probably the biggest opponents of Roosevelt. They voted against the unemployment insurance act, they voted against Medicare, they voted against racial integration. There wasn't a thing that they didn't vote against. Bilbo and Rankin. They were very powerful. So we combined these two fellows into Billboard."[34]

At Northwood Institute, Yip further explained his concept of the *villain,* and how he manipulated that idea to change evil into good in *Finian's Rainbow*: "I don't want to say 'villain' because I don't like villains in stories—out and out villains. I don't believe there are villains. I believe that people are products of their tradition, of their education, their environment and their upbringing. And let's be truthful about it—nobody's black and white in the sense of anything . . . People are [a] paradox. The worst of people have some good in them. The best of people have some bad in them. Honesty is an important thing in writing a play, if you want to make it a real play, a fair play, and something that is, in the highest sense of the word, civilized and educational. People that write plays where the villain is all villain and the hero is all hero are nonsense. There are no such people. We've got to find out what makes people act the way they do . . . Billboard Rawkins is a product of his environment . . . He's just a product of his age. He can't help it; we all do that. We're all caught in it in some way or another . . .

"So money is this thing that rules us, really. Money is this thing that almost dictates everything we do in life . . . Well, [Rawkins] . . . now he asserts his influence, the power. And now we see how legislation works for power, even though the power is wrong, even though the legislation is wrong. As you know, at a certain point it took a lot of fighting, it took a bloody Civil War and it took a hundred years even after that war to say that people, whether they're black or white or yellow or red, have a right to live unbothered . . . Now, by invoking that law he also invokes the wrath of Sharon, this girl who doesn't understand our mores, doesn't understand the Civil War. She came here because there's this little constitution that says everybody's born free and equal and everybody has the right to the pursuit of happiness.

"[She asks,] 'Haven't you ever read it [the us Constitution]?' And he says, 'No, I have not time to read it. I'm too busy defendin' it.' Well, behind every kind of inhuman motive, you will find some rationalization like that: 'I'm defendin' it.' . . . Again, by a joke I'm defending the Constitution. This is the way of employing humor and employing satire to make universal points, eternal points, with laughter. Anybody hearing that line . . . has a different idea about tradition and defense of human rights . . . We made them laugh at themselves. And when you make people laugh, people will feel that they're superior, and when people feel superior they are ready to ingest a new idea. But if you demean a person by arguing down, why then, he gets mad. But if you do it with humor, I'm saying he feels superior, he laughs at something and he accepts the idea.

"Anyhow, he employs the restrictive covenant to get the people off the land and the little Irish girl who comes from a highly different milieu, doesn't know our mores, our folklore, our philosophy, is baffled by it. She says, 'You mean to say you're chasing these people off because their skins are black?' And she says something now that isn't a curse, and that isn't mean, and that isn't vengeful at all, but is bewilderment. 'Good God, I wish you knew what it's like to be black in a country where it is wrong to be black. I wish you were black (so you) would know what (it would) feel like to be in their skin.' And she doesn't do it mean, she doesn't do it to be vengeful . . . she wants to be rational . . . and before you know it there's big Senator Billboard . . . black. And now he has to live the life going through all the laws that he himself legislated . . . [it's] high humor, high fun to see what it's like to make laws that are against humanity that finally must come back and be against yourself . . .

"Now you must have some feeling for the race problem. Now here are beautiful sharecroppers, black and white, and working together on this property . . . There was an injustice done and I think you can touch the (root of that) injustice. And so we've got feeling for the people up there on that stage. Something's happened that has touched you deep down emotionally to the very instincts of your human soul. That's the important thing . . . So I come back to the original proposition that if you're going to do something, you must do something that has worth, that has passion, that has feeling, and dramatically, technically, we've arranged that play so that at the end of the first act, this man, this senator, this white man, this powerful man, is a black man, and whoever has done this to him is in deep trouble because you know something is going to happen to that little girl and the boy that she likes."[35]

Yip also illustrated how he used Og to explore the issue of racism: "Notice how much is packed into this scene, of more than meets the ear or the eye. A wooded section in the hills. Og is lying on a fallen tree stump, eating an apple and singing 'How Are Things in Glocca Morra?'

. . . And as he's singing, we see Rawkins enter . . . He's all disheveled, shabby from hiding out in the forest away from his dog and people. He doesn't want anybody to see him in this terrible condition. He's hopeless. He steals up behind Og, lying there peacefully singing . . . grabs the apple out of his hand, 'Gimme that!' And Og says, 'You needn't grab; there's plenty of apples around.'—'Well, I don't see 'em!'—'Well, naturally you don't. Mortals never can see all the apples they could have.' A very important line. We don't see all the apples . . . We don't see all the crops that we could produce if we do the right things . . . And he says, 'An apple here, an apple there, little green apples everywhere,' and he . . . says, 'My, you must be hungry. Would you care for a sandwich?' . . . Rawkins says, 'Wouldn't you be hungry if you'd been hiding out in this forest two weeks like a hunted 'possum?'—'Well, what were you hidin' from?'—'My wife, my people, my friends. You think I want them to see me in this condition?'—'I see nothing wrong with you.'—'Ya don't? Ya must be blind! Can't ya see I'm black?'—'Oh, yes. And I think it's very becoming'—Rawkins says, 'But I'm a white man, dammit, a white man . . . At least I was a few weeks ago.'—'Well, that's a coincidence. I was green a few weeks ago . . . Don't you find an occasional change of color interesting?'—'No, I don't. But they won't get away with it—I tell ya, ya can't get away with it.'—'Oh, you needn't get so excited, Mister. I think it's just ridiculous makin' such a fuss about a person's color.'—'Why, you moron, don't you realize what it is to be black?'—'Aren't you still a human bein'? You can still hear bird music and smell honey! A rose is still a rose despite the color of your nose.' And Rawkins says, 'But you can't get in a restaurant, you can't get on a streetcar, you can't buy yourself a cold beer on a hot day, you can't walk into a church and pray.' . . .

"Og says, 'Who says you can't?' Rawkins: 'The law says you can't.'—'The law? Hm. That's a silly law. Is it a legal law?'—'Of course it's legal! I wrote it myself!'—'Why don't you change your color again?'—'How the hell am I gonna do that?!'—'Well, you said you had a change two weeks ago.'—'I did nothing of the kind. Some witch wished it on me' . . . And Og says, 'Oh, a witch. . . . Well, in that case I can help you. What kind of a witch was she?'—'How do I know? I didn't look her up in *Who's Who*.'—'Sure we can find her in—[Og brings out a little book] in

Which is Witch. The book has a list of all the witches, their curses and their cures.' He starts walking back and forth . . . Rawkins gets mad and [says], 'Go away, will you?' He sees him mad. 'Oh, I think I understand your trouble now. You're too unfriendly.'—'I'm in no condition for friendship.'—'And it's all that witch's fault.'

"Now here's an important point," Yip added, "'She gave you a new outside, but she didn't give you a new inside. Very incompetent. This will give witchcraft a bad name . . . It takes our entire profession back a hundred years. I'm afraid I may have to alter your whole personality. My whole reputation is at stake.' And now he's got the senator sort of hypnotized. 'Why don't you leave me alone?'—'Oh, this won't be a bit hard. All we have to do is broaden out that narrow mind a little. Reduce some of that bigotry and your pomposity won't show at all. Wait til they see you in your new spring psyche. People will say you're in love! Now for the magic cure.'"[36]

Then Yip described how Og throws magic powders into the tree stump and a puff of smoke comes out as he recites:

"Fiddle faddle foil and fiddle
Cure this fuddled individdle
Rise, ye vapors, and unwind
This tangled medieval mind.
Breath of bee and bluebird wing,
Make this scowling spirit sing.
Balm of briar and sandalwood,
Season him with brotherhood.
Magic vapors, make this person
A better person, not a worse 'un.

"Now you see that we employ all the tricks of Shakespeare, and all the things that I've learned in literature, and plagiarizing them, bringing them to a new use, the use of my satiric satire, and this is how things go . . . And of course Rawkins . . . falls asleep and [Og says], 'The cure is beginnin' to work!' And he skips off with 'How are things in Glocca Morra this fine day?'"[37] Rawkins awakens in a positive mood, and soon becomes the fourth voice in a black gospel group.

Finally, Yip returned to discussing the love story between Sharon

David Wayne as Og in *Finian's Rainbow*, January 10, 1947.
Courtesy of Eileen Darby Images, Inc.

and Woody, and its deeper meaning to the plotline concerning xenophobia. "The point I'd like to make is that you'd never like a song without its having some integrated, logical reason . . . A song is never just something that you work in and just all out . . . sing for the sake of singing. A song has as much exposition . . . character, entertainment, enlightenment, and [must] be a part of the scene. In other words, we're not just going to sing a song to entertain you but to advance the story, advance the characterization.

"Now we have one . . . We come to a scene which is a love scene. Woody and Sharon have to get together at some time and the time is right, the moonlight is right and what kind of a love song shall we have for Woody, who is this kind of a southern guy. He's not just a Broadway ingenue. He's a real character. He's a fellow with sharecroppers, he's of the soil, he's an honest person. He's not just a guitar player or a singer or a Broadway juvenile. So we've got to give him a song that [will] be part of that character, be honest. And she, a girl, a colleen, from Ireland, rather unique, interesting, isn't the kind of girl you meet every day. She's Irish with her Irish folklore, a little bit strange . . . and he's in love with her. And he wants to tell her he's in love with her but the good writer, the writer who has some respect for his skill and his trade, wants to stay away from the cliché writing . . . A good writer wanting to write a lasting song and wanting to keep away from clichés tries to think of an original idea.

"Now, the situation presents itself here to the writer. All right, there she is and he wants to tell her he loves her. And the first thing that comes to his mind at this point is that 'you've bewitched me.' Which is what love really does, isn't it? Love is . . . sort of a witchcraft. You meet a person who is chemically on your beam, who vibrates the way you do. Something happens to you that doesn't happen when you . . . go out and buy a banana . . . He wants to express that idea and he says . . ."[38]

I look at you and suddenly
Something in your eyes I see
Soon begins bewitching me
It's that old devil moon
That you stole from the skies

It's that old devil moon
In your eyes

You and your glance
Make this romance
Too hot to handle
Stars in the night
Blazing their light
Can't hold a candle
To your razzle dazzle

You've got me flying high and wide
On a magic carpet ride
Full of butterflies inside
Wanna cry, wanna croon
Wanna laugh like a loon
It's that old devil moon
In your eyes

Just when I think I'm
Free as a dove
Old devil moon
Deep in your eyes
Blinds me with love.[39]

Yip continued, "It's a little tongue in cheek, isn't it? He's trying to tell her that there's something about her, 'you've bewitched me, you bedeviled me, you made me feel something I never . . .' And he's doing it almost with a twinkle in his eye so that we don't take it too seriously and at the same time the real emotion is there . . . [In the second part] . . . you notice there's a mixture there of honest emotion and yet fun and lightness. There's nothing gooey about it. No treacle, no sentimental junk there. It's a real love song. It's an honest love song . . . It's imitative of nothing else. It's a new idea . . . And notice that the tune, too . . . You must give the tunesmith credit. What an unusual tune it is.

"Now why did we write a witchcraft song there? That wasn't done just . . . to be original and just . . . to say, 'You've bewitched me.' We have a purpose. In the second act, if you remember, at one point the bigots, the rednecks . . . are going to blame Sharon for having turned a senator black because she's a witch, because there's witchcraft in her, she comes from a foreign place. Anybody that comes from a foreign place with a foreign accent, and the prejudice is all there, is evil, has witchcraft, is a witch . . . So what we want to do is telegraph in the first act that there's something bewitching about our heroine. Later on in the second act, bango, there it is. And then when he wants to reprise, when Woody, the hero, wants to reprise, he says, 'Yeah, you turned that senator black, I told you you were a witch . . . didn't I? Didn't I always say that "[You and] your glance / Make this romance / Too hot to handle?"' And you've got a great reprise. But the reprise comes in in a situation in the second act that again is not foreign to the song. It's part and parcel, integrated into that song."[40]

Yip added an interesting story about the origin of "Old Devil Moon." He said, "Everything is fair in war, in love, and in songwriting. Because the creative spirit is one that isn't just logical and there isn't just thinking out a thing mathematically. Much of the creative spirit depends upon luck, grabbing things out of the air, a word, anything that will give you a handle for creativity. Now, Burton Lane and I were writing movies before we wrote *Finian's Rainbow*. And when you're writing movies you're always writing songs that get left out of movies, songs that you have left over. And we were writing a song for Fred Astaire. [Lane claimed it was for Lena Horne.] . . . We needed a song for Astaire and Burt had written this lovely tune which had always intrigued me. And the lyric I had written for this song for Fred Astaire and for the particular situation in the picture went like this.

> Came to give you back that ring
> Came to drop the whole damn thing
> And to take it on the wing.
> But now you're standing there
> With that moon in your hair
> And I swear this is where I came in.

. . . And luckily, when we were doing *Finian* we needed a witchcraft song at this point." So Yip and Lane used the tune from "This Is Where I Came In" for "Old Devil Moon."[41]

At the conclusion of Yip's interviews on *Finian's Rainbow*, he explained that the end of the musical leaves a great many unanswered questions. "And now here is Finian who came to this great land of wealth and plenty and gold and what's happened to his gold crock? What's happened to all of his great promises and dreams? His dreams are all shattered because if you're in the audience and you've been living this man's dream and you've been living the life for these two hours, you've lived a lifetime with these people and you hate to see his dreams shattered, but the author's very happy that you're feeling miserable because [you're] waiting on him to solve the problem for [you]. And here's where you [the author] feel like a god. You've got an audience here and unless you give them the answer, they're going to walk out very miserable and they won't sleep for nights and they're going to kill you for having a society like this that could do these things. All right.

"So now we come from what we call climax to resolution, okay? . . . Now we make a big, big point that the man who's poor, that the man who has nothing, he can be born as free and as equal, fifty times as anybody, and he can pursue happiness, and then we push the very Constitution of the U.S. We are all born free and equal, we have the right to the pursuit of happiness, but *are* we born free and equal? And can we pursue happiness? And shouldn't there be one little word stuck into the Constitution, that says, yes, we are born free and equal and we all have the right to the *means* for the pursuit of happiness. Now, unless you are given the *means* for the pursuit . . . you don't have the means, you cannot pursue happiness. And this is what our whole situation right now is all about, as we evolve as human beings, as we evolve as a nation, as we evolve, does Congress realize . . . that human beings must be given the opportunity, not only in words, but in practicality, to have the tools with which they can go to work and then on their own free enterprise, do the things. And that stage we have not reached yet. And this is why *Finian* is still maybe 25 years ahead of its time, even though it was written in 1946. We still have to find out that we've got to give people the means for the pursuit of happiness. What are the means? Free education. Free opportunity for a job. Free opportunity to be equal and to get good jobs. Now that's not being communistic and that's not being socialistic and that's not being a (rebel). It's being honest and democratic . . ."[42]

There is no doubt that *Finian's Rainbow* has had universal appeal. In New York alone, there were four major revivals, in 1955, 1960, 1967, and 2009. A film version, which Yip hated, was made in 1968 starring Fred Astaire and Petula Clark and directed by Francis Ford Coppola. Yip himself told a few stories to confirm the show's popularity. As early as 1949, he told the following stories at a Philadelphia author's luncheon held "in defense of dignity":

"When *Finian's Rainbow* opened in this city of brotherly and sisterly affection, I overheard a conversation in the lobby of the Erlanger during intermission. (An author loves to eavesdrop on his audience for uninhibited criticism.) The dialogue I overheard was between two rugged individuals with mint julep accents. First mint julep man said, 'Jim, cain't understand why the sheriff don't come right on down and close dis here show up.' Second mint julep man: 'Beats me too, Bill, but I must say I'm having a right good time.' First M.J.M.:—'That's the trouble, Jim, ah am too, but they sure oughta get the sheriff to close it down.' At this point, there came the signal for the curtain going up, and Jim reckoned as how they better hurry back in if they didn't want to miss any of it.

"I am happy to state that the conscious mass appeal culture dished out by Finian McLonergan brought thousands of Southerners to the Box Office and we haven't lost a Dixiecrat yet.

"It is pleasing to note that *Finian* has been playing for three solid years in the United States. It is playing to packed houses in Prague after two years, and will be performed in Paris and Tel Aviv next year. It is being made into a movie which more millions will see . . ."[43]

And in February 1970, Yip told a radio audience, "I had a funny experience just about a half year ago. I was at a party and there was a Czechoslovak anthropologist there. He could barely talk English but he talked enough. And somebody asked me to sing 'Glocca Morra.' So I did and his face lit up and he came over and he says, 'How do you know that song?' I said, 'Why, it's an American song and it was written for an

American musical.' He says, 'Really? I thought this was an old Czecho-slovakian folk song because every Christmas that show is revived and that song is the big song out of it.'

"In Czechoslovakia they had a wonderful trick. They had a fella come in who was the Senator and who was made up half black and half white. His right side was white and his left side was black and he played the whole scene before he turned black facing the audience with his right profile. And all he had to do when the shock came was to turn around and there he was and he played to the audience with the left profile and it worked beautifully. We didn't do that in New York, our opening. What we did was we got a stand-in for the Senator who had his height, his shoulders, his stance, and everything else, and he fell to the ground in a sitting position with his back toward the audience and his great big white hat and talking to Buzz, the Sheriff, who was facing the audience. So from the Sheriff's reactions and facial expression the audience learned everything without facing the actual Senator. The audience got the reflected actions of the Sheriff without ever showing the Senator's face."[44]

But perhaps one of the most entertaining recollections came from Lena Horne, herself a noted civil rights activist, who told this story about deciding to perform for a demonstration in Birmingham, Alabama, held by Dr. Martin Luther King: "And when I went to Birmingham, I—You know what I sang in Birmingham? I sang 'Begat' because Martin Luther King was a preacher and I didn't know any religious songs."[45] One imagines that Yip would have been amused by that story.

Finally, it seems appropriate to end this chapter with a small tale of another of Yip's major successes in 1947. On June 24 of that year, he was finally awarded his bachelor of science degree from the City College of New York. His final four credits were granted as what today we would call "life experience," for public speaking and professional playwriting.[46]

12 | A Pause for Burton Lane

There are times when collaborators have mixed feelings about their partners. This was certainly the case with Burton Lane. In 1929, when Ira Gershwin introduced the sixteen-year-old Lane to Yip Harburg, Yip was thirty-three years old, so according to Lane, there was a bit of a "father-son thing" in their relationship. As a result, perhaps, Lane was slightly hesitant with Yip. His memories of their work together on *Finian's Rainbow* seem to bounce between feelings of exuberance and intimidation.

"And when I write songs with him," Lane told Max Wilk, "I don't think there's a more satisfying creative experience in anything I've ever done . . . I mean, he has a tremendous *ear*—catches every nuance that's in a tune—fits it with lyrics that are right, and it's a joy. He makes *me* like my own tunes better."[1]

But as Lane indicated, there was a constant tension between him and Yip, which Lane tried, somewhat unsuccessfully, to figure out over the years. His comments about Yip illustrate his problems with this "father-son thing," a relationship that might have recalled his conflicted feelings about his own father. "I had a very pushy father," Lane told Wilk. "Whenever my father saw a piano, he'd say to me, 'Go over and play.' It was so painful for me—and to this day, when people ask, 'Will you play?' my first reaction is 'no.'"[2] Some of his unhappiness working with Yip centered around what could be called Yip's "pushiness."

One of the qualities that Lane liked so much about Yip was that he was "a socially conscious person." But at the same time, Lane wanted interviewers Bernard Rosenberg and Ernie Harburg to know that, although he was interested in *Finian's Rainbow* from the start, he did not want to be caught up in writing a message musical, as Yip and Fred Saidy did. He was attracted to the project for its entertainment value; its meaning was a valuable add-on: "You want to do an entertainment . . . With *Finian*, Yip came to me . . . when he and Fred had written a first draft of the show . . . It happened that that show was about things which are socially significant, but it wouldn't have to be. It could have been anything . . . Yip brought an idea which I liked tremendously. I liked it because it had something to say, but I might have liked it if it didn't have something to say—if the idea was a good one. In other words, I was not primarily interested in only doing a socially significant show. Yip was."[3]

So they built a musical together, but later, when Lane reflected back on the experience, he commented, "And one has to wonder, why two people who did a show like *Finian* never did another show. Because when I would bring things to Yip which I thought had great value, unless you could get social significance into it, he didn't want to do it. I think if you could come up every time with an idea that has something to do with life—whether it deals in a funny way or a serious way or any way—with the realities of life, where people leave the theatre feeling they've been upgraded a little bit, that is preferable to me than to do a show about *Annie*, which is a show one can enjoy, but limitedly . . .

"I thought it [*Finian's Rainbow*] was the best idea I'd ever heard in my life—I loved it tremendously . . . [But] the second act, when I saw it, started to get very heavy handed, very angry. [Lane does not specify what the issue at stake was.] When you lose your objectivity, it becomes heavy. In terms of satire, you've got to look down on the silliness of things people do as if you were on the moon, with great tolerance and love of what's on the earth. Look at those silly people killing each other, what are they killing each other for? You make fun of war.

"But once you get involved in it in a subjective sense, you can't make fun of it anymore, and Yip got angry in the second act, and very heavy, and I was able to get him out of that . . . it's no secret, I had a lot of ambivalent feelings with Yip because it was like father and son, there was a big age difference and it was up and down . . . I loved writing songs with Yip. He was the best, the best. And worth the pain of other things just to sit in a room and write songs with him, but Yip and I were not talking after *Finian*."[4]

Rosenberg and Ernie Harburg went on to ask Lane about his collaboration with Yip. "First of all," he waffled, "everybody has their own personality and everybody has their own egos and they all have their own strengths and insecurities and I finally, after many years of analyzing, came up with what I thought was really the crux of his [Yip's] difficulties . . . when I would say to Yip, 'That line's not clear,' or 'It doesn't seem right,' he never argued, he would change the line. He respected my judgment on that and he would change it and there was no problem. . . .

"I don't think I ever worked with a more flexible composer. I think one of the reasons Yip liked working with me is that I never objected if by accident he added notes that shouldn't have been there. But to me the lyric was more important than the tune because you had to say it right—that was the first thing an audience was conscious of, what was coming out of their mouths. The music was subjective. They would get that later."[5]

As Lane noted in another interview, "Yip would get very excited when he heard a tune. He'd bounce all over the room, and he'd write. He was already clicking with lyrics. He'd go home and brush it up a little bit but he would write while he was there, while he was all excited . . . Yip was all joy. He bounced. He was enthusiastic. As a matter of fact, one of the things that worried me working with Yip when I was improvising was that he'd write something too fast and a lot of times I was right, and it wasn't good enough. He would get carried away with enthusiasm. We all do . . . But the point is, with Yip, he was always enthusiastic—except if something was terrible, but he was really a very enthusiastic writer."[6]

Still, Lane seemed to fear Yip's assertiveness. "But if you were to say one word about the book, he'd [Yip] tear your head off. He used to attack people. When we had readings, we had about 40 readings of *Finian* while we were working on it, just to write it, to get an audience reaction to it, on Bentley Drive in California, we went out to 25 or 30 people every couple of weeks and we wrote a couple more songs, and it was a workshop, it was a Broadway workshop. A great way of doing it. But if anyone, later sitting around and talking, said something, Yip said, 'What?! What do you mean?!' He'd get angry. That was the one area where he was insecure. Yip had never written a book before. That was his first book. He had made contributions to books, but he had never written a book."[7]

When asked about Saidy, Lane gave a brief response before returning to Yip: "Fred was always in the background. He would be insecure too, but not as insecure. Yip was the one who would be aggressively antagonistic. Couldn't take any criticism at all. When you're not on top of something, when you're frightened, then you really don't know. A couple of years later in California Arthur Freed asked me if I would work with Yip. He knew we had problems . . . Yip had no respect for me; before *Finian* went into rehearsal we played a couple of benefits where we did some songs for the show, and Yip would introduce me as his piano player or 'the guy who plays the piano.' He never introduced me as the composer . . . I said to him . . . 'Yip, the next time you introduce me that way, you're going to be singing a capella. I'm walking off the stage and you're going to do it alone.' So working in a studio, nobody's the boss, we're both getting what we're getting, and . . . we're on equal footing. On that basis, I would work with him."[8]

For all the questions he had about his relationship with Yip, Lane still wished to identify with him. "Yip's a loner," he told Wilk, "like me. He's worked with lots of marvelous composers, but he's never really tied himself permanently to any one. He's always wanted to try new things with different talents. The results are usually fascinating."[9]

One is left to wonder about Lane's feelings toward Yip. Did he love him as a friend, a father figure, a composer? Did he fear Yip's strong opinions? Was he nervous about being criticized by this man he so admired? These are intriguing and unanswered questions, and they open up a hundred more about the unique relationship between collaborators. As the next episode in Yip's life illustrates, however, Burton Lane was a loyal and true friend.

13 | Anger, Frustration, and Persistence During the McCarthy Years

The sense of ambivalence and confusion toward the Soviet Union, and toward communism in general, that had persisted in the United States from 1917 through World War II ended with the surrender of Japan in August 1945. Fear of Soviet incursion into Asia, Eastern Europe, and then the rest of the world now set the United States on a relentless path to stop communism wherever it appeared or threatened to—at home or abroad. So intense was this crusade that in 1947, President Harry Truman ordered the FBI to investigate the backgrounds and activities of more than 3 million US government employees. By 1950, Uncle Sam's henchmen began firing people they deemed to be security risks. Further, when the Soviets successfully tested their first atomic bomb in 1949, the Cold War nuclear arms race took off, and with it, a Red Scare that was fiercer and longer lasting than that of the post–World War I era.

Yip Harburg, like so many other show business personalities, was swept into the phenomenon that became known as McCarthyism. Named after its chief proponent, the Red Scare became an epidemic when in February 1950, Senator Joseph McCarthy of Wisconsin accused the US State Department of employing communists—all-American, Ivy League–educated "Reds." From there came the panic over the accusation that spies had been feeding atomic bomb secrets to the Soviets ever since the early 1940s. The most publicized case was that of New York–born Julius and Ethel Rosenberg, who were executed in the electric chair in Sing Sing prison on June 19, 1953, after having been found guilty of conspiring to transmit secret national defense information to the Soviet Union. By 1954, millions of US citizens were feeling the effects of McCarthyism. Communism was seen as such an evil that in that year, the Communist Control Act made party membership illegal in a nation that prided itself on being the world's protector of freedom of speech. The House Un-American Activities Committee (HUAC) hearings that were so prevalent during the early 1950s continued into the 1960s as well.

Hollywood, no stranger to censorship as we have already seen, hopped onto the Red Scare bandwagon as early as 1947, when the industry blacklisted what are now called the "Hollywood Ten," banning these writers, directors, and actors from working on films. In that same year, the conservative writer Ayn Rand told HUAC that Yip and Jerome Kern's song "And Russia Is Her Name" was a good example of Hollywood writers' pro-Soviet sentiment. Yip was also mentioned, as were many others, in the publication *Red Channels*, whose aim was to expose so-called un-American work in the media. The result of this poisonous atmosphere was that in 1950, Yip was removed from the creative team working on the musical film *Huckleberry Finn*; he did not return to film work for a full decade.

Within the context of the McCarthy years (and beyond), it's important to look at what Yip had to say about his own beliefs and feelings, and about the Red Scare's effect on his career. For example, in a 1977 interview with radio personality Jack O'Brien, he responded to questions about his personal creed:

"I was never any doctrinaire kind of a fellow," he began. "First of all, when we talk about right and left, Jack, don't you find that what was right twenty years ago now has become middle of the road . . . All these things are really . . . flexible and they're changeable. And I don't think anybody knows what right is or what left is. I think [it is] confusion we make, and especially people about me, when I tirade against injustice or with satire. I feel there's no such thing as right and left. There's forward and backward. Now, in the evolution of man, he has to go forward, which means he has to make change or else he would stay where he was when he was a Neanderthal, but every change involves a trauma, and we all hate change and we are all afraid of the fellow who wants a little more change . . .

"For example, when Roosevelt was President, who ever thought of unemployment insurance? That was considered a communist idea, but now we accept the thing. I don't think we ought to label anything with isms. We ought to go slowly and advance ahead and change as the society calls for change. Now the poet, the artist, is always a little bit more passionate about change than the average guy and so he's mistaken always for the way-out rebel and things of that sort.

"I never considered myself a rebel. I always considered myself a fellow who, when I had a script and I felt it could be better, I tore the script up and rewrote. And that's what makes a good artist. That's what makes a good songwriter . . . The artist always wants a change. He feels there's something better . . . But you've got to do that politically too. If the system doesn't work—and if there's bigotry, if there's racism, if there's injustice, if there's one guy with all the wealth in the world, and another guy starving and nobody does anything for this guy, you've got to want to say, 'I want a change. That's why I want to tear up this lyric, get something better.'"[1]

When asked if he thought that communism could work anywhere in the world, Yip responded, "I don't think communism, or anything, or socialism, or even democracy has ever had a chance to function . . . democracy is the most advanced, the most civilized, because every man has to pitch in and do something. Communism, as we know it, right now, under Stalin and the guys that are running it now, is a bureaucracy . . . a dictatorship . . . But Karl Marx never said that. Karl Marx, if you read it, was a humanist . . . Karl Marx said it's the individual and freedom for the individual, and how he can become free of the tyranny of working too long and too hard and everything else . . . We all confuse these things. I think . . . the history of the world is the history for freedom, the fight for freedom . . .

"I'm not looking for leadership in any esoteric form. The only thing I know is people. I know I'm living with you. I know I'm facing you, Jack O'Brien. I want to have a good relationship with you. I want to see you well dressed, well clothed, well fed, and a decent human being that I can communicate with, and I'd like to see that extended to the whole world and how to do that is a very tough job and under what rules we use and what societies we form, man must be educated so that he will know what this earth is, how to distribute the wealth, how to work with one another, how to cure neurosis and neuroticism, one man from another, which is the best form of society and we are groping; we are at the foothills of civilization. Man hasn't been here for a long time; [he was] a Neanderthal just a few thousand years ago. And we're still groping . . .

"Where there's no freedom, then there's no spirit. And you cannot progress and you can't do anything. The number one thing is man's freedom and any kind of system that takes away man's freedom is dead, but you must realize too that freedom is not an absolute word. It's like everything else . . ."[2]

As we have already seen, for these beliefs, Yip had been carefully watched in Hollywood for years. As he explained in 1971, "Always. Always. . . . every lyric was fingerprinted and the history of it taken and the microscopes were applied to every word to see what hidden meanings there were. And I lost many a job and people were afraid to write with me. But the fella who's always in advance of his social awareness always goes through that. That's a historic repetition—all the ages. I mean, whether you're a little minor poet like myself or you're a major scientist like Galileo . . . I went through that all the way through. I was canceled out everywhere. I was blacklisted from Hollywood because . . . I was president of the Hollywood Democratic Committee which was a society to advance the cause of Roosevelt and the New Deal, so immediately you were termed a Red or what the hell ever. Sure, we were blacklisted and we were hounded. But it doesn't matter if you write the truth and if you write beautifully, those things will live much longer than the big hit songs that came out at the time."[3]

So it happened that in December of 1950, Yip was called into the office of J. Robert Rubin, head of MGM's legal department, and questioned about his political activities and beliefs. Nothing describes that meeting better than the follow-up letter Yip wrote to Rubin on December 25, 1950:

It is Xmas day. The world is celebrating the birth of a saint who was crucified as a sinner. And today people are still crucifying each other in the same obfuscated manner. On this day, it is especially grim and ironic that I should be defending myself against the scurrilous and unwarranted charges made by Counter-Attack, the Pontius Pilate organization of our day. This vicious group, hell-bent on crucifixion and a little money, makes poor Judas with his puny thirty pieces of silver seem a harmless fellow indeed.

It is ignominious to be placed in a position of having to ask you to believe that I have no evil intentions toward a country which was a refuge for my parents and a land of rich reward for me. To think that I would belong to any organization which has for its purpose the violent overthrow of our form of government, its constitution, or its institutions, is palpably absurd.

At your invitation I came down to see you last Thursday at your office. I had no advance notice of the purpose of our meeting. You asked me whether I was a communist, or ever had been a Communist, or was ever a member of any communist organization. Each of these questions you will recall I categorically, and without qualification or attempt at evasion, answered in the negative. I am ready at any time to repeat the above under oath.

Since I believe that the Federal Constitution is the firmest guarantee of human rights, it would be supremely irrational to wish to see it overthrown. In the final years of my life, it is not likely that I would want to see the world in a state of chaos and turmoil. Of course I realize that Loew's Inc. relies upon the truth of the statements herein contained and . . . I am also willing that this declaration of mine be made a part of any agreement entered into. You may consider any statements made as not only statements of principle, but as warranties as well, upon which you have the right to reply.

In reference to organizations to which I belong, and which you inform me are on the Attorney General's list as being subversive—I believe I joined the National Council of Soviet-American Friendship because since the politicians had failed so miserably I hoped the poets might succeed in bringing about understanding and peace. It was the only way that I could communicate with the artists, writers, and poets of the Soviet Union at a time when communication is desperately needed. This organization numbers among its membership some of the country's most conservative business and professional men, as well as scientists, artists and intellectuals of the highest stature.

You mentioned the Hollywood Writers Mobilization and the League of American Writers. Without criticism or repudiation I do not remember belonging to either of these organizations.

None of the organizations to which I have belonged have ever, so far as I know, advocated or promulgated anything but democratic principles. If at any time it is ever proven to me that any organization to which I belong is in reality subversive of the best interests of this country or owes allegiance to a foreign power which threatens this country, I would of course, sever connections forthwith.

Finally, to clarify my position, let me say this. I am a Franklin Roosevelt Democrat, believing firmly in everything he stood for. I know, as an intelligent person, that the world is not static, that change is the law of all life. It is cruel and unfair to label communist all those who wish to help bring about healthy needed change. Our constitution provides for the possibility of change. The machinery is there. As long as we have ballots, it would be criminal to join groups who would use bullets.

I am, like you, confident of the final judgment. But in reference to that, let me assure you that unless we all, *now* while there is time, fight the evil men of Counter-Attack and their ilk, instead of one another, we shall end up, together at last, in the same lime pit . . .[4]

In 1976, Yip reflected more on this McCarthy era experience and what it meant to his career. As he told Celeste Wesson of WBAI radio in New York City, "Well, I was working in Hollywood . . . I got a call from Metro's lawyer, Mr. [J. Robert] Rubin and [he] said, 'Look here, what are your politics?' and so on, so on, so on, so on, and all that nonsense, you know. I had never . . . joined the Communist Party . . . I'd just been one of those nice, vociferous guys who was fighting injustice and join-ing all the good movements at the time, that saw ahead and were pro-phetic and prophesied many things that are now happening today . . . I was just a member of the human race, doing my little bit for it, and they wanted me to do all sorts of crazy things . . .

"At first they didn't want anything. They just wanted me off the picture [*Huckleberry Finn*]. They wanted no facts, no anything. And they paid me, they paid me my contract and I got off the picture. The picture was done . . . And evidently, atheist that I am, there must be some divine providence that took care of me . . . because it was a big flop. I hate chuckling over things like that, but in a case like this, I mean, you can't help being a little mystical.

"After I was dismissed from the picture, blacklisted in TV and radio . . . and of course nobody would dare touch us or even mention our names, but I was not barred from the theatre. I was able to do *Flahooley* and other things later on . . . It was harder to get backers. I had to be checked out on everything, but I will say in my case my plays made money, and anything that makes money . . . you overlook. You can have as black a heart and as red a face as possible. As long as you make money they'll forgive you a little bit. They fine combed my stuff a little, but I will say that the theatre was great, though. The theatre was the one place that had the guts to stand up and say things.

"Now, but what happened in Hollywood, after I was blacklisted, a picture came up, this was about two or three years later . . . *Hans Christian Andersen*, and Goldwyn wanted me, and he sent his wife Frances over to New York and she asked me to her hotel and I came to see her; [they] wanted me to do the lyrics for the picture and I said, 'Fine.'

"We had almost signed the contract and before a few weeks were up, bango, suddenly the contract, the verbal contract, was absolved and I didn't get the picture, and—she made it clear to me that they'd have trouble clearing me . . . I got from the agent, Louis Schur, that Goldwyn wanted me very badly but he didn't want to have any trouble with the powers and the critics and so on. Then the next thing that happened, I was in Martha's Vineyard, my summer home, and I got an emergency call. They want[ed] Harold Arlen and myself to do the Judy Garland picture, *A Star Is Born*, and she wanted us, and naturally, a star, having had such a big hit with *The Wizard of Oz* always has some feeling . . . well, we're her good luck stars. Let's get Harold and Yip to do the picture. Of course I was willing . . . [I went to New York]. And everything was set . . . And I said [to Harold], 'Well, I'm going to pack up, go back to the Vineyard, pack up, come back here.' And I did. I came back and was ready to get on. Everything was set—airplane, everything. And I got a telegram, an out-and-out telegram from Sid Luft [Judy Garland's husband]: 'Sorry, we can't clear you now.' And, 'Judy heartbroken. We're certainly going to do the next big [thing] and we're going to fight to get you cleared,' and so on and so forth. But finally, Harold had to get Ira Gershwin to do the thing for me.

"All the way through the fifties. This was about five, six years later, seven years later. And so I lost one picture after another like that. In fact, I never got back to Hollywood for ten years . . . Ten years later the thing had sort of died down a little bit and the studios were getting a little more aggressive . . . they realized that they were going to ruin without the good guys who had all left.

"Anyhow, what happened was the thing, like every blackguard thing, boomerangs. It boomeranged on the studios. How did it boomerang on the studios? Here's how: Arthur Freed, who was the head of the best musical comedy group or segment in all of Hollywood . . . was terribly mad that he couldn't get me for a picture. He wanted me to come out and . . . do a picture on the life of . . . the first woman journalist, Nellie Bly. They had a whole script written on Nellie Bly; they were writing it; they wanted Harold and myself to do the picture. Of course, Arthur Freed knew that that would be a subject that interested me. And he actually got me over. This time they sent for me, paid my fare, and we had started work on it . . .

"And Mr. Brewer, Roy Brewer, who was the head of the IATSE [International Association of Theatrical and Stage Employees] . . . and also a high muck-a-muck in the Legion of Honor . . . the American Legion. Notice how he worked it both ways. Head of the union and head of the legion, see? So with that kind of power, he held a scepter and a club over the studios. They couldn't move. Here was a man who was always in the ignominious position of having to fight for a two dollar raise for his men, you know, calling out strikes, being beaten the hell out of by the studio, and now he becomes head of all the studios. What a joyous, dramatic turn of events this was. The man who had to crawl now was getting Louis B. Mayer and Jack Warner to crawl to him and say, 'Please, can we use So-and-So? Can we use [Dalton] Trumbo to write two scenes, or a paragraph? Can we use Yip Harburg? Just one lyric, please?' What a joyous position he had now. And he was taking it all out on the studios. So when he found out that I was on the picture of *Nellie Bly* [he said,] 'Uh-uh. Nothing doing. This picture will be boycotted.' And Arthur Freed, Louis B. Mayer, got me in the office, apologized to me. 'Can't help it, we're in a terrible spot. Will you please go and see Roy Brewer and talk to him? We've talked to him and he said, we can clear things up if you just go there and [soothe] them up a bit.'

"So I went to see Roy Brewer one day. Well, I wish I had a tape of that meeting . . . Number one, he called in a fellow by the name, I think, of Cardigan. Cardigan was an ex-Communist. He came in with a file of papers on me that was thicker than all my works, and . . . I said, 'What did I do in pictures that was subversive? Can you tell me that?' He says, 'Look, we know all the tricks . . . [but] we must say this. We don't have anybody who has ever directly mentioned your name, who said you were in a cell or said you were a Communist.'

"I said, 'All right. Number one, I am not a Communist. Now what the hell do you want of me?' . . . He said, 'But you did things.' I said, 'Like what?' He said, 'Well, did you write a song called "Happiness Is a Thing Called Joe?"' I said, 'Yes, for *Cabin in the Sky*. A big hit.' He says, 'Which Joe were you talking about? Was it Joe Stalin?' Now, this is what I had to contend with. Either you bust out laughing, or you throw the desk at him. Well, I just broke into laughter, and this got them mad.

"And finally, the outcome of this whole meeting with Roy Brewer, Cardigan and the list [of] things like 'You gave money to China?'— 'Yes, I gave money to China.'—'Did you give money to the Spanish Loyalists?'—'Yes, I gave money to the Spanish Loyalists.'—'Why did you give money to the Spanish Loyalists?'—'They were fighting for my freedom. Did you want Nazi Germany to win?' You know, crappy, silly things like that. They were so idiotic. Finally they couldn't get anything on me, really, except these idiotic things where I had given my money to—'Are you a member of the Hollywood Democratic Committee?'— 'Not only am I a member, I started it.'—'Why did you start it?'—I said, 'There was a fellow, Roosevelt. We wanted to get him in. I liked Roosevelt.'—'Weren't there a lot of Communists in there in the Hollywood Democratic Committee?'—I said, 'If there were, I wouldn't know it. They don't have hammers and sickles on their foreheads. I don't know a Communist from another guy. All I know is the guys I worked with are all great, good guys, and thought the way I did. And I was the founder, one of the founders of it.' Well, we went on. All the silly old things, you know. 'What is democracy?'

"'All right,' I said, 'Why don't you want me to write *Nellie Bly*? I could get you a great score out of that and maybe we'd have some hit songs and it'll make you happy, too, and then you wouldn't have to sit around here with all these grim faces. I could write some funny songs for you. Your lives are very grim now. Don't you want a little happiness? Another "Over the Rainbow" maybe, or something like that?' Well, this got them madder and madder. I said, 'What do you want me to do?' They said, 'Do you know the newspaper that the American Legion gets out?' I said, 'Yeah.' . . . They open up . . . 'Here is an article by a good friend of yours . . . Here it is.' I took a look at the headline: 'I Was a Dupe for the Communists.'—'He was in your position. He was not a member of the Communist Party, but he was a dupe for it. Would you just write us one article along similar lines?'

"I said, 'No, I will not write one article. It's got nothing to do with politics. I've read your *Legionnaire* many times and I think it's a fourth-rate magazine and I will not write for anything that isn't a first-rate magazine. This is purely a literary idiosyncrasy of mine.' Well, they never got the article. I refused to write the article and the show was called off. I never got to see *Nellie Bly*. We have a couple of good songs, and that's it. Maybe the songs will come out at some time . . .

"It was one ignominious thing after another. Now, as I tell it, it sounds almost hilarious and funny, but it wasn't then. It was frightening and it was not only frightening, but it just took all your dignity away and you realized what it is to live in a police state and to have the fear that we understand people in certain countries have about not knowing what's going to happen next . . .

"First of all, it not only keeps hitting you, but you know that all around you that some of the fellows like my friend [Philip] Loeb did commit suicide, that [Joseph Edward] Bromberg did die, that this was taking a toll of my best friends, whom I was supporting at the time, like Henry Myers who had done all these beautiful shows and couldn't make a living, that he had just sold a pilot to one of the networks for a thousand dollars a week and the contract was abrogated and he went from a thousand dollars a week to penniless, couldn't work anywhere. And that you had to support him and you had to support ten others. And all around there was misery and heartbreak . . . They borrowed from each other. Dalton Trumbo borrowed a lot of money. If you read his book, I gave him some money and others gave him money which he returned later on . . . I was lucky. I had royalties from shows. And I had good songs out that were making money. And I had made a lot of money in Hollywood so I had some investments. I was a lucky guy. I was one of the lucky people."[5]

So Yip went home to Broadway, where during the next decade he launched three musicals with human rights messages: *Flahooley* (1951), *Jamaica* (1957), and *The Happiest Girl in the World* (1961). Of these, *Flahooley* was the angriest and in an interesting way, a continuation of some of his *Finian's Rainbow* concepts. The main plot of *Flahooley* concerns a young toy inventor who develops a laughing doll for his company's Christmas season. The doll's name is "Flahooley," a word that Yip credited as "a Gaelic thing, an Irish thing. It's anybody who talks to little people, you know, is a flahooley."[6] The script, written by Yip and Fred Saidy, explains that the doll laughs to set it apart from all other dolls, who cry. (In a draft version of the libretto, the doll clearly said, "Dirty Reds!" but that was soon changed.[7])

At the same time, a group of leaders from the Middle East bring the toy company's CEO, B. G. Bigelow, an ancient magic lamp to fix; it seems the genie will not come out and grant wishes. The two stories collide when the hero, Sylvester, produces the genie; wishes for success so that he can marry his girlfriend, Sandy; and then witnesses the genie making so many dolls that it drives the prices down and threatens the company's very existence. The company sets out to destroy the surplus of dolls, to get the genie back into the lantern, and to return to normal production.

Among the themes that Yip carried through from *Finian's Rainbow* were the dangers of overconsumption, the greed and inequities of the capitalist system, and the very real threat of overpopulation. The genie, whose name is Abou Ben Atom, is like Finian, an optimist who wants only good in the world and to see people happy. In addition, the libretto includes references to industrial spying and efforts to silence creativity. In effect, as the spirit of the genie is squelched, so was Yip's.

In a 1969 interview on the radio program Chappell's Broadway, Yip and composer Sammy Fain spoke about the show's message and its problems during the McCarthy era. As Yip explained, "I liked *Flahooley* very much because again, it was my métier, it was dealing with a social problem, of surplus, of why does a country that produces surplus have poverty? But it was done humorously. It was done with a toy factory and a toy tycoon who was a very funny man . . . And [some Arabs] bring [the broken lamp] to this toy and magic factory, America being the land of know-how and mechanical wizardry. They bring this problem to America to see if they can get the genie out of the lamp because they like the old ways better than the new. And this idea of shipping oil and getting oil and oil wells drying up was not as pleasant as just rubbing a lamp and getting everything they want, and they'd like to go back to the old days.

"The hero has invented a doll that laughs, but it couldn't be produced for price, and the laugh couldn't be produced either so that it'd really be a human laugh. The genie does happen to come out of the lamp and solves the problem for the factory, produces all the dolls at once at a price that was so ridiculously low that it outsells all the other toy houses, and comes Christmas this genie keeps on producing dolls, and he's so imbued with the loveliness of the idea of providing a doll for every child, and a child is born every half a second, and he won't have to get back into that claustrophobic lamp and he wants to stay out. He likes the world. He likes a world where he can produce dolls and distribute them to children at [a] low cost.

"Well, comes a point where the abundance of dolls causes the price to fall and recession sets in. The tycoon wants the genie to stop producing the doll. The genie won't stop producing. He wants to keep on going in this beautiful way and spreading happiness and laughter in the world, but happiness and laughter that the genie wants to produce produces nothing but unemployment. So we have to close our factories and the genie now becomes a subversive character who's imported into the United States to overproduce in order to cause a recession, or depression. Therefore, things must be done to the genie.

"Well, they start breaking up his doll and getting rid of the surplus the way we do in order to save our economy, which throws the genie into a psychological tailspin. He goes into a coma, becomes schizoid, and an international complication is started because the Arabs now claim that we have ruined their source of supply.

"So you see how the whole humorous idea of economics is brought out with great laughter, great fun, and the situation is never really resolved to the perfection of international relationships, but it is resolved politically, in that they withdraw the genie; we withdraw with face, with honor, and poverty continues, so that there will be a shortage of supplies, so that the price can be kept up, and so that laughter is kept out of the world.

"I think that people did not quite understand the significance of the thing and I think the show had a few complications which were not ironed out . . . But there was great laughter. But I think by that time the McCarthy era had set in and we had gotten notices on the show before we even opened up. Miss [Dorothy] Kilgallen . . . and even Mr. Ed Sullivan called this a Red show . . . that we are using brazen propaganda. And they lost the whole point of the thing . . . And instead of understanding that it was pro-the United States, pro-letting us see where we are blind and that we are better patriots than those that just blind themselves and wave a flag for everything that's bad and that's silly and that is unproductive."[8]

Yip continued this discussion with another interviewer in 1976: "Showing how the economy works, that we cannot afford to have lower prices and we cannot afford to lose the profit system even if it means giving people everything they want. Great point. But it was 1950 with the McCarthy committee on. I mean, this was a most unpatriotic show, and even a man like Brooks Atkinson, after it got to New York, I mean, gave it a horrendous notice.

"Some who were more diplomatic couched it in dramaturgical analysis like, 'It's too cluttered . . . There are too many themes this takes up and we don't know which theme they're whacking away at.' A man like Ed Sullivan, who had a column, came out brazenly and said, 'Mr. Har-

The collaborators of *Flahooley*, 1951. Included clockwise from left: Bil Baird, Jerome Courtland, Yip, Ernest Truex, Fred Saidy, Irwin Corey, and Beth Logue. Courtesy of the Yip Harburg Foundation

burg, who is a real pro in the theatre, he got away with *Finian*, but now he's really trying to get away with something more brazen, and that's *Flahooley.*'

"Well, word had gotten around, word had gotten around. A man . . . on the *News* at that time . . . gave it a rave notice when it first came out. He was unaware of what was happening . . . [But] when the Sunday thing came out, his headline was, 'Politics and Laughing Dolls . . . Make Strange Bedfellows.' But his first review was great, but . . . evidently somebody had gotten to him."[9]

During the out-of-town previews, Yip noted, there were lines of "people around the block, just around the block at the box office, couldn't get seats. As soon as the notice came out, the lines ended, and we could barely make it through the summer, and we had to close finally . . . [After that] you had to censor yourself. You had to do things in a much more roundabout way, but I always thought that writing shows that were political ought to be censored from a satiric point of view. I don't think agit-prop straight on is good showmanship. I mean, that's just too realistic, transposing things from life right on to the stage. The stage is a place for imagination and entertainment and always should have what Churchill called 'a tactic through the soft underbelly,' you know, with humor and entertainment . . . But, so, I would say it affected things like when we'd have a show ready to go and get a backers audition, a lot of the backers would 'look out for Harburg' or 'look out for Saidy' and go through this with a fine comb, 'What does it mean?'"[10]

A couple of lyric examples illustrate what Yip brought forth in *Flahooley.* Perhaps most indicative of his sense that the nation had become a land of followers of McCarthy and his ilk was the opening number, "You Too Can Be a Puppet," a song presented with the assistance of a chorus of Bil Baird marionettes. The lyrics are simple and to the point, for as Yip told Deena Rosenberg in 1976, "Sammy Fain is much nearer the simple, the unsophisticated, pure heart and pure loveliness of a very simple kind. I'm not deriding him . . . but I have to write a very, very simple lyric with [him], but it's a loveable kind of gaiety."[11] The first part of the song includes these lyrics:

Verse

The world is full of a number of things,
And one of them is people,
People is the thing that the world is fullest of.
Among the number of things that people do
Is make a number of other people.
And this makes enemy number one a thing called love.

The world is full of a lot of escape, red tape and indecision,
But people is the escape that people escape from most.
They take to gin and to histamine,
To aspirin, Picasso and television,
And some take Consolidated Gas or the Saturday Ev'ning Post.
We pity you, we do, for all the ills that ail yur,
But here's good news for you, you needn't be a failure.

Chorus

Tiddlee aye, tiddlee aye,
Tiddlee all your trouble away,
You too can be a puppet,
You too can be a puppet.
Tiddlee swell, tiddlee grand,
Science has just discovered a gland,
And now you too, you too can be a puppet, a puppet.

Man, man, silly man,
Full of human folly,
Why be Grable fan,
Ku-Klux Klan,
When you can
Be Kukla, Fran and Ollie?

Tiddlee aye, tiddlee dee,
You can be just as happy as we,
Be a puppet, not an also ran,
Come out of the woodwork, brother,
And join the brotherwood of man,
The brotherwood of man.[12]

Yip's persistent concern about the values that are inculcated in children came through in some of the lyrics of "B. G. Bigelow, Inc.," the song that describes the toy company's many products. Here are a few lines:

A boy cannot grow up a gigolo
With toys from Bigelow, Inc.,
For what a man will fill his future days with
Depends upon
In childhood
What he plays with.

A Bigelow drum can make you run to battle,
A Bigelow fife can make you want to fight,
When Bigelow sells a kid a sword to rattle,
That kid grows up an Eisenhower Dwight, Dwight, Dwight.[13]

And about Yip and his colleagues being decimated by McCarthy, in the title song are these lyrics:

Show me a land where a feller can't laugh,
And I'll sell you that land for a buck and a half.
Show me that land where they jail your wit,
And I'll show you a land where no songs git writ.
Show me a land where they gag ev'ry gag
And they choke ev'ry joke with chains,
And I'll show you a land
Without Donald Ducks,
And a land without Mark Twains.[14]

In 1969, Yip explained why the song "The Springtime Cometh" pleased him so: "I thought 'The Springtime Cometh' was as lovely a thing as I could write. It was a take-off on all such Elizabethan, madrigal, sentimental, over-saccharine songs . . . It came in when the genie was ill, sick, he was out. The little girl who had posed for the doll, the laughing doll, dresses herself up as the doll, comes in at a moment in the play when the dolls were being burned and broken in order to get rid of surplus. And this is the thing that broke the genie's spirit. Even though he was a spirit himself, it broke his spirit. She came in telling him there are things to be done, there's a thing called Christmas and that during Christmas time people enjoy giving things to children for nothing, free, and that if he dresses up as Santa Claus, stands in front of Macy's, he'll be able to give his doll away and nobody'll hit him over the head. And nobody'll say that he's breaking the economy of the city. And so this is a joyous moment and even though it's winter, for him 'the springtime cometh, hummingbird hummeth, the sugar plum plummeth,' and, as he says, 'to summeth up, the springtime cometh for the love of thee,' so that the whole thing, even though it has a fine emotional value, to bring the spirit back to the genie whose spirits have been broken at this time, it also does it again with tongue in cheek on all such songs, cheer-up songs, Pollyanna songs; yet it is a Pollyanna song, but it's a Pollyanna song that doesn't take itself seriously."[15]

Flahooley opened on May 14, 1951, and closed after only forty-eight performances. Yip and his collaborators revised it for a version titled *Jollyanna*, which played short runs in Los Angeles and San Francisco the next year. Over the years, various small companies revived it for a few performances, including the Equity Library Theatre in 1964, London's Lost Musicals series in 1997, and an off-Broadway mounting in 2009. However, after the 1951 effort, it was not until 1957 that the next E. Y. Harburg musical hit Broadway. *Jamaica*, which Yip wrote with his old friends Harold Arlen and Fred Saidy, was designed as an intimate story about the Caribbean island that had made the word *calypso* so popular in the United States. It was also designed as a musical called *Pigeon Island* to showcase Harry Belafonte, the actor-turned-singer the record industry had nicknamed the "King of Calypso." Belafonte, however, had to undergo vocal chord surgery and could not do the show; in his place, producer David Merrick signed on the singing sensation Lena Horne, and as Harold Meyerson and Ernie Harburg put it, "*Pigeon Island* became *Jamaica*, a largely plotless evening of theater that was a triumphal revue for Lena Horne. Songs written for other characters were rewritten and reassigned. What was potentially a notable musical play became instead an evening of terrific entertainment."[16]

Two years after its opening, Yip spoke about his travails with the show. His words resound with a raw, non-reflective tone, his anger and disappointment at having to surrender his creative voice to the power of the director, Robert Lewis, and the producer, Merrick, most palpable. "It's not because I'm a writer," Yip explained, "but I believe the important fellow in all these things is the fellow with a word. Nothing else matters, really. It's the fellow who starts with the empty page and fills it and says, 'Here's what'll happen, here's what they say, here's how they do it'—he's the fellow that counts. Then when the director takes it, believe me, if there's nothing there he's got nothing and he can make nothing out of it. If the rice isn't there, he hasn't got the patty. The director sometimes will give you plus, most of the time will give you minus. Sometimes you thank heaven that he's just neutral, just puts the thing on a little bit the way it is.

"There's a lot of psychological things that go on with a fellow directing. The director always feels frustrated that he is not the creator of the thing, he is only an interpreter, and therefore he has great hostility towards the writer. Most directors want you out of the theatre, don't want you there.

"We went through a terrible thing with Robert Lewis, who is supposed to be a big name in the theatre and is actually a phony—unbelievable, knows nothing. He takes your material; you don't know what's going on in his mind, and he stages something—like in this show *Jamaica*, which was an adorable, charming, lovely thing like *Finian* on a small folk-tale basis—and he makes it a huge extravaganza for Lena Horne, with dancing and things, that destroys the very meaning, the tapestry of the whole thing. It's a travesty on everything we wrote.

"I felt so brokenhearted about it, I never went back to see it. I never saw it the opening night, or ever. I won't go to see that show. That it's making money is a tribute to the powerful material we have in there, the wonderful songs by Harold, and I've got some real socky lyrics there. If *Finian* had been done this way, it would have been the same horrible thing that this is. In other words, they took a sweet, darling show, with intimate songs, with a charming idea—and made this of it.

"This is something I think is important, more than the memories of Hollywood or anything else. Naturally, one has a financial interest in the show. You're on royalty, and you own part of it. Sure. Every good writer gets a small interest, some interest in the show, a percentage. We have a percentage. I wouldn't write a show at this point without that. No, having a percentage doesn't entitle you to a voice; being the author entitles you to the *entire* voice, but there are ways of getting around that. The author has the final say, theoretically, allegedly—but not practically, not actually. For example, what happens in a show like *Jamaica*? *Jamaica* is written with a certain style, with a certain meaning. Also, when you write a show, you over-write, because you cannot guess at everything while you're in your room, in your little tower putting it down on paper. You've got to see it in action. You've got to hear it with a live audience. Then you sit back, and there are a lot of things that you have prophesied in your writing that come true, and there are a lot of things that you've had doubt about that also show up, one way or another. Your doubts are verified, or sometimes you get surprises. The things you loved are falling and the things you didn't, show up. Therefore you over-write. You expect to make certain changes. The good trouper knows that when he goes out of town—and for that reason, he goes out of town five or six weeks—he will have to make those changes. And he prepares himself with changes.

"Now, the fellow who wrote the book of *Jamaica*, Fred Saidy, and I, as old-time showmen, did exactly that. We over-wrote also on songs, and we had one or two songs in the background that we were going to employ. Now, when you get a man like David Merrick, who is probably now the strongest impresario on Broadway, by virtue of quantity, of having more shows than anybody. He grew up as assistant on the bookkeeping end of the business, as business manager. It's a business mind, shrewd enough to know the theatre, to know how to get people to come into the theatre—new packaging methods, new publicity stunts, new promotion, how to manipulate theatre owners to get better bookings—in other words, the business of the theatre he's a shark at. This makes him now a producer.

"Now. He comes to a man like me. 'Everybody speaks of you as a great musical comedy man, you know your business, I want a show from you.' I tell him this idea for *Jamaica*. The idea was mine. When I tell him the idea, he loves it. He says, 'Go ahead, I'll produce it if you write it.' So Fred Saidy and I wrote it. We had a contract. He wasn't obligated to produce it if he didn't like it—he'd lose his advance, that's all. If he didn't like it, we'd have the right to sell it somewhere else, and he'd lose his advance. He doesn't gamble very much, really. It's we that are doing the gambling. Sure. We spend a year writing this thing. Most of the time I do it without any producer.

"But, in the case of Robert Lewis, he took this sweet, intimate, meaningful little thing, and made it into a big extravaganza musical comedy with people coming out and dancing old-fashioned dances like in the twenties, and big revolving things in front of your eyes. What we got there is a big extravagant entertainment thing which fights the book at every instance, and in which the book had to be chopped and cut and the meaning gone, the joy gone, the sweetness, the characters, the love—everything is out. And all you have is empty entertainment, with here and there, the songs. Of course, the songs we write always have some kind of punch or wallop or commentary.

"The critics don't know what goes on. All they know is the finished product. They all say: 'Bad book; great production.' That's all they will see. They will know nothing at all of what has been cut, of how the director has amputated coarsely, has done surgery of a butchering nature on this thing. They will know nothing of what went into it. All they will see is Lena Horne is great, Lena Horne is a wonderful thing—even though she doesn't at all represent the character we wrote. I would never have cast her in the role. But when Merrick got the book, he said, 'Well, I've got to have a big star, to get money. I will get Lena Horne.' The Hollywood business. 'I'll get Lena Horne, because if you don't get Lena Horne, who have we got to sell it?'

"Now, this is regardless of whether the part is for Lena Horne. It was never written for that type of person, who is just a singer. This has nothing to [do] with the songs, nothing to do with the lyric quality. But she's a big box-office attraction. That's all Merrick is worrying about. As soon as he got her, you see, she says, 'I want Robert Lewis to direct me, because he has a big name.' Now, she and Robert Lewis become one, and Robert Lewis, he's a little—how shall I say?—a queer. Look, I know a lot of homosexuals, and there are all degrees of homosexuals, and they have as much right to live as they do as the big masculine guy has. I have no intolerant attitude toward them, but—a lot of them have attributes that just hit certain values of life completely wrong. For example, sex relationships between men and women, love relationships or romantic relationships, such as we write, which have twinkle and fun, even though there is conflict, which always makes for drama. It's earthy. They interpret it as violent, and mayhem, and embarrassment. Their approach to sexuality is a mechanical one, because they don't know what [hetero] sex is, therefore they theorize about it—that sex must be this, this is what it does to the human being. Therefore you act this out on the stage.

"So our wonderful love thing, the relationship, say, in *Jamaica* between this boy Koli and this girl Savannah, now becomes a horrendous and violent mayhem thing of such anger and such bitchiness: that was not included in the thing! That's only one aspect of the thing. But the whole show takes on a frenetic frenzied thing that this guy sees in it that we don't. We see in it charming folk people, not doing dances, but living up to an anthropological fact of earthiness and saltiness. I would say, as *Finian* was done—it was done with sweetness and lovableness. The sharecroppers were dancing. These were Jamaicans dancing. But you don't get that here. You get Cotton Club, 1920, with all the brashness and everything thrown at you. Therefore the story is destroyed.

"But with this guy, this Robert Lewis, he was so frightened of authors. What he does is a common trick in the theatre, divide and conquer. In other words, what he does is this. He goes to Lena Horne and says, 'I will present you as the great artist you've never been on the stage—provided I will not be troubled and bothered by the authors, who always will throw this thing off-gear if they have anything to say.' She's frightened. She goes to the director and says, 'I want the authors out of the theatre. I want to do everything Bobby Lewis says.' You see? It's a Svengali relationship. This is what this little man does, and this is a known trick. Before you know it, the authors are out. They can't say anything. The show goes on the way these two see it.

"Now, when you get a producer like Merrick who knows nothing about the literature of the theatre or the soul of the theatre, but only the business—he says, 'I've got to play [it] safe. Lena is my star. A million and a half dollars in the box-office. The way she wants it, this is how it is. Don't touch, boys. If you touch, we close the show.' So then we open in Philadelphia, and I say, 'If this show goes on the way it is, I demand to maintain my prerogative. I close the show.'

"Well, I wanted to close the show then. Then comes the big ethical question. Sixty Negroes working; you throw them out of business. Now, who will get his head into the noose? The author? Or do you want to throw these fellows out? You see?

"For a thing like *Jamaica* you get all kinds of money. Any author who has had success can go out and get money. In this case, Merrick has a couple of backers, oil well men, who will put money into anything he wants them to. There's a fellow, big oil well man, who has nothing to do—he'll be behind Merrick, help him in any show—it gives him prestige, he knows girls, etc. Well, what the hell, there'd be no theatre if there weren't chorus girls going out with the backers. There'd just be no theatre. You would have goddamned socialism, that's what you'd have—government subsidy. Is that as good? Never! Because that's bureaucracy, that's terrible. [The oil man] is the one who supplies Merrick with the money, and Merrick is the one that makes or breaks you.

"It cost about $300,000 to do *Jamaica*. I had no money in it, nor Merrick. Merrick has no money. That comes from maybe two backers who put up the main amount, and then a lot of friends that want to come in on the kill, you see, who'll offer money. I imagine they [the main backers] put in about $200,000, then $100,000 he gives to his friends. It's a sort of a favor to friends, you see. This is better than the horse races. The writer is the little jockey they're betting their money on. That's all we are, we're stable boys."[17]

Yip was also angry at the critical response to *Jamaica*. As he continued, "I don't mean to deliver 'messages' in these things, I mean to deliver myself of a humorous idea in a satirical way, a laughable way, and make people enjoy it—and they do enjoy it.

"For example, there's a song in *Jamaica* called 'Leave De Atom Alone,' which is done Calypso, in which this girl says: 'If you don't leave it alone, you'll have terrible trouble with it—you'll burn your fingers, it'll singe your hair, it'll ruin your sweet disposition.' But she does it in a way that gets laugh after laugh after laugh. Mr. [Walter] Kerr comes out and says that Mr. Harburg, who's a jimdandy lyric writer, ought to lay off these ideas in musical comedy. Now, why should I lay off these ideas in musical comedy? Because Mr. Kerr thinks that the stage is a sanctified place, and you must not desecrate this sacred platform that must be for sheer entertainment, with no thought, with no controversy, with nothing to think about, with nothing that will stir your juices to say right or wrong—that it must be used for pleasure and for just unadulterated entertainment. So we have 'Goldilocks' now, which does not defy or disturb the tranquility of Mr. Kerr's Jesuit soul.

"I don't work that way. When there's something without conflict in the theatre, when there's something without big drama, I am not stirred. I can't write, I can't be funny, I can't write a lyric, I can't write a song, unless it has some meaning. Mr. Kerr is completely against that, so that I am behind the eight ball with Mr. Kerr no matter what I do. He is generically against me, you see.

"So, I don't really have Mr. [Brooks] Atkinson on my side. He's always leery, and he took great trouble with *Jamaica* to say, 'Well, at last a show that has nothing but sheer joyous entertainment, doesn't try to say anything,' and skipped over 'Leave De Atom Alone,' and skipped over another wonderful song called 'Napoleon's a Pastry,' and skipped over another wonderful song called 'For Every Fish There's a Little Bigger Fish.' He forgot those completely, which jampack this *Jamaica* thing, which say all the things I want to have said."[18]

In 1959, Yip revised the Broadway script of *Jamaica* in cooperation with the Karamu Playhouse in Cleveland, Ohio. Their script represents the closest existing version to Yip's original idea. The main plot tells the story of the small community of Pigeon Island just off the coast of "mainland" Jamaica. Savannah, a young woman, has dreams of moving to another island, called Manhattan. She is particularly entranced by the idea that, as the song "Push De Button" illustrates, she can "Push de button; Up de elevator; Push de button; Out de orange juice . . . Push de button, Wipe de window wiper; Push de button, Rinse de baby diaper," and so on.[19] Her long-term boyfriend Koli, a fisherman, wants to stay put. Along comes imperialistic Joe Nashua, a Harlem businessman, who wants to exploit the rich pearl oyster harvest to be found in the waters off the island. The islanders initially believe that Joe is just one of hundreds of tourists who will bring "the beautiful Yankee dollar" to their shores.

The subplot involves the people of the island who live simple lives until they hear they can make good wages by going into the dangerous coves to retrieve the pearls. Then ideas of competition and greed set in. It takes the appearance of a gigantic hurricane to set things right. At first, the inhabitants of Pigeon Island believe that there has been an atomic bomb explosion, leaving them alone on the earth. To survive, they begin to use the pearls as currency to purchase Koli's fish. He, in turn, becomes rich. Once their misunderstanding is set to rest, the inhabitants return to their more communal life, while Joe loses his business venture and Savannah returns to Koli.

Besides pushing buttons and cheering for the Yankee dollar, Yip ensured that the people of Pigeon Island had great wisdom about the current state of the world's affairs. As he explained in a 1979 interview, "the show said some very . . . meaningful things. You know, the plot of that show was that a big hurricane, storm, lashed a little island, Pigeon Island, off the coast of Jamaica, and they thought that the world had blown itself up and they had to start from Genesis and start all over again, that the white man had blown the world up. That was the idea of the show. You can see how modern it was. It's futuristic, even. And I had some great idea[s] to say in it. The heroine was a girl who . . . wanted material things. She wanted to go to that other island, New York. The hero was a guy who was satisfied with the naturalness of that island. He says, 'I've got everything I want now. I don't want to go to that other place, make a lot of money, get a heart attack and come down here to recuperate. I'm already recuperated.' So we made a mockery of the whole business-success cycle thing.

"Then there was another great point in that show that this girl, who is really in love with this poor fisherman, boy, now in order to get to New York, falls [for] . . . another guy who's going to get her to New York with money, and after the storm . . . by the luck of nature . . . fish is the only commodity you could eat on the island, so now all the jewels [pearls] come [Koli's] way. Everybody trades their jewelry, [even] the tourists, for his fish. Now he has all the jewelry to show the transitory power of money, you know. But now she comes back to him not because she wants the jewelry, the money, but because she really realizes that he was the one she loved. But now his love for her . . . runs the terrible acid test now of the capitalist system: Does she love me for me, or for my money? Now he doesn't know if her love is real or not. And the whole problem of today, is it me or my money he's after, or she's after? . . . Right, so each of these shows [including *Finian's Rainbow*] had powerful themes which nobody's doing now. Nobody! They were well in advance not only of their day but of today."[20]

Jamaica is chock-full of beautiful and interesting songs, but two in particular illustrate Yip's concerns about the state of civilization. The first is "Monkey in the Mango Tree." As Yip once said, "Now, I don't know if these statistics are accurate, but I read them somewhere, but it's been figured out by mathematicians that if ten thousand monkeys were each given an electric typewriter and left to pound away at them day and night for ten years, that the sum total of their literary output, if it were ever put together, we could extract every word included in Shakespeare's *Hamlet*. But I dare say it would probably take only three monkeys one half hour to write the song I would now like to sing for you . . . which took me several days."[21]

Yip then sang these lyrics:

Three monkeys in the mango tree
Were indulging in philosophy
And as I walked by the mango tree
One of them addressed himself to me

Hey man, is it true what they say?
Hey man, is it true that today
They claim that my brothers and me
Are the predecessors of humanity?

Hey man, why you give us bad name?
Hey man, it's a blight and a shame
To claim this uncivilized cuss
Could have been descended from the likes of us

How can you have de brazen face
To scandalize our noble race?
Don't identify yourself with me,
Said de monkey in de mango tree

Would a monkey do what silly man will do?
Live in de jungle of Madison Avenue
Fight his neighbors with a gun and knife
Love his horses and divorce his wife?

Would de monkey love a girl in zipper pants
Mud packs, girdles and deodorants?
Falsies fillin' out de vital spot
How de hell de feller know just what he got?

Hey man, why you give us bad name?
Hey man, it's a blight and a shame
To claim most unbiblically
That this chump could once have been a chimpanzee

Dat de monkey language
De monkey very clever
Which is to say in his own way
Would a monkey ever

Analyze his psyche, amortize his soul,
Tranquilize his frontal lobes with alcohol?
Televise his follies and the life he lives
Eulogize his gargles and his laxatives?
Simonize his teeth, lanolize his hands
Harmonize his chromosomes with monkey glands?
Mechanize de Greeks, modernize de Turks
And then with one little atom (poof!)
Atomize de works?

Hey man, do you call it fair play?
Hey man, is it cricket to say
Dat de monkey and his uncles and his cousins
And his aunts
Are de parents of such foolishment and decadence?
Don't identify yourself with me,
Said de monkey in de mango tree.[22]

The other song that also addressed Yip's concern with the nuclear age was "Leave De Atom Alone." As he explained it, the song was "inspired by the late Senator [Richard B.] Russell of Georgia . . . who always pushed for more and more atomic bombs [and] missiles, even when he knew that we had two bombs for every child and when asked if he wasn't worried about a world destroying itself, he replied, 'If there's goin' to be a nuclear showdown, with only two people left on this planet, ah want this new Adam and Eve to be Americans.' Now wouldn't it be social justice if these two lonely leftovers happened to be Dick Gregory and Jane Fonda?"[23]

The song, as Yip also noted, was "ahead of [its] time . . . It bothers me that people aren't aware that a song was written like that in 1957 when it wasn't quite the thing to be against the nuclear [bomb]."[24] Audiences often received "Leave De Atom Alone" with great enthusiasm. As Yip remarked in 1979, "And that stopped the show cold with laughter. Now, the trick of taking a cataclysmic idea like this, you know, which may destroy the whole human race, and make people laugh at it, to do that lyrically and musically is an art form that I don't find now at all, that's gone."[25]

The lyrics to "Leave De Atom Alone" are as relevant today (perhaps more so) as they were in 1957 when Yip wrote them:

Verse
Ever since de apple
In de garden wid Eve
Man always fooling wid things
That cause him to grieve
He fool wid de woman
De rum and hot blood
And he almost wash out
Wid de forty day flood

But not since de doom day
In old Babylon
Did he fool wid anything so diabolical
As de cyclotron

So if you wish to avoid
De most uncomfortable trip to paradise
You will be scientific
And take my advice

Chorus
Leave de atom alone
Leave de atom alone
Don't get smart alecksy
With de galaxy
Leave de atom alone

If you want to keep riding in Cadillac car
If you don't want to surely
Go to heaven prematurely on a shooting star
If it pleasure your heart
To keep smoking that big fat cigar
Let me drive de point home
Leave de atom alone

If you want Mississippi to stay where it is
If you want to see Wall Street
And General Motors continue in biz
If you want Uncle Sam to keep holding
What's yours and what's his
If you're fond of kith and kin
In their skin and bone
Don't fool around with hydrogen
Leave de atom alone

Bad for de teeth
Bad for de bone
Don't fool with it
Leave it alone

If you like Paris in the Springtime
London in de Fall
Manhattan in de Summer

With music on de mall
Stop fooling with de fallout
Above de cosmic ball
Or you will soon be fissionable material

Bad for de teeth
Bad for de bone
Don't fool with it
Leave it alone

Don't mess around you dopes
Lay off the isotopes
Don't you fuss with the nucleus
Don't go too far with de nuclear
Don't get gay with de cosmic ray
You'll burn your fingers
And you'll lose your hair
And you leave big smog
In de atmosphere

You most exasperated
When radioactivated
And cannot be located
On telephone
Go back to rock'n'roll-a
Rum and Coca-Cola
Go back to Eve
But leave de atom alone

Bad for de teeth
Bad for de bone
Spoil your complexion
Tie up de traffic
Jam up de plumbing
Lose your sweet disposition
Don't fool with it
Leave it alone![26]

For all its troubles and the fact that Yip boycotted the Broadway version of *Jamaica*, it was a big hit, opening on October 31, 1957, and running for 558 performances. It was also nominated for seven Tony Awards, including Best Musical. But, as mentioned earlier, Yip was so unhappy with the show that two years later, he worked on a revision of it out of town. He also began creating another Broadway musical, this one with the unlikely source material of Aristophanes' great Greek comedy *Lysistrata*, and the most unlikely composer, the long-deceased nineteenth-century Jacques Offenbach. It should be noted, however, that Yip had help from Fred Saidy and Henry Myers with the book (with a "bow" to Thomas Bulfinch's 1855 compendium on mythology), and from Jay Gorney, his first collaborator, who aided in choosing which of Offenbach's music to use.[27] As Yip later told interviewer Paul Lazarus, he "thought of *Lysistrata* as the oldest comedy in the world, something like 2,500 years. And at that time Aristophanes was concerned with reducing war to absurdity. Of course you could see that there was a kinship there."[28]

Lysistrata tells the story of a coalition of Greek women from Athens, Sparta, and other towns, cities, and islands, who withhold sexual relations from their warrior husbands until the men sign peace accords to end war forever. In Yip's *The Happiest Girl in the World*, Lysistrata and her cohorts are aided by the goddess Diana and the god Pluto. In this version, romance is more pronounced than in the original Greek comedy, and sex is more of a banter between the celestials than between the humans. In the end, the "good" goddess and the "evil" god decide that they must coexist in the world, and then all live happily ever after.

It's rare to have an interview that Yip gave before one of his musicals was even in production. But in February 1959, a good two years before *The Happiest Girl in the World* opened, Yip spoke about the show to an interviewer from the Popular Arts Project through the Columbia University Center for Oral History. He particularly emphasized the complexities of funding a musical:

"Now, Fred and I are writing this thing for over a year and half, this new show we're doing, *Lysistrata*, with Offenbach music. We're drawing no money. We're doing it on spec, completely. Every show is done on spec. The guys that do this are the real adventurers in this business, you know. But we get no capital gains. It's the oil well fellows that get them. Just as if we don't speculate at all! It's terrific speculation. And if you have a hit, the government takes it, right off the top. You're on the 75 or 80 per cent bracket with *Jamaica* money, but they don't count the three years that went into making it. That was not 'speculation' but oil wells is. That's why fellows cannot afford to invest the time in writing good shows—or in writing a show, period. You're speculating completely, you're betting on yourself and your work, for a year and a half or two years. It's really two years goes into it, before it goes on.

"Now, we're going to audition *Lysistrata* next week, for example. We'll have a group of people, and some producers we like, that we'll choose. We'll sing the songs. We'll put on the whole show. They will see this show come to life probably a lot better than it ever will [be] on the stage, because the meaning will be there, everything will be there—right from the beginning, from the curtain, with all directional indications, everything; designing of the show, everything, right from the beginning. We'll have the manuscript and everything ready to go, for people to take over. All they have to do is mechanically put it on. And if we, by some great fortune, have a director who can take our stuff and give it a little plus value, a little extra meaning, we will thank heaven. But if he just doesn't ruin it, we will be grateful.

"It has Shavian aspects, let us say, in the content. I've taken Offenbach's music, which is semi-classical, yet down to earth, so that I have to have somebody who will appreciate that. I took all his popular gems from his different operas and telescoped them into one show, which was quite a hard job to do—some from [*La*] *Belle Helene*, [*The Duchess of*] *Gerolstein*, *Tales of Hoffman*, *Orpheus*—I took the best of each, those that fitted the mood for different songs in this show. As you can see, it is a wild acrostic—more than that—it's a puzzle within an enigma. It took a lot of working. Now it's done.

"Also, this show, which has universal meaning today—because naturally, it's anti-war, you know, done with great humor and fun, great satire—it could be done in different cities of the world, which would give this something. There are international possibilities."[29]

Again, Yip spoke about the show just a few days before it opened in the spring of 1961: "This is a funny show with the stress on comedy and laughter and entertainment, of how to bring about peace in the world . . . if anybody is interested in a thing like peace and having some fun with it and laughing at our absurdities and how to bring it about and really wanting to get the solution of it, I say let's all see *Happiest Girl* . . . We got wonderful reviews, both in New Haven and in Philadelphia. And the only way an author can judge a play is because he's so near it and it's always his baby, so it's always beautiful . . . But the way to be objective [is] to stand behind the audience, back of the theatre, and clock the waves of laughter. Either they're there or they're not. And to see audience reaction . . . The last night in Philadelphia, Saturday night, we had a packed house, standing room only, turning away people—by word of mouth. And the audience actually cheered, yelled 'bravo,' so I felt pretty good."[30]

Unfortunately, Yip's optimism was misplaced. *The Happiest Girl in the World* ran for only ninety-seven performances on Broadway. However, audiences who saw it could not miss Yip's attack on war and imperialism. Those who remembered publisher Henry R. Luce's 1941 *Life* magazine article "The American Century" also understood Yip's subtle references to the United States' leadership role in the Cold War world. "The Glory That Is Greece," an early number sung by Pluto, the hero Kinesias, and the chorus, introduces those themes:

Pluto:
    Strike up the cymbals for the glory that is Greece
    The land of pottery and poetry and peace
    Where children speak
    In classic Greek
    Where everything we make is pure antique

    We're here to celebrate with music and with mirth
    The one and only great democracy on earth
    So make it known
    With baritone
Kinesias:
    That we're the on—
    Only Great Democ—
Pluto:

Souvenir program for *The Happiest Girl in the World*, 1961. The upper image shows Cyril Ritchard as Pluto; the lower shows Janis Rule as Diana. Courtesy of the Yip Harburg Foundation

Cracy to give to history
The sandal and the smock
The vase and Odyssey
Chorus:
And Slaves with Ph.D.
And all because we're free
We're free

Kinesias:
Each backward nation is our protégé and ward
We bring them culture
With our cultivated sword
We set them free from tyranny
Pluto:
And woe to the foe
Who refuses to be free

Chorus:
Sing glory to his name
It belongs to history now
Solidify his fame
With his laurel on his brow
With laurel wreath
This brow we crown
He brought the Spartan
Temples down
Pluto:
Classic ruins
Nobly laid
Good for future tourist trade
Chorus:
Sing glory to his fame
Kinesias his name

Pluto:
Oh well. (Spoken)
Strike up the cymbals for the glory that is Greece

The land of lute and lyre and the golden fleece
We give you sex
That's ambi-dex
We give you Oedipus for future wrecks.

Chorus and Pluto:
This is the Grecian Age, the Grecian Century
With Grecian gold and Grecian gods to keep us free
On every isle
On every sea
Gold—Grecian!
Gods—Grecian!
For all time to be.

Long may her fame increase
The glory that is Greece
It's all the truth and peace
The glory that is Greece
There's joy and peace in Greece
And Golden Fleece in Greece
We're up to here in Greece
In Greece, in Greece
In Greece, in Greece
The glory that is Greece.[31]

Yip's favorite song in the show was "Adrift on a Star." As he described it, "I started off falling in love with [Offenbach's] 'The Barcarole' so much and when I got that lyric I felt the whole show could be that way and I thought it would be a great tour de force to take the lovely, bouncy, beautiful, brilliant music of Offenbach and give . . . some of those old-fashioned lavender and lacy romantic, chintzy lyrics out of them and give them some modern meaning . . . When you are working on anything it's more on your mind than you think; it's on your subconscious . . . And every little word you read and every little note you get or a little thing a person says somehow or other goes through a computer sieve in your mind and rings a bell if you're working on a song.

"Well, . . . [when] I was working on 'The Barcarole' thing, the lyric, [I] couldn't quite get it. I knew that 'The Barcarole' was a boat song. I got this lovely little note from my wife who had just stepped out of the house for a few hours and I came home and I saw no dinner on the table but I did see this humorous note. I wish I could remember it. She always writes humorous notes. She knew I was working on this very tough lyric and she said, 'Don't worry, . . . I know you're a man who's valiant enough to always swim against the tide and keep your eyes on the . . . universal stars and your hand on the eternal plow. It'll come to you and you will find one meatball in the ice box.'

"Well, keeping your eyes on the universal stars and your hand on the eternal plow . . . I said, 'Well, why can't this boat, this boat song, instead of being a gondola, be the earth which is a universal boat that's roaming around in space.' So I wrote the song 'The Barcarole' with a lyric that was fitting . . . for a rather more cosmic boat. And . . . it made this wonderful point, the point that all the youngsters now . . . are saying, 'Who am I, where am I, where am I going, what am I doing here?' Well, that's not a new question. That's an old, old, old question. Every century, every age, every religion has asked that and every person asks that of himself. If you try to really even think of infinity you can go crazy, so the best thing you do is to go into marijuana. So instead of going crazy into marijuana, we go into philosophy and I said, 'Well, what is this boat?' And I'll say, I know why I'm here. I'm here because I'm on a boat. I'm a little astronaut in a great big astronautic vehicle called the World. Here we are Adrift on a star . . . And it fits the tune."[32]

Here we are
Adrift on a star
Alone in a silent sky.
Lost in space
Together we face
The wonder of where and why.
Why a sky without an end
A sea without a chart?
Why the wind and why the rose
And why the trembling heart?

The moon, the tide, the years,
They go drifting along
Oh, music of the spheres
Are there words to your song?

Is there a bright, gleaming goal
Ending this brief barcarole?

Here we are,
Adrift on a star,
And what is the journey for?
Can it be
The heart is the sea
And love is the golden shore?

That wherever we are
In this star-sprinkled dome,
If there's love in your star,
You're home
You're home.[33]

"In other words, the question is answered. You make the star your own home by finding love . . . Doesn't matter where we're going. It's nice to know, be curious about it, but you don't go into tailspins over it."[34]

Yip added a beautiful thought to this in 1980, and it is especially revealing because he was not one to speak much about his personal life: "I think every writer has . . . some theme that runs all . . . through everything he does. I think you can recognize it in Shaw, you can recognize it in Gilbert, you can recognize it even in some of our lyric writers like Cole Porter and [Ira] Gershwin. And each one contributes his own hallmark and I don't think they can be compared as to who is the better. Each one has his own technique and his own contribution. I think what moves me, of course I'm very conscious of social injustice and the use of satire and humor . . . as a weapon against these follies and foibles. But I suppose like everybody else I think basically we all go around trying to find out who we are. The kids today think they're the only ones that . . . are in quest of that search. And I think we all want to know how we're related to the universe and how we are related to people.

"And . . . I sometimes go up the Empire State and look at the stars and see how I'm related to the universe. Well, I can't reach those stars. So I go down, then I try to see how I'm related to people and there are too many people, too many stars. So I go home. And no one's at home. And my thesaurus is gone. So I tiptoe into my bedroom where the lady of the thesaurus usually has it and I find her in bed asleep with her arms folded over George Bernard Shaw. Well, there's a man I'm never jealous of and she has [a] benign look on her face, so I know she has just been able to tell Androcles how to handle that lion. And her face is usually one that makes me feel that behind those eyelids are the stars that I finally can touch, that I couldn't reach, but now that I can touch. And behind those eyes are always the people I couldn't reach, but now I can touch. And I think it's summed up in this song."[35] At this point, Yip sang "It's Only a Paper Moon," but the sentiments also echoed those he described when talking about "Adrift on a Star."

Yip Harburg's Broadway career more or less ended with *The Happiest Girl in the World*. Between 1961 and 1968, he had little output. In 1962, he collaborated with Harold Arlen on the animated film *Gay Purr-ee*, which featured the voices of Judy Garland and Robert Goulet. He also wrote lyrics for Garland's final film, *I Could Go on Singing* (1963). In 1966, Yip's last hit song, "Hurry Sundown," written with Earl Robinson for the Otto Preminger film of the same name and rejected, was recorded by Peter, Paul and Mary. Their version achieved the thirty-seventh slot in the January 21, 1967, issue of *Billboard* magazine's "Top 40 Easy Listening Chart." Then, in January 1968, Yip's final Broadway musical, *Darling of the Day*, written with Jule Styne, opened and closed after a mere thirty-three performances. Yip blamed the critics for the failure, but there had been problems throughout the show's creation, and the theme of a famous but reclusive artist adopting the identity of his deceased valet just did not captivate audiences.

Yip made one last attempt at writing a commercial musical, this one titled *What a Day for a Miracle* or *The Children's Crusade*. It was about the Children's Crusade of 1212–1213, made up entirely of youth whose fate has never been recovered. Yip saw this as yet another way to present the idea of world peace to audiences. As he told David Frost in 1972, "Well, history has a way of repeating itself, they say, and it's true . . . The children were born into a world of war. They had heard nothing but the clang of armor and people going off to fight the heathens. The world was broken up into two parts—the heathen east and the Christian west, and we were the goodies and they were baddies and of course that never existed after that, did it? No. Never had another situation like that. And children have a way of, when they come into the world, seeing the world as a playground. It's a place of beauty and when suddenly it becomes a battlefield they get terribly . . .

"And something happens to them. They rebel in their own way, and they rebelled then. They said the elders have spoiled the world and the elders cannot save the savior. It is up to the uncorrupt, the pure in heart and of one little boy by the name of Stephan of Cloyes, actually a real, historic character [who] amassed 50,000 children and the Fifth Crusade [*sic*] took place and it was a children's crusade. And they said, we are going to bring love back into the world without spears and without armor. And the adventures of this little boy who at this point had both the church and the state, the king, completely tied up because the people were all with him. They wanted to believe in a miracle at this time. They were so . . . despairing of paying taxes and being tyrannized by war that the people wanted to accept any miracle just as most people today want to accept Aquarius and want to accept astrology. Anything to hang on that will get us way out of the real world of hypocrisy and evil. And these children, these children, actually taught the church and the state a great, beautiful lesson, that faith in the love of life rather than the fear of death is everlasting power . . ."[36]

What a Day for a Miracle opened on April 29, 1971, at the University of Vermont for a brief run. It never made it past Burlington. In later years, Yip expressed his disappointment that his Broadway career was at an end: "I'd love to write more shows but I don't think one is able to any more. I don't think my craft is of any use at this present age. Number one, you couldn't get it on for less than a million dollars, and to get the backing of a show for a million dollars, unless it's rock 'n' roll, unless it's raucous, unless it's porno, and unless it has all the fulminations and insanities of today, it's very hard to get on. A publisher won't publish a song by Harold Arlen."[37]

In a lecture at the University of California, Los Angeles in 1977, Yip gave more insight into his disappointment at the way that lyrics and music were being written for the theater. As he explained, "A song is when you hear it you associate it with some idea. And you bring it back at any time when you're alone, when you're in a mood or when you're happy. And you can sing it back. I can sing back any of the songs of [Cole] Porter or [George and Ira] Gershwin, [Jerome] Kern. 'Old man river, that old man river,' Or 'A foggy day in London Town, had me low and had me down.' I can sing any one of those songs whenever I need it to comfort me but I cannot sing the songs of today. Because the songs of today depend upon percussion, beat, instrumentation, gyration, weird sounds, clownish garments, hair-do, all the gimmicks and tricks to cover up and disguise the non-song, the non-lyric, and the non-communication. Because the music has to be so high to cover up the little lyric.

"There are no roots. My roots go back to Gilbert and Sullivan. The roots of today, they go back to gibberish and salivate . . . the children today and the youth of today and the song writers today pride themselves on having lost their innocence and their purity. But with it they lost their spirit, and above all they've lost their humor. I find no humor in today's songs. Without humor, you've got no courage. Without courage, there's no nation, and there's no happiness. We wrote love songs, we wrote songs that were risque. But we had twinkle, we had an attitude."[38] This is not to say that Yip did not appreciate some of the newer musical writers. He had great admiration for Stephen Sondheim, for example, and appreciated such musicals as *Fiddler on the Roof*, but for the most part he found the new generation lacking.

During this time, Yip could have chosen to retire on his laurels and his royalties, but he did not. Rather, he began the process of reinventing himself into a published poet, storyteller, performer, and lecturer. As a result, he was more in the public eye than he had been in a long while and much appreciated for it.

14 | A Pause for Friendship During Hard Times

It was Burton Lane who first alerted Yip Harburg that he was about to be blacklisted. At the time, the two were working together on *Huckleberry Finn*. The concern and mutual care for each other is clearly illustrated in the following two letters written in 1950.

The first letter, written on November 22, was from Lane, then in Hollywood, to Yip:

Dear Yip,

I had a bit of a blow the other day which I'm going to tell you about as it concerns you so that you can be prepared if and when you are confronted with it. However, I must swear you to secrecy as no one must know that I told you about this. Should my name become involved at this time it could do me great damage, and since my only interest concerns you, I'm sure you wouldn't want to do anything which could hurt me. So please be careful.

Last Friday night there was a preview of my picture, *Royal Wedding*, and Arthur Freed told me he had something important to talk over with me and asked me if I would drop in to see him on Monday. I did, and this is what Mr. Freed sprung on me, "Burt, we're faced with a serious problem. I don't think Yip and Don Stewart will ever be able to work in a studio again." I asked him why, knowing full well what he would tell me and the inevitable answer came out,—"because they've been accused of being communists."

After the first shock was over I told him you were not a communist and that your whole life had been devoted to making America a better place and that you had no intention of ever trying to over-throw the government by force. I went on in that vein about you. He reminded me how much he thought of you and your talent, but he said the pressure was on and anyone who is not a communist had to prove that he wasn't one, and if a person was a communist he was a traitor and should be treated as one. I challenged him as much as I could without putting myself in a spot and at one point in the conversation he asked me would I like to work with a lyric writer who was a communist. I told him that up to now I had never thought in those terms, that I had never thought when I was about to start writing with a collaborator to ask him what his politics were, that the important thing was could we do a good job. Of course, you know Freed and you know how useless it is to talk logic to him, and so I finally dropped it.

Even though you and I had discussed this possibility so many times when we were together, it still was a shock to me to suddenly be confronted with the actuality. Freed made a point that I should not mention this to anyone as it wasn't definite yet. That's why you must protect me and not let on that I have warned you. But, after thinking this over for the last couple of days I decided to let you know so that you can protect yourself instead of waiting for them to act.

I have a suggestion to make to you and, at this moment, it seems like the best course of action for you to take. Should the studio suddenly cancel your contract there is no doubt in my mind that ugly publicity would result and you would be hurt very badly. You know as well as I that an accusation that someone is a communist gets all the publicity and the denial none. Therefore you must not allow this situation to go that far. It is my suggestion that you use some ruse to beg out of doing the picture. Your reasons must have nothing to do with politics. They should not give the impression that you have any idea what is going on at the studio. I believe this is the only way you can keep yourself from being smeared.

Please before you do anything, let me know what you intend to do so that I can be prepared should Freed send for me again. This is a shocking situation and I do hope that it will work out without you being hurt.

As ever,
Burt[1]

Yip, then in New York, responded just a few days later, on November 28. In a most caring way, he tried to give Lane some comfort and absolve him of feeling any sense of guilt. His letter read in part as follows:

First, accept my heartfelt thanks for your letter and for the friendship and courage you showed in writing it. Your information will be kept secret, confidential and entre nousish. Let me add my warning to your own awareness—you must do everything possible this side of decency in this hysterical climate to protect yourself and your income. Of course, sooner or later, this kind of hysteria will, barring miracles, reach everybody. Eventually, even . . . Dore Shary will be swallowed up, (and all his crawling, all his recanting and throwing his friends to the lions will avail him nothing.) Finally, Arthur F. [Freed] himself will be engulfed by virtue of circumstance and circumcision.

Certainly trying to prove you are not a Communist Party member these days is inviting Ordeal by Slander . . . The time comes, however, when you can no longer throw up the sponge, when principles involving something more important than your own nervous system, impel you to action and you must then take up arms against the (toads) [replaced with (Louis) "Budenzes" in pencil].

In reference to the Metro thing specifically, there is nothing, at this point for me to retreat from. It would be irrational of me to withdraw without motivation. Nothing has been said to me. [Kenneth] McKenna phoned, asking me to postpone, to which I agreed. The next move is theirs . . . The situation was ignited, I am sure, by an article which was printed in the American Legion magazine, in which [Louis] Budenz referred to me as having just completed the lyrics for *Huck Finn* at Metro. Haven't seen the article, but assume that it included the usual name-calling, and Metro fell for it, as planned. This may rebound on them unpleasantly, however . . . Nothing is ever achieved unless somebody fights. This is abundantly shown by the entire difference in feeling between the [West] coast and New York. There, all the

Liberals live in fear and trembling. Here, because they fight, take action, oppose, speak out, the situation is quite different. You would be amazed at the people, heretofore unheard from, who are now fighting for freedom of the writer, the performer in all the arts and crafts.[2]

Lane continued to defend his lyrical father figure in the years following Yip's initial blacklisting. As he told Deena Rosenberg in a 1985 interview, "We were in the hands of maniacs. I became, later, a producer at Paramount where the head of the studio, Y. Frank Freeman, was the man that all the studios cleared whoever they wanted to employ with. This guy was like the . . . voice of the blacklist. He had all the so-called books from the Congressional committees and, what was it, 'Red' something [*Red Channels*], a magazine . . . that had a list of all the people who should be blacklisted. And when I was there for about six months when I wanted to do *Finian's Rainbow* [as a film], and I had a meeting with Y. Frank Freeman and he said to me, 'Well, that was written by that "comma-nist."' He would say, not 'communist,' but 'comma-nist.' He said, 'That was written by that "comma-nist" Harburg.' And I said, 'Well, Yip wrote it but he was no communist.' And he said, 'Oh, yes he was.' I said, 'Oh, no he wasn't.' And he swiveled around in his chair and started to look through the volumes he had, stacks of volumes all behind his desk. And I said, 'Mr. Freeman, I'm going to take a gamble and I'll bet you my year's salary that you won't find Yip's name listed or named as a communist by anybody. There's no way. I've known Yip all my life and I know that he was never a joiner; in fact, he didn't even want to join the automobile club.' He looked . . . and said, 'I'll be in touch with you later.' He couldn't find it in my presence.

"So a few days later his right hand man came to me in the commissary and slipped something into my hand, and said, 'Don't look at it now—look at it later.' And when I left the commissary I took out this piece of paper and on it it had 'Russian War Relief,' some joint antifascist committee. I'd belonged to every one of these myself. [They] had nothing to do with communism. Russia was our ally and we were helping, just as they were helping, to win the war. But this was the information they had, and I wanted to hire Fred Saidy when I first became a producer there, and he was unemployable. And a year later the head of the studio, Don Hartman, called me and said, 'If you want Fred Saidy now you can have him. We made a mistake. A mistake was made.' So these were the crazy things and the outrageous things that were going on in Hollywood at that time . . ."[3]

15 | The New Old Yip

In 1966 Yip Harburg turned seventy, an age when people often frame their lives around retirement. Times had, in a way, forced Yip to do the same. As he himself reported, the cost of mounting a musical was so high that funding was difficult to raise, and he was seen not only as a political hot potato but also as old-fashioned. In addition, his collaborators were retiring or dying, leaving him more and more isolated. None of this stopped Yip from pursuing his creative or human rights work. He still wrote songs and involved himself in the musical community, but as the years passed, he placed more stress on writing light verse (much of it political), giving talks and interviews, and working for causes he believed in. In the process, he created the image of himself he wanted future generations to embrace. Much of what Yip has said, quoted throughout this book, in fact, is a result of the numerous public appearances and radio and television interviews he participated in during the 1970s.

There were particular issues that Yip considered of utmost importance to address. Education was one. In recognition of the excellent education he had received even though he had been so poor, Yip gave back and was recognized for it. In 1967, for example, he funded a scholarship for a boy at the Oakwood School in North Hollywood. This was not the first time he did so. He also consistently gave money to his alma mater, City College; indeed, in 1968 he made a large donation, pledging $1,000 annually for five years and then a bequest of $10,000 in his will. From this funding came the E. Y. "Yip" Harburg Alumni Association Scholarship. In appreciation and recognition of his own success, in 1972 he received the James K. Hackett Medal for "distinguished alumni achievement in drama." His name appears on a special plaque in City College's North Academic Center honoring accomplished alumni. In 1979, Wayne State University, not part of Yip's education, also honored him with a Humanity in Arts Award. Yip often donated money to support work in Israel, for example that of the Givat Haviva, an institution of higher education dedicated to building

Jewish-Arab friendship and understanding. This was one activity that led to his receiving the 1977 Negev Peace Award from the Israeli government.

Yip also supported outreach and education in his own field—musical theater. In 1970, he was instrumental in launching the famous Lyrics and Lyricists series at New York's 92nd Street Y. Two years later, he was inducted into the Songwriters Hall of Fame and continued to give one interview after another. Most important, in late 1980, Yip joined Leonard Bernstein, Arthur Laurents, and Sheldon Harnick at a news conference announcing the creation of a new musical theater program at New York University's Tisch School of the Arts, a program that has gained international renown.

As expected, Yip continued to work for peace and human rights. In 1964, he and Burton Lane wrote "Freedom is the Word" for a huge, closed-circuit telecast for the NAACP, celebrating the tenth anniversary of the Supreme Court decision in *Brown v. Board of Education*. Yip kept up his support of the Civil Rights Movement, and with it, the antinuclear and then the anti–Vietnam War movements. During 1967 and 1968, two of the most dramatic years in US history, Yip worked on a tribute to Dr. Benjamin Spock at New York's Town Hall. Sponsored by the National Committee for a Sane Nuclear Policy (SANE), the event honored the pediatrician who had put his career on the line to speak out against the Vietnam War and the effects of nuclear bomb testing on the earth's people. Yip also performed at various antiwar rallies and donated money to several organizations, including the Congressional Peace Campaign Committee and the Student Mobilization Committee in New York. In July 1968, in response to the mobilization committee's appeal for a donation to support its inclusive networking, Yip sent in $20 and this response: "I found your position ethical, democratic, and logical . . . I have been through too many decades of good movements which were blown into oblivion on the winds of inflexibility and fanaticism both from the right and from the left . . . You younger people, I hope, will have learned from our struggles, that if the goal is good, nothing must divide you."[1]

Writing poetry gave Yip great pleasure. It was through this art form that he reached his old fans as well as new readers and listeners. His first two volumes appeared about eleven years apart: *Rhymes for the Irreverent* in 1965 (which he frequently referred to as his "guru" book) and *At This Point in Rhyme* in 1976. (The former was reissued in 2006 as a compilation of Yip's poems, including those from the latter.) As he told the great oral historian Studs Terkel the year after his second book was published, "Well, life, it seems, Studs, is a combination of everything, isn't it? It's an ability to see life and all our follies and to know that we're here in a great big void, spinning around, an insignificant planet in a still more insignificant solar system, in a still more insignificant galaxy . . . And we've got to see ourselves humorously and at the same time we *are* here to see ourselves courageously and we do know that the end of everything is death of some kind. What happens after that we don't know. We're here on a short cruise and so the cruise might as well consist of laughter and consist so as to have courage to withstand this bigger idea, this bigger disaster that awaits us all, of nothingness. And in order to do that, we've got to have a lot of laughter while we're doing it."[2]

And laugh he did—at himself, at others, about the world. The most serious matters became fodder for his pen, and in the process, his readers and listeners learned some things about Yip himself. As he told an audience in 1973, "See . . . when Einstein says 'E' equals MC-squared, you know where you are. It's clarity. But when Lewis Carroll says, 'Words are only what you want them to mean,' that's Mad Hatterism, and in an age of verbal deception and duplicity it is only natural that confusion should become the fashion. Fashion becomes fad, fad becomes a commodity. So to supply the demand for confusion, I have been asked by my publisher to write a sequel to my guru book, *Rhymes for the Irreverent*, which proved to be so confusing they had to print several editions . . . and I thought it might be appropriate tonight to take you on a junket tour to the looking glass into this land of rhymes. It's a land where all the banks look like cathedrals and the cathedrals look like banks and the only way the natives can tell the difference is by the worshipful faces in the banks and the bankrupt faces in the cathedrals. Well, in this land the godfather is called President and [the] saint is called Traitor and the murderer is called Patriot and peace through genocide is called Peace with Honor. So let's meet a few of these natives and their problems, out of this little book of rhymes. And the first native we meet is the agnostic.

> No matter how much I probe and prod
> I cannot quite believe in God
> But oh, I hope to God that He
> Unswervingly believes in me.

Ah, there's a fellow for you [the atheist].

> Poems are made by fools like me
> But only God can make a tree.
> Yet only God Who makes the tree
> Also makes the fools like me.
> But only fools like me, you see,
> Can make a God Who makes a tree.

So now we come to a fellow who calls himself the realist.

> Where Bishop Patrick crossed the street
> An X now marks the spot.
> The light of God was with him
> But the traffic light was not."[3]

Yip also wrote of his feelings about aging. As he related in 1977, "Well, this is growing older, as I am and as we all are. But I seem to be growing older a little faster than everybody . . . Anyhow, to comfort myself, in 'Springtime for Senility' I say:

> At forty I lost my illusions
> At fifty I lost my hair
> At sixty my hope and teeth were gone
> And my feet were beyond repair

> At eighty life has clipped my claws
> I'm bent and bowed and cracked
> But I can't give up the ghost
> Because my follies are all intact.

And I hope they continue to be intact," he added. "Because it's only with follies that we can make life acceptable and a little comfortable."[4]

As Yip noted in another interview, "For eighty springs and summers I have been tiptoeing through the tulips, oblivious of clocks, calendars and autumn leaves. All around me science—now there's a *schlamazel* word—was having its heyday. Atoms were moving mountains, dissolving empires. Amazing miracles were happening all around me while I was trying to find a rhyme for 'orange juice.' I had always hoped when reaching this venerable time of life to be a warehouse of wisdom, an oracle of aphorisms with the young eagerly at my feet catching my pearls, but to quote Oscar Wilde, 'The youth of today are monsters. They have no respect for dyed hair.' Why should they? What have our scientific miracles given them?

> Air, polluted.
> Milk, diluted.
> Lives, computed.
> Homes, uprooted.
> Mates, ill-suited.
> Sex, disputed.
> Incomes looted
> And psyches booted."[5]

Yip maintained his criticism of the love of money and the capitalist system in the United States. In his poem "Heavenly Vaults," for example, he reflected once again on religion, but with a twist: "If somebody were to come down on a flying saucer and look at the world as it is, or our world, or the American world . . . this is how he would view it . . .

> Where banks all look like temples
> And temples look like banks
> Where does one count his blessings
> Where does one offer thanks?
>
> You sense the holy places
> By the faces in the ranks

The bankrupt in the temples
The worshipful in banks.

We don't know whether we're in a temple any more . . . or in a bank."[6]

In his poem "Of Thee I Sing—Babel," Yip reflected on the bigness that capitalism and modernity brings. He explained the poem this way: "Well, I'm talking about bigness now. I mean, I've seen New York City now become canyons, canyons, shutting out our light. I see people running up and down elevators, rabbit-like, into rabbit hutches and acting like ants, and I have an office on the 35th floor . . . and as I look down, it's a frightening sight and I don't know where we're going with our bigness. I don't know what the building of skyscrapers and the hubbub of traffic is doing to us. *The Bible*, with its parables, with its funny little stories about the Tower of Babel, suddenly the jibberish and everything else, has great meaning for us, these little parables. What are we building? Where are we going? We have . . . outsmarted and outwitted ourselves by shutting out our sun, polluting our air and making our lives miserable in air-conditioned rooms that never open a window and when you really see the sight from the 35th floor window, it's frightening that man goes up, stays there eight hours a day, and comes down, takes him two hours in a traffic jam, two hours to get home. I don't know what his life is nor does he. In other words, we're building another dinosaur. Well, we know that anything that becomes over powerful and over big, what happens to him, whether it's the albatross or the dinosaur.

Build thee more stately mansions, little man
More grandioso, more gargantuan.
But as towers rise and the derricks roar,
Remember there was once a dinosaur."[7]

And, for Yip, what did all this building and overcrowding and overpopulating bring?

"Riots up in Harlem
Death in Alabam'
Famine in Biafra,

War in Viet Nam.
Holocaust in Ireland,
Bloodshed in Araby,
God is in His heaven,
Watching football on TV."[8]

Yip wrote many poems about the Vietnam War era. In one, published in *At This Point in Rhyme* and discussed with Studs Terkel, Yip expressed his anger at Richard Nixon and the Watergate affair. However, the poem called "Black Night at the White House" was originally written about Lyndon Baines Johnson in 1964:

A . . . Baines Lyndon, in his boudoir royal,
Awoke one night from a deep dream of oil —
And saw within the moonlight of his room
A shadow with a Peace Plaque glowing in the gloom.
He could not discern the form or face,
But he knew 'twas someone from outer space.
A damned dissenter! A long haired poet!
A dirty peacenik, — the peace words show it.
"You," cried Lyndon, "may be Keats or Shelly,
But to me, you're nothin' but a Nervous Nellie!"
Just then Lady Bird ups and wheezes —
"Lyhndon, babeh — yoh tawkin' to *Jesus*."[9]

Renamed "Identity Crisis," the poem appeared in a section of *At This Point in Rhyme* called "Little Drops of Watergate," and read this way:

Milhous Ben Nixon in his royal tower
Awoke one night from a deep dream of power
And saw within the moonlight of his room
A shadow with a peace plaque glowing in the gloom
He could not discern the form or face
But he knew it was someone from outer space,
Some long-haired peacenik, some pinko poet,
The weird beard tells it and the peace words show it.

"You," cried Nixon, "may be someone from Berkeley,
  Harvard or Kingdom Come,
But to me you're nothing but a campus bum."
Just then Pat rubs her eyes and wheezes,
"My God, Dickie, you're talking to Jesus!"[10]

In two poems Yip shared with Terkel, he lambasted the military establishment and people's willingness to buy into war fever. The first reads,

Mass the missiles,
Draft the boys,
Pile the rockets high.
Build the bombers,
Load bombs,
Till they span the sky!

The Armageddon days have come,
But one thing's very clear—
There's no defense that's strong enough
To save a folk from fear.

Build pentagons and armories
From Boston to La Jolla;
There is no fortress strong enough
To placate paranoia.[11]

The second poem echoes the same sentiments.

We've licked pneumonia and TB
And plagues that used to mock us.
We've got the virus on the run,
The smallpox cannot pock us.
We've found the antibodies
For the staphylo-streptococcus
But oh, the universal curse
From Cuba to Korea
That bug of bugs
That bugs us still

And begs for panacea
Oh, who will find the antidote
For Pentagonorrhea?[12]

Another of Yip's constant concerns was what he saw as the younger generation's too-serious nature. He spoke often about wanting to infuse young people with humor, and to move them back to the time when songs were hummable and pleasant to the ear. This was a rather nostalgic stance and, in 1972, as the interview transcript for the following quotation noted, was met with only "moderate applause."

"There must be hope. If there's no hope there's no use writing anything and I wish the youngsters of today would understand this and that no matter how dismal, how despairing things are, and I've lived through cycles and cycles, now, of ups and downs and wars and things, but built into the darkness of the human dust is always the light of the human spirit and we must never forget it. We must never despair to a point where things are hopeless . . .

"I'm very sad that those beautiful, sweet songs with architecture and structure are not being played now and that they've been pushed off the air by songs that are rather vituperative and convulsive, and I understand why. The young people are angry, they're lost, they're outraged. But I do wish that they'd take another look at themselves, now that they've gone through the 60s, and written these songs of the 60s, to see how far it's gotten them. Really, it hasn't gotten [them] very far . . .

"It's all about bringing back sweet songs with hope and romance. I don't say imitate us. But I say, let's get a happier point of view and let's get out, organize ourselves in songwriting and in political action and do something about the world with a happier sense of humor. And this is my sad song, in their own terms. [Yip then sang to the tune of "Where Have All the Flowers Gone."]

Where have all the sweet songs gone
Long time passing.
Where have the good songs gone
Long time ago.

Who are they that dare to spurn
Gershwin, Porter, Rodgers, Kern?
When will they ever learn?
When will they ever learn?"[13]

The poems just quoted were those that Yip stressed in interviews, but his books contain many others that readers can enjoy. Less well-known and unpublished are political parodies of his own or others' popular standards. It's interesting to look at a few examples of these songs, for although they were very much in the humorous political mode that Yip tried to encourage younger songwriters to emulate, they also had a bitter edge.

Richard Nixon was the brunt of several of Yip's barbs. Nixon was particularly notorious because of his participation on HUAC, his handling of the Vietnam War, and the Watergate scandal that led to his resignation as president. To the tune of Cole Porter's "Anything Goes," Yip wrote this:

For getting votes, no one's as tricky
Or dirty, as Tricky Dicky,
For Dicky knows,
Anything goes.
To get the vote he'd stoop to mayhem
Or Carswell, or Billy Graham's
Fatuous prose,
Anything goes.
He'd push angels and men aside,
Commit genocide,
Bomb the fleet away,
Deal the wheat away,
Make the Bill of Rights
Just a swill of rights,
Where the old Potomac flows.
The I.T.T. is easy pickin'
Through Kissinger or ass lickin'
Dicky boy knows,
Anything goes![14]

The same sense of anger that the Sixties/Seventies generation felt about the seemingly endless war in Vietnam came through in Yip's parody of his own song from *Finian's Rainbow*, "If This Isn't Love." In the new version, the title was altered to "If This Isn't Peace."

A secret, a secret,
He said he had a secret,
A war-ending, peace-pending,
Nation mending secret.
He's dying to reveal it,
And lay it in our lap,
But says he must conceal it
Until Vietnam
Is wiped right off the map.

If this isn't peace,
The whole world's psychotic,
If this isn't peace,
You're unpatriotic.
With napalm and love,
With missiles and kisses,
You're hissed off the list;
You're a communist, if this
Isn't peace.[15]

A final example of Yip's disdain for the Nixon Administration is based on Alan Jay Lerner and Frederick Lowe's "I've Grown Accustomed to Her Face" from the musical *My Fair Lady*. Parodied in 1970, Yip's version, "I've Grown Accustomed to Disgrace" had these lyrics:

I've grown accustomed to disgrace,
And let me make it very clear,
I've grown accustomed to the stink
I hear from Huntley Brink
The grime, the crime, the slum, the slime,
We're getting richer every year,
But let me make it very clear,
My lungs are full of emphysema

And my hyper-tension grows,
When the rhetoric starts running
From the Presidential nose.
Alas, it seems I'm not alone,
We all of us have grown
Accustomed to disgrace.

[Spoken quote from Alexander Pope]
"Vice is a monster of so frightful mien,
As to be hated needs but to be seen;
Yet seen too oft, familiar with her face,
We first endure, then pity, then embrace."

I've grown familiar with that face
Whose hope is all in outer space,
The face that makes it very clear
To live upon this sphere,
We'll arm the goon, pollute the moon.
I've grown accustomed to that face
That buys and sells the human race,
That quotes the latest market values and the latest football score,
As glibly as the body count of boys who die in war.
I've grown accustomed to despair,
Accustomed to disgust,
Accustomed to disgrace.[16]

It seems more in Yip's spirit to end these examples of his lyrics on a lighthearted note, using his own favorite symbolic image—the rainbow. References to rainbows proliferate throughout Yip's work. They appear in *Bloomer Girl, Flahooley, Jamaica, Darling of the Day,* the verse of "Happiness Is a Thing Called Joe," and of course, *The Wizard of Oz* and *Finian's Rainbow.* In a 1951 interview with radio host Jinx Falkenberg, Yip claimed that "Look to the Rainbow" was his favorite song. "I don't think I can improve on it," he said, "I don't think we can improve on it. I kind of take a little heartfelt joy in that song."[17]

Author John Lahr explained Yip's connection with rainbows as "a visual bridge between Earth and the galaxy." As he quoted Yip, a rain-

bow was a "symbolic link between man and the heaven of his imagination . . . I've laid great store in man's imaginative ability, on man's
ability to be bigger than death, bigger than life in his imagination.
Man's imagination is what takes him out of his misery."[18]

Yip spoke of his connection to rainbows in several interviews. In
1979, he told a Canadian audience that "Look to the Rainbow" expressed it all. "Because after all, that's all man has, can look to," he explained. "There's nothing else. And the rainbow being that symbol, the
same symbol that Noah had when he made his covenant with God . . .
it's not religious, it's not, you know, fanatic, it's . . . I think, something
we all understand. It's symbolic."[19] In 1978, Yip told Studs Terkel that
the song was "my real theme, formula, no matter what happens. I think
the human species has a life force that's got to prevail and survive and
no matter how many follies, foibles, it will. It always has and will. And
so my theme song, the theme that keeps me going all these years, is
'Look to the Rainbow.'"[20]

Yip often connected the rainbow with the United States. As he put
it in 1971, "So I, as a lyrical son of an immigrant, saw this country
with the eyes of a worshiper and the heart of a Shavian poet, a trouba-
dour. I capsulated its follies, twitted its foibles, chronicled its fears and
sang its hopes. Always I saw this land under a rainbow umbrella, and
a banner that waved with humor and humanity."[21] In another interview, he expanded on this idea: "Let me introduce myself. I belong
to a special tribe of what used to be called troubadours—sometimes
they were called minstrels, now we're called songwriters—who were
not ashamed of a thing called romance, emotion, humor, and especially the English language. We lived in a world that knew the difference between sentiment and sentimentality. In this world we brewed
coffee and savored the aroma as it percolated. In this world we took
time off to woo a girl; it wasn't instant, like the coffee, but it was good
to the last drop. Ecology was still intact. We had not yet zapped the fish
out of the waters, nor smogged out the bluebird or the rainbow out of
the sky. We worked for, in our songs, a sort of better world, a rainbow
world. Now, my generation, unfortunately, never succeeded in creating
that rainbow world so we can't hand it down to you. But we could hand
down our songs which still hang on to hope and laughter . . ."[22]

In 1972, during George McGovern's unsuccessful run for the presidency against Richard Nixon, Yip scripted this adaptation of "Look to the Rainbow":

On the day he was born
Said McGovern he did
What in hell kind of planet is this for a kid?
And he cried from his crib
At his first interview
This world must be fixed
For a dream to shine through

So look, look, look to McGovern
With eyes on the future and heart on the beam
Look, look, look to McGovern
Follow the fellow who follows the Dream.

Well he sharpened his wits
And he polished his prose
And he challenged the vultures, the hawks and the crows
To clear the pollution
And brighten the skies
So a kid can see rainbows again with his eyes

Vote, vote, vote for McGovern
Let's get the crooks and the quacks off our backs
Vote, vote, vote in McGovern
Vote out brain-Washington's brainwashing hacks.

Let's banish all bombs
Let's get rid of all slums
And congressional chums with their double-talk gums
Your dream is your ballot
The dream is at hand
And here is McGovern to govern this land.

Look, look, look to McGovern
Why vote for the skim milk when you can have cream

Look, look, look to McGovern
Follow the fellow who follows the Dream.

Follow the fellow, follow the fellow
Follow the fellow who follows the Dream.[23]

In 1979, two years before his death, Yip once again reminded an audience about the importance of his rainbow dream. Upon accepting an award from the Horatio Alger Association of Distinguished Americans, he reiterated, "We've got to stop thinking of me and thinking of us and you. And so, being a songwriter, I changed my philosophy of writing from 'Brother, Can You Spare a Dime?' to 'Somewhere Over the Rainbow' because even though we were all down and out, that American dream that my immigrant parents came over for was still there. In spite of the fact that we had gone off the track, it was still there and that was behind the greatness of this country, that the ideal of that dream is symbolized in the rainbow, the rainbow that Noah spoke about . . . that rainbow is still there. But our dream is not accomplished. That rainbow still has to be reached. We've got to find out what we are going to do with the wealth and the affluence and the good luck and gifts that God has given us . . .

"What is the good of scientific advancement and nuclear energy when it is being used for genocide and for global destruction? What are the good of our Cadillacs and our automobiles and those other great inventions when they pollute the air? Are we using our wealth, our scientific advancements properly? Have we a goal? Have we an ideal? We cannot congratulate ourselves yet on having achieved success because our success now must be the beginning of a new and better world. We've got to find out what our values are. What are we going to do with all the success that we have accumulated? What are our moralities?

"And so I leave you, not on a negative note, but that same grit and guts that went into the Horatio Alger idea . . . from rags to riches, must now go from riches to humanity, to beauty in life, to see to it that our songs are now uplifting and to make the American spirit work for us as our forefathers had planned, not for economics alone, but for this

Yip with Frankie McCormack, assistant curator of the Songwriters Hall of Fame, December 1980. Posters for the musical *Jamaica* can be seen on the left. Courtesy of the Yip Harburg Foundation

greater thing that is more, as Shakespeare said, in heaven and earth, Horatio, than your philosophy has dreamed of."[24]

On March 5, 1981, Yip Harburg was in Hollywood to discuss a film version of Robert Louis Stevenson's *Treasure Island*. On his way to a meeting, he was struck down by a massive heart attack. The car he was driving drifted slowly across Sunset Boulevard, hitting an approaching vehicle but harming no one in it.

Yip had ended *At This Point in Rhyme* with this "Epitaph":

I've whittled my wit,
And whipped my rhymes,
For a small obit
In the New York Times.[25]

But of course, his many obituaries were far from small. For years after his death, in fact to this very day, E. Y. "Yip" Harburg has been remembered in various ways. A month after his leaving, a memorial service was held at the large Shubert Theatre in New York City. Three years later, he was posthumously inducted into the American Theatre Critics Association's Theatre Hall of Fame, whose plaques audiences can appreciate when they attend performances at New York City's Gershwin Theatre.

In 1993, Harold Meyerson and Ernie Harburg published their full-length biography of Yip, *Who Put the Rainbow in The Wizard of Oz?* Then in 1996, the 100th anniversary of his birth, an exhibition of Yip's works that included a video of him performing some of his own songs was mounted in the Billy Rose Theatre Division at the New York Public Library for the Performing Arts at Lincoln Center. In 2001, results of a poll conducted by the Recording Industry Association of America and the National Endowment for the Arts named Judy Garland's "Over the Rainbow" the top recording of the twentieth century. In 2004, in a television special sponsored by the American Film Institute to honor the 100 greatest film songs, "Over the Rainbow" took the number-one slot with "Ding-Dong! The Witch Is Dead" following as number eighty-two. And in April 2005, the US Postal Service issued a 37-cent stamp commemorating Yip. Today, even if people don't quite remember his name, his songs are played, hummed, and loved somewhere on this earth every day of the year.

Acknowledgments

When I was growing up, my parents had strict rules about bedtime. No matter if the sun had not yet set in the summer or if I was still wide awake, by 8:30 (at the latest, 9:00) I had to be in bed with the lights out. I was usually still keyed up from my busy schoolgirl day, so instead of trying to count sheep, I sang . . . and not softly. I pretended I was onstage, in a film, or on the radio as I belted out "Over the Rainbow," "How Are Things in Glocca Morra?" or "April in Paris." (Yes, I even belted out that number.) I thought I sounded great, but my parents and sisters never appreciated my efforts. "Shut up and go to sleep" was all the response I received.

Nevertheless, I grew up appreciating and memorizing E. Y. "Yip" Harburg's lyrics and his collaborators' tunes, so I was truly pleased when Parker Smathers of Wesleyan University Press and Music/Interview series editor Daniel Cavicchi asked me if I would like to write this book on Yip. Once I started work, I also received care and attention from Suzanna Tamminen, the press's wonderful director. For their faith in me, their support, and the opportunity to fulfill a long wished-for dream, I thank them. Thanks also to Leslie Starr, Stephanie Elliott, Lys Weiss, Peter Fong, Sara Evangelos, and Joanne Sprott for expertly (and kindly) taking the book through the production process.

I could not have completed this book by the requested deadline, or perhaps ever, had it not been for the support I received from Ernie Harburg and Nick Markovich of the Yip Harburg Foundation. Their generosity knows no bounds. Both Ernie and Nick supplied me with interviews, supporting details, and interesting tidbits of information throughout the research and writing process. Ernie told me stories not only about Yip, but also about himself as Yip's son. Nick helped to clarify details and constantly provided documents and photos and lots of interesting stories as well. I owe each of them my deepest gratitude. The contents of the book are, however, my own . . . and, of course, Yip's.

At the City College of New York, where I am a faculty member, I owe a big thank-you to Thomas Sabia and Fred Matcovsky for recovering Yip's college transcripts from the registrar's archives. During a most pleasant afternoon, Tom and I analyzed the transcripts and the old college catalogues that existed during Yip's time there. It was a truly interesting venture. I'd also like to thank Dean Geraldine Murphy and Deputy Dean Mary Ruth Strzeszewski for granting me travel funds for my research trip to Yale University. While I was there, Richard Warren kindly guided me through Yip's papers in the music library's archives. I am also grateful for a PSC-CUNY research award.

For their immense help in securing permission to quote from Yip's lyrics (and what would this book be without them?!), I'd like to thank Monica Corton of Next Decade Entertainment, Michael Worden of Alfred Music Publishing, Julie McDowell of Hal Leonard Corporation, Sebastian Fabal of Imagem, Aida Garcia-Cole of Music Sales Corporation, and Steven Winogradsky, Sam Arlen, and the Harold Arlen Estate. For other wonderful quotations, I thank Lynn Lane, Anthony Saidy, David Wilk, Craig Tenney of Harold Ober Associates, Kay Duke Ingalls, Deena Rosenberg Harburg, the Columbia University Center for Oral History, Columbia University Press, University of Michigan Press, and Scarecrow Press.

For the photos from *Bloomer Girl* and *Finian's Rainbow*, I am most grateful to Alex Teslik and Virginia Teslik of Eileen Darby Images, Inc. I thank Ken Golden for the cover photo.

Finally, I'd like to thank Gela Kline, Carolyn Beck, Lydia Shestapalova, Bonnie Anderson, Gregory Williams, Doris Cintron, Catherine Franklin, Suzanne Wasserman, Aria Hendricks, and Victor Alonso (as always) for their support. And Miguel, Lucinda, Joe, and Fern . . . just for being.

Appendix Musicals, Films, and Songs

This is a chronological listing of the key E. Y. "Yip" Harburg works discussed in this book. Extensive lists, which are continuously being updated as new items are discovered, are available at the Yip Harburg Foundation website (www .yipharburg.com).

1932
Americana
"Brother, Can You Spare a Dime?" (Music by Jay Gorney)
The Great Magoo
"If You Believed in Me"; later titled "It's Only a Paper Moon"
   (Music by Harold Arlen)
Walk a Little Faster
"April in Paris" (Music by Vernon Duke)

1934
Ziegfeld Follies of 1934
"I Like the Likes of You" (Music by Vernon Duke)
Life Begins at 8:40 (Music by Harold Arlen; Co-lyricist: Ira Gershwin)
"What Can You Say in a Love Song?"
"Quartet Erotica"
"Let's Take a Walk Around the Block"
"Fun to Be Fooled"
"You're a Builder Upper"

1935
"Last Night When We Were Young" (Music by Harold Arlen)

1937
Hooray for What! (Music by Harold Arlen)
"Down With Love"
"Hooray for What"

1939
The Wizard of Oz (Music by Harold Arlen)

"Ding-Dong! The Witch Is Dead"
"Over the Rainbow"
"The Jitterbug"
"If I Only Had a Brain"
At the Circus (Music by Harold Arlen)
"Lydia, the Tattooed Lady"

1940
Hold on to Your Hats (Music by Burton Lane)
"There's a Great Day Coming, Mañana"

1942
"The Son of a Gun Who Picks on Uncle Sam" (Music by Burton Lane)

1943
Cabin in the Sky
"Happiness Is a Thing Called Joe" (Music by Harold Arlen)

1944
Song of Russia
"And Russia Is Her Name" (Music by Jerome Kern)

"Don't Look Now, Mr. Dewey (But Your Record's Showing)"
    (Music by Arthur Schwartz)
"Free and Equal Blues" (Music by Earl Robinson)
"You Gotta Get Out and Vote" (Music by Earl Robinson)

Bloomer Girl (Music by Harold Arlen)
"Sunday in Cicero Falls"
"Grandma Was a Lady"; later renamed "It Was Good Enough for Grandma"
"The Eagle and Me"
"Man for Sale"
"When the Boys Come Home"
"Right as the Rain"

1945
"The Same Boat, Brother" (Music by Earl Robinson)

1947
Finian's Rainbow (Music by Burton Lane)

"How Are Things in Glocca Morra?"
"Look to the Rainbow"
"That Great Come-and-Get-It Day"
"Necessity"
"When the Idle Poor Become the Idle Rich"
"The Begat"
"When I'm Not Near the Girl I Love"
"Something Sort of Grandish"
"Old Devil Moon"

1951
Flahooley (Music by Sammy Fain)
"You Too Can Be a Puppet"
"B. G. Bigelow, Inc."
"Flahooley"
"The Springtime Cometh"

1957
Jamaica (Music by Harold Arlen)
"Push De Button"
"Monkey in the Mango Tree"
"Leave De Atom Alone"

1961
The Happiest Girl in the World (Music by Jacques Offenbach)
"The Glory That Is Greece"
"Adrift on a Star"

1968
Darling of the Day (Music by Jule Styne)

1971
What a Day for a Miracle / The Children's Crusade (Music by
    Henry Myers, Larry Orenstein, Jeff Alexander)

Notes

Many of the sources used in this book came courtesy of the Yip Harburg Foundation. I have designated these as YHF. Complete citations for lyrics appear in the Lyric Credits.

PREFACE AND A NOTE TO THE READER

1 Facts on *Over the Rainbow* adapted from "A Yip Harburg Chronology," Yip Harburg Foundation (YHF).

2 "Yip at the 92nd Street YM-YWHA, December 13, 1970," typed transcript 1-10-3, p. 3, cassettes 7-2-10 and 7-2-20, YHF.

3 "Yip at the Y #2, February 1, 1972," typed transcript, p. 3, archive tapes 7-2-50 and 7-2-60. YHF.

4 Denny Martin Flinn, *Musical! A Grand Tour* (New York: Simon & Schuster Macmillan, 1997), p. 363.

5 Ibid.

6 Wilfrid Sheed, *The House That George Built* (New York: Random House, 2008), p. xxv.

7 "Yip at the Y #2," p. 10. The song from *Finian's Rainbow* is titled "When I'm Not Near the Girl I Love."

8 "Table 1: Yip's Composers and Number of Songs Published with Yip and Registered at American Society of Composers, Authors, and Publishers (ASCAP)," in Harold Meyerson and Ernie Harburg, *Who Put the Rainbow in The Wizard of Oz?* (Ann Arbor: University of Michigan Press, 1993), p. 39; also "Yip Harburg's Composers" with explanation by Nick Markovich, July 18, 2008, YHF.

9 "Appendix 4: Alphabetical List of Yip Harburg's Song Titles (537)," Meyerson and Harburg, pp. 393–405.

10 "Something Sort of Grandish–Paul Lazarus, WBAI-FM, March 2, 1980," typed transcript 1-9-8, p. 16, recording 7-1-100, YHF.

11 "Over the Rainbow: Yip Harburg interviewed by Deena Rosenberg, 1980," typed transcript from video documentary, p. 11, archive audio cassette 7-1-220, archive video cassette 5-1-41, YHF.

12 E. Y. Harburg, "Lecture at UCLA on Lyric Writing, February 3, 1977," typed transcript, pp. 5–7, tape 7-3-10, YHF.

1. WHAT'S IN A NAME?

1 Much of this material has been gathered into "The Evolution of E. Y. Harburg's Name" collected by the Yip Harburg Foundation (YHF).

2 "Speech by E. Y. 'Yip' Harburg: Oral History Luncheon, Waldorf-Astoria, May 17, 1980, Moderated by Martin Bookspan," typed transcript, pp. 2–3, recording 7-2-201, YHF.

3 City College transcript for Edgar Y. Harburg, courtesy of the registrar's office of the City College of New York.

4 Ibid. The transcript is currently available only on microfilm and is difficult to read in places. Yip's father's name could be "Leivin" or "Lewis" or "Louis."

5 Ibid.

6 Interview with Studs Terkel, n.d., quoted in Harold Meyerson and Ernie Harburg, *Who Put the Rainbow in The Wizard of Oz?* (Ann Arbor: University of Michigan Press, 1993), p. 10.

7 "Yip Harburg interviewed by Michael Jackson, KABC Radio, California, post-1976, n.d.," typed transcript 1-9-1, p. 10, tape 7-1-20, YHF.

2. EARLY YEARS

1 "Reminiscences of E. Y. 'Yip' Harburg" (February 1959) on p. 1 in the Popular Arts Project through the Columbia University Center for Oral History.

2 "Speech by E. Y. 'Yip' Harburg: Oral History Luncheon, Waldorf-Astoria, May 17, 1980, Moderated by Martin Bookspan," typed transcript, pp. 2–3, recording 7-2-201, Yip Harburg Foundation (YHF).

3 "Reminiscences of E. Y. 'Yip' Harburg," p. 2.

4 Yip Harburg in Bernard Rosenberg and Ernest Goldstein, *Creators and Disturbers: Reminiscences by Jewish Intellectuals of New York* (New York: Columbia University Press, 1982), pp. 135–54.

5 "Brief Interview with Yip Harburg: Canadian Broadcasting Company (not confirmed), n.d.," typed transcript 1-9-22, pp. 1–2, tape 7-1-200, YHF; probably from the late 1970s or 1980.

6 "Reminiscences of E. Y. 'Yip' Harburg," p. 3.

7 Rosenberg and Goldstein, pp. 139–40.

8 Max Wilk, *They're Playing Our Song: Conversations with America's Classic Songwriters* (New York: De Capo Press, 1973, 1991; reprint 1997), p. 229.

9 Rosenberg and Goldstein, pp. 140–41.

10 "Over the Rainbow: Yip Harburg interviewed by Deena Rosenberg, 1980," typed transcript from video documentary, pp. 1–2, archive audio cassette 7-1-220, archive video cassette 5-1-41, YHF.

11 Rosenberg and Goldstein, pp. 138–39.

12 Wilk, p. 229.

13 "The David Frost Show—February 23, 1972, Guest: Yip Harburg," typed transcript 1-9-25, p. 2, VHS 185, audio cassette 7-1-260, YHF.

14 Rosenberg and Goldstein, p. 140.

15 Ibid., pp. 141–42.

16 "Over the Rainbow: Yip Harburg interviewed by Deena Rosenberg, 1980," YHF.

17 "Reminiscences of E. Y. 'Yip' Harburg," pp. 4–6.

18 Ibid., pp. 8–9.

19 Ibid.

20 "Yip on the Dick Cavett Show, WNET-TV, New York City, 1978," typed transcript, audio cassette 7-1-240, pp. 5–7, video cassettes 5-1-23 and 5-1-24, YHF.

21 "Reminiscences of E. Y. 'Yip' Harburg," pp. 8–9.

22 "Yip on the Dick Cavett Show," YHF.

23 Rosenberg and Goldstein, p. 142.

24 John Lahr, "The Lemon-Drop Kid," *New Yorker*, September 30, 1996, pp. 68–74, accessed August 11, 2010. http://archives.newyorker.com.

25 Yip Harburg interviewed by Deena Rosenberg, June 1978, as quoted in Harold Meyerson and Ernie Harburg, *Who Put the Rainbow in The Wizard of Oz?* (Ann Arbor: University of Michigan Press, 1993), pp. 20–22.

26 Rosenberg and Goldstein, p. 142.

27 "Reminiscences of E. Y. 'Yip' Harburg," pp. 8–9.

3. BROTHER, CAN YOU SPARE A DIME?

1 Yip Harburg interviewed by Studs Terkel, *Hard Times: An Oral History of the Great Depression* (New York: Random House, Inc., 1986), pp. 19–20.

2 "Yip Interviewed by Jack Sterling: The Jack Sterling Show, WCBS Radio, NYC, Spring: 1961," typed transcript, p. 6, Yip Harburg Foundation (YHF).

3 Yip Harburg, as quoted in Bernard Rosenberg and Ernest Goldstein, *Creators and Disturbers: Reminiscences by Jewish Intellectuals of New York* (New York: Columbia University Press, 1982), p. 144.

4 Rosenberg and Goldstein, p. 144.

5 "Yip Harburg at the Y—January 27 and 28, 1980," typed transcript 1-10-5, pp. 7–8, audio recordings 7-2-140 and 7-2-150, YHF.

6 Terkel, *Hard Times*, p. 20.

7 "Something Sort of Grandish—Paul Lazarus, WBAI-FM, March 2, 1980," typed transcript 1-9-8, pp. 2–3, recording 7-1-100, YHF.

8 Rosenberg and Goldstein, pp. 144–45.

9 "Brother, Can You Spare a Dime?" words by E. Y. Harburg, music by Jay Gorney, 1932. See lyric credits for full citation.

10 Terkel, *Hard Times*, p. 21.

11 Harold Meyerson and Ernie Harburg, *Who Put the Rainbow in The Wizard of Oz?* (Ann Arbor: University of Michigan Press, 1993), p. 47.

12 Rosenberg and Goldstein, p. 145.

13 "Something Sort of Grandish—Paul Lazarus," p. 2, YHF.

14 "Yip at the 92nd Street YM-YWHA, December 13, 1970," typed transcript 1-10-3, p. 6, cassettes 7-2-10 and 7-2-20, YHF.

15 Terkel, *Hard Times*, p. 21.

16 John Lahr, "The Lemon-Drop Kid," *New Yorker*, September 30, 1996, p. 72, accessed August 11, 2010. http://archives.newyorker.com.

17 Yip Harburg, as quoted in Lahr, p. 70.

18 "Chappell's Broadway, April 2, 1971—Guest: Yip Harburg," typed transcript 1-10-17, pp. 5–6, recording 7-10-400, YHF.

4. A PAUSE FOR JAY GORNEY

1 "E. Y. Harburg, Lecture at UCLA on Lyric Writing, February 3, 1977," typed transcript, pp. 5–7, tape 7-3-10, Yip Harburg Foundation (YHF).

2 Background information and several of the quotes in this chapter are adapted from Sondra K. Gorney, *Brother, Can You Spare a Dime? The Life of Composer Jay Gorney* (Lanham, MD: Scarecrow Press, Inc., 2005).

3 Ibid., p. 12.

4 Ibid., p. 13.

5 Ibid., p. 14.

6 Author interview with Ernie Harburg, October 5, 2010, New York City.

7 Gorney, p. 106.

8 Ibid., pp. 105–6.

5. YIP'S PATH TO SHOW BUSINESS SUCCESS

1 Brooks Atkinson, *Broadway* (New York: Limelight Books, 1970, 1974; reprint 1990), p. 289.

2 John Bush Jones, *Our Musicals, Ourselves: A Social History of the American Musical Theatre* (Lebanon, NH: Brandeis University Press, 2003), pp. 81–83.

3 John Lahr, "The Lemon-Drop Kid," *New Yorker*, September 30, 1996, pp. 68–74, accessed August 11, 2010. http://archives.newyorker.com.

4 Yip Harburg in Bernard Rosenberg and Ernest Goldstein, *Creators and Disturbers: Reminiscences by Jewish Intellectuals of New York* (New York: Columbia University Press, 1982), pp. 135–54.

5 "Yip Harburg interviewed by Jonathan Schwartz, WNEW-FM, New York City, February 17, 1980: Subject: Harold Arlen's 75th Birthday," typed transcript, pp. 20–21, Yip Harburg Foundation (YHF).

6 Ibid.

7 "It's Only a Paper Moon (If You Believed in Me)," words by E. Y. Harburg and Billy Rose, music by Harold Arlen, 1933. See lyric credits for full citations.

8 "Canadian Broadcasting Company interview with Yip Harburg, November 26, 1979," typed transcript, p. 5, tapes 7-1-60 and 7-1-80, YHF.

9 "Yip Harburg, Speech at University of Vermont, April 21, 1975," typed transcript, pp. 34–36, recording 7-2-230, YHF.

10 Max Wilk, *They're Playing Our Song: Conversations with America's Classic Songwriters* (New York: Da Capo Press, 1973, 1991; reprint 1997), pp. 232–33.

11 "April in Paris," words by E. Y. Harburg, music by Vernon Duke, 1932. See lyric credits for full citation.

12 "Yip Harburg, Mark Taper Forum, February 5, 1973," typed transcript, p. 16, tapes 7-2-70, 7-2-80, and 7-2-90, YHF.

13 "Brief interview with Yip Harburg: Canadian Broadcasting Company (not confirmed), n.d.," typed transcript 1-9-22, p. 6, tape 7-1-200, YHF; probably from the late 1970s or 1980.

14 "Yip Harburg interviewed by Deems Taylor, *The Kraft Program*, January 25, 1934," typed transcript, YHF.

15 "Something Sort of Grandish—Paul Lazarus, WBAI-FM, March 2, 1980," typed transcript 1-9-8, p. 5, recording 7-1-100, YHF.

16 "I Like the Likes of You," words by E. Y. "Yip" Harburg, music by Vernon Duke, 1933. See lyric credits for full citation.

17 "Something Sort of Grandish—Paul Lazarus," pp. 18–19, YHF.

18 Yip Harburg, as quoted in Harold Meyerson and Ernie Harburg, *Who Put the Rainbow in The Wizard of Oz?* (Ann Arbor: University of Michigan Press, 1993), pp. 75–76.

19 Wilk, pp. 144–46.

20 "The Revue: Yip Harburg with Deena Rosenberg and Mel Gordon, November 15, 1980," typed transcript 1-9-11a, pp. 2–9, tape 7-7-270, YHF.

21 "Yip Harburg at the Y—January 27 and 28, 1980," typed transcript 1-10-5, pp. 9–10, audio recordings 7-2-140 and 7-2-150, YHF.

22 "Let's Take a Walk Around the Block," "What Can You Say in A Love Song?"

and "Quartet Erotica," words by E. Y. Harburg and Ira Gershwin, music by Harold Arlen, 1934. See lyric credits for full citations.

23 "Yip Harburg interviewed by Jonathan Schwartz," pp. 23–24, YHF.

24 "A Visit with E. Y. 'Yip' Harburg: A Musical Life in Concert, from CBC Television Broadcast, ca. 1979," typed transcript, p. 5, VHS 5-1-95, cassette 7-2-220, YHF.

25 "Last Night When We Were Young," words by E. Y. "Yip" Harburg, music by Harold Arlen, 1937. See lyric credits for full citations.

26 "Canadian Broadcasting Company interview with Yip Harburg," pp. 13–15, YHF.

27 "Canadian Broadcasting Company interview with Yip Harburg," pp. 18–19, YHF.

28 *Hooray for What!*, book by Howard Lindsay and Russel Crouse, lyrics by E. Y. Harburg, music by Harold Arlen, 1937, 1938; typed manuscript, pp. 1–2, YHF. See lyric credits for full citation.

29 "Chappell's Broadway, April 2, 1971–Guest: Yip Harburg," typed transcript, 1-10-17, pp. 1–2, recording 7-10-400, YHF.

6. A PAUSE FOR VERNON DUKE

1 The information in this chapter derives from Vernon Duke, *Passport to Paris* (Boston: Little, Brown and Company, 1955).

2 Duke, p. 223.

3 Ibid., pp. 267–68.

4 Ibid., p. 272.

5 Ibid., pp. 273–74.

6 Ibid., p. 276.

7 Ibid., p. 276.

8 Ibid., p. 287.

7. FROM HOLLYWOOD TO OZ AND BACK

1 Yip Harburg, as quoted in Bernard Rosenberg and Ernest Goldstein, *Creators and Disturbers: Reminiscences by Jewish Intellectuals of New York* (New York: Columbia University Press, 1982), p. 149.

2 "Reminiscences of E. Y. 'Yip' Harburg" (February 1959) on pp. 23–29 in the Popular Arts Project through the Columbia University Center for Oral History.

3 Rosenberg and Goldstein, pp. 150–51.

4 Max Wilk, *They're Playing Our Song: Conversations with America's Classic Songwriters* (New York: Da Capo Press, 1973, 1991; reprint 1997), p. 234.

5 "Yip Harburg interviewed by Aljean Harmetz, Spring, 1975," typed notes, Yip Harburg Foundation (YHF).

6 Ibid.

7 "Ding-Dong! The Witch Is Dead," lyrics by E. Y. "Yip" Harburg, music by Harold Arlen, 1938. See lyric credits for full citation.

8 "Yip on the Dick Cavett Show, WNET-TV, New York City, 1978," typed transcript of audio cassette 7-1-240, pp. 16–17, video cassettes 5-1-23 and 5-1-24, YHF.

9 "The Revue: Yip Harburg with Deena Rosenberg and Mel Gordon, November 15, 1980," typed transcript 1-9-11a, pp. 4–5, tape 7-7-270, YHF.

10 "Something Sort of Grandish—Paul Lazarus, WBAI-FM, March 2, 1980," typed transcript 1-9-8, p. 10, recording 7-1-100, YHF.

11 "Yip Harburg interviewed by Aljean Harmetz, Spring, 1975."

12 Ibid.

13 "Yip Harburg Interviewed by Studs Terkel, undated—probably January or February, 1977; Topic: Yip's New Book, *At This Point in Rhyme*," typed transcript 1-9-23, pp. 26–27, tape 7-1-50, YHF.

14 "Something Sort of Grandish—Paul Lazarus," pp. 8–9.

15 "Canadian Broadcasting Company interview with Yip Harburg, November 26, 1979," typed transcript, pp. 7–9, tapes 7-1-60 and 7-1-80, YHF.

16 Aljean Harmetz, *The Making of the Wizard of Oz* (New York: Alfred A. Knopf, 1977; reprint New York: Hyperion, 1998), pp. 80–81.

17 "Over the Rainbow," lyrics by E. Y. "Yip" Harburg, music by Harold Arlen, 1938. See lyric credits for full citation.

18 "Yip Harburg, Speech at University of Vermont, April 21, 1975," typed transcript, pp. 37–41, recording 7-2-230, YHF.

19 "Yip Harburg, Mark Taper Forum, February 5, 1973," typed transcript of tapes 7-2-70, 7-2-80, and 7-2-90, p. 22, YHF.

20 See, for example, *The Wizard of Oz: 70th Anniversary Special Edition*, DVD, Warner Brothers and Turner Entertainment Co., 2009.

21 Wilk, p. 235.

22 "World of Music—N.E.T.—E. Y. Harburg: Lyrics for the Musical Theatre— Host: Morton Gould, January 27, 1965; broadcast March 10, 1965," typed transcript, p. 8, YHF.

23 "Yip at the 92nd Street YM-YWHA, December 13, 1970," typed transcript 1-10-3, pp. 14–15, cassettes 7-2-10 and 7-2-20, pp. 6–7; partial lyrics of songs from "World of Music," pp. 8–9, YHF. "If I Only Had a Brain," lyrics by E. Y. "Yip" Harburg, music by Harold Arlen, 1938. See lyric credits for full citation.

24 Wilk, p. 234.

25 Wilk, p. 239.

26 "Reminiscences of E. Y. 'Yip' Harburg," pp. 32–33.

27 "Yip on the Dick Cavett Show," pp. 17–18.

28 "Lydia, the Tattooed Lady," lyrics by E. Y. "Yip" Harburg, music by Harold Arlen, 1939. See lyric credits for full citation.

29 For details on Will Hays, Joseph Breen, and censorship, see Harriet Hyman Alonso, *Robert E. Sherwood: The Playwright in Peace and War* (Amherst: University of Massachusetts Press, 2007), pp. 83–86, 180–83.

30 "A Visit with E. Y. 'Yip' Harburg: A Musical Life in Concert, from CBC Television Broadcast, ca. 1979." typed transcript, pp. 6–7, VHS 5-1-95, cassette 7-2-220, YHF.

31 "Lydia, the Tattooed Lady." See lyric credits for full citation.

32 "Reminiscences of E. Y. 'Yip' Harburg," pp. 29–31.

33 Wilk, p. 235.

34 "There's a Great Day Coming, Mañana," lyrics by E. Y. Harburg, music by Burton Lane, 1940. See lyric credits for full citation.

35 "Happiness Is a Thing Called Joe," lyrics by E. Y. "Yip" Harburg, music by Harold Arlen, 1942. See lyric credits for full citation.

36 "Canadian Broadcasting Company interview with Yip Harburg," pp. 25–27, YHF.

8. A PAUSE FOR HAROLD ARLEN

1 "Yip Harburg interviewed by Jonathan Schwartz, WNEW-FM, New York City, February 17, 1980: Subject: Harold Arlen's 75th Birthday," typed transcript, pp. 9–10, Yip Harburg Foundation (YHF).

2 "Yip Harburg Interviewed by Deena Rosenberg, November 22, 1976," typed transcript, pp. 3–4, archive tape 7-1-70, YHF.

3 "Over the Rainbow: Yip Harburg interviewed by Deena Rosenberg, 1980," typed transcript from video documentary, pp. 8–9, archive audio cassette 7-1-220, archive video cassette 5-1-41, YHF.

4 Max Wilk, *They're Playing Our Song: Conversations with America's Classic Songwriters* (New York: Da Capo Press, 1973, 1991; reprint 1997), pp. 146–47.

5 Ibid.

6 Ibid., pp. 147, 151–52.

7 "Canadian Broadcasting Company interview with Yip Harburg, November 26, 1979," typed transcript, p. 7, tapes 7-1-60 and 7-1-80, YHF.

8 "Yip Harburg interviewed by Jonathan Schwartz," p. 11, YHF.

9 "The 20th Century: The Songs of Harold Arlen, Narrator/Interviewer: Walter Cronkite," n.d., typed transcript, pp. 3–4, YHF.

10 Edward Jablonski, *Harold Arlen: Rhythm, Rainbows, and Blues* (Boston: Northeastern University Press, 1996), p. 133.

11 Ibid., p. 178.

9. HUMAN RIGHTS ACTIVISM TAKES CENTER STAGE

1 Max Wilk, *They're Playing Our Song: Conversations with America's Classic Songwriters* (New York: Da Capo Press, 1973, 1991; reprint 1997), p. 236.

2 Edward Jablonski, *Harold Arlen: Rhythm, Rainbows, and Blues* (Boston: Northeastern University Press, 1996), p. 195.

3 Ibid., p. 194.

4 "Yip Harburg Interview with Deena Rosenberg, November, 1980," as quoted in Harold Meyerson and Ernie Harburg, *Who Put the Rainbow in The Wizard of Oz?* (Ann Arbor: University of Michigan Press, 1993), p. 219.

5 E. Y. Harburg to Mayor Fiorello La Guardia, April 24, 1941, Series II, folder 23/195, MSS83. The E. Y. Harburg Collection in the Irving S. Gilmore Music Library of Yale University.

6 James R. Page, Paul K. Yost, and Olin Wellborn to Gentlemen, November 13, 1941, Series II, folder 23/195, MSS83, Yale University.

7 "The Son of a Gun Who Picks on Uncle Sam," lyrics by E. Y. Harburg, music by Burton Lane, 1942. See lyric credits for full citation.

8 "Tribute to Russia Day" souvenir program, June 22, 1943, Series I, folder 20/152, MSS83, Yale University.

9 "And Russia Is Her Name," lyrics by E. Y. Harburg, music by Jerome Kern, 1943. Sung in film *Song of Russia* by Walter Lawrence, 1944. See lyric credits for full citation.

10 "Yip Harburg interviewed by Michael Jackson, KABC Radio, California, post-1976, n.d.," typed transcript 1-9-1, p. 2, tape 7-1-20, Yip Harburg Foundation (YHF).

11 "Don't Look Now, Mr. Dewey (But Your Record's Showing)," lyrics by E. Y. Harburg, music by Arthur Schwartz, Program for Liberal Party Rally for FDR, October 31, 1944, Series I, folder 20/153, MSS83, Yale University. See lyric credits for full citation.

12 "Free and Equal Blues," lyrics by E. Y. "Yip" Harburg, music by Earl Robinson, 1944, 1947. See lyric credits for full citation.

13 "Get Out and Vote," lyrics by E. Y. Harburg, music by Earl Robinson, 1944, typescript, Series I, folder 20/153, MSS83, Yale University. See lyric credits for full citation.

14 E. Y. Harburg to David O. Selznick, May 18, 1944, Series II, folder 23/195, MSS83, Yale University.

15 Wilk, p. 236.

16 "Canadian Broadcasting Company interview with Yip Harburg, November 26, 1979," typed transcript, pp. 28–30, tapes 7-1-60 and 7-1-80, YHF.

17 "E. Y. Harburg, Lecture at UCLA on Lyric Writing, February 3, 1977," typed transcript, pp. 7–8, tape 7-3-10, YHF.

18 "Sunday in Cicero Falls," lyrics by E. Y. "Yip" Harburg, music by Harold Arlen, 1944, *Bloomer Girl* typescript, 1944, pp. 2-1-1 and 2-1-2, YHF. See lyric credits for full citation.

19 "Grandma Was a Lady" ("It Was Good Enough for Grandma"), lyrics by E. Y. "Yip" Harburg, music by Harold Arlen, 1944, *Bloomer Girl* typescript, 1944, pp. 1-3-5 and 1-3-6, YHF. See lyric credits for full citation.

20 "The Eagle and Me," lyrics by E. Y. "Yip" Harburg, music by Harold Arlen, 1944, *Bloomer Girl* typescript, 1944, p. 1-3-9, YHF. See lyric credits for full citation. Note that some publications say "Ever since *that* day / When the world was an onion." Others say "Ever since *the* day . . ."

21 "Yip Harburg interviewed by Studs Terkel, June, 1978," typed transcript, p. 19, YHF.

22 "Chappell's Broadway, April 2, 1971–Guest: Yip Harburg," typed transcript 1-10-17, pp. 6–8, recording 7-10-400, YHF.

23 "Something Sort of Grandish—Paul Lazarus, WBAI-FM, March 2, 1980," typed transcript 1-9-8, pp. 11–12, recording 7-1-100, YHF.

24 Stephen Sondheim, *Finishing the Hat: Collected Lyrics (1954–1981) with Attendant Comments, Principles, Heresies, Grudges, Whines and Anecdotes* (New York: Alfred A. Knopf, 2010), p. 99.

25 "Man for Sale," lyrics by E. Y. "Yip" Harburg, music by Harold Arlen, 1944, *Bloomer Girl* typescript, 1944, pp. 2-3-22 and 2-3-23, YHF. See lyric credits for full citation.

26 The "Civil War Ballet" can be viewed on YouTube. Search "Agnes de Mille," "Civil War Ballet," or "Bloomer Girl."

27 "Yip at the Y #2, February 1, 1972," typed transcript, p. 17, archive tapes 7-2-50 and 7-2-60, YHF.

28 "When the Boys Come Home," lyrics by E. Y. "Yip" Harburg, music by Harold Arlen, 1944, *Bloomer Girl* typescript, 1944, pp. 1-1-2 and 1-1-3, YHF. See lyric credits for full citation.

29 E-mail from Ernie Harburg to author, February 28, 2011.

30 "Yip Harburg Interview with Deena Rosenberg, November, 1980," in Meyerson and Harburg, p. 201.

31 "Right as the Rain," lyrics by E. Y. "Yip" Harburg, music by Harold Arlen,

1944, *Bloomer Girl* typescript, 1944, pp. 1-3-19 and 1-3-20, YHF. See lyric credits for full citation.

32 E. Y. Harburg, "'Till We All Belong, n.d.," typescript, YHF.

33 "The Same Boat, Brother," lyrics by E. Y. "Yip" Harburg, music by Earl Robinson, 1944, 1945. See lyric credits for full citation.

34 Albert Einstein to E. Y. Harburg, June 29, 1946, Series II, folder 23/195, MSS83, Yale University.

10. A PAUSE FOR AGNES DE MILLE

1 Agnes de Mille, *And Promenade Home* (Boston: Little, Brown and Company, 1956, 1957, 1958, 1984, 1985, 1986), pp. 194–95.

2 Ibid., p. 196.

3 Ibid., pp. 196–97.

4 Ibid., p. 197.

5 Ibid., p. 198.

6 Ibid., p. 200.

7 Ibid.

8 Ibid., p. 202.

9 Ibid., pp. 202–3.

11. YIP'S CASE STUDY OF *FINIAN'S RAINBOW*

1 Max Wilk, *They're Playing Our Song: Conversations with America's Classic Songwriters* (New York: Da Capo Press, 1973, 1991; reprint 1997), p. 236.

2 Yip Harburg at Northwood Institute, as quoted in Harold Meyerson and Ernie Harburg, *Who Put the Rainbow in The Wizard of Oz?* (Ann Arbor: University of Michigan Press, 1993), pp. 222–23.

3 Wilk, pp. 236–37.

4 "Yip Harburg interviewed on Chappell's Broadway, February 27, 1970," typed transcript 1-10-16, p. 1, recording 7-10-390, Yip Harburg Foundation (YHF).

5 "Yip Harburg interviewed by Professor David M. Keller, 'The Dramatic Experience,' Program 1: The Musical Comedy Theatre, WNYC-TV, 1968," typed transcript, pp. 7–8, YHF.

6 "Yip on the Dick Cavett Show, WNET-TV, New York City, 1978," typed transcript, audio cassette 7-1-240, p. 21, video cassettes 5-1-23 and 5-1-24, YHF.

7 "Yip Harburg interviewed by Professor David M. Keller," pp. 8–9, YHF.

8 "Yip Harburg, Speech at University of Vermont, April 21, 1975," typed transcript, pp. 1–4, recording 7-2-230, YHF.

9 "Yip Harburg at the 92nd Street Y, December 15, 1974," typed transcript, pp. 2–3, recording 7-2-110, YHF.

10 "Yip Harburg, Speech at University of Vermont," pp. 1–8, YHF.

11 "How are Things in Glocca Morra?" lyrics by E. Y. "Yip" Harburg, music by Burton Lane, 1946. See lyric credits for full citation.

12 "Yip Harburg, Speech at University of Vermont," pp. 4–9, YHF.

13 "Yip Harburg, Lecture at Northwood Institute, 1978," typed transcript, pp. 5–6, tapes 7-3-30, 7-3-40, 7-3-50, 7-3-60, and 7-3-70, YHF.

14 For example, see James Stephens, *The Crock of Gold* (New York: Dover Publications, Inc., 1997; reprint of 1912 ed.), pp. 52–53.

15 Eleanor Roosevelt, "My Day" column, March 31, 1948, YHF.

16 "Yip Harburg, Speech at University of Vermont," pp. 8–10, YHF.

17 "Look to the Rainbow," lyrics by E. Y. "Yip" Harburg, music by Burton Lane, 1946. See lyric credits for full citation.

18 "Yip Harburg, Speech at University of Vermont," pp. 11–12, YHF.

19 "Yip Harburg at the 92nd Street Y, December 15, 1974," p. 18, YHF.

20 "Yip Harburg, Speech at University of Vermont," pp. 13–14, YHF.

21 "That Great Come-and-Get-It Day," lyrics by E. Y. "Yip" Harburg, music by Burton Lane, 1946. See lyric credits for full citation.

22 "Yip Harburg, Speech at University of Vermont," pp. 14–17.

23 "Necessity," lyrics by E. Y. "Yip" Harburg, music by Burton Lane, 1946. See lyric credits for full citation.

24 "Yip Harburg, Speech at University of Vermont," pp. 16–17, YHF.

25 "When the Idle Poor Become the Idle Rich," lyrics by E. Y. "Yip" Harburg, music by Burton Lane, 1946. See lyric credits for full citation.

26 "Yip Harburg, Lecture at Northwood Institute, 1978," p. 25, YHF.

27 "The Begat," lyrics by E. Y. "Yip" Harburg, music by Burton Lane, 1946, 1952. See lyric credits for full citation.

28 "Yip Harburg, Speech at University of Vermont," p. 18, YHF.

29 "When I'm Not Near the Girl I Love," lyrics by E. Y. "Yip" Harburg, music by Burton Lane, 1946. See lyric credits for full citation.

30 "Yip Harburg, Speech at University of Vermont," pp. 18–19, YHF.

31 "Yip Harburg at the 92nd Street Y, December 15, 1974," p. 21, YHF.

32 "Something Sort of Grandish," lyrics by E. Y. "Yip" Harburg, music by Burton Lane, 1946. See lyric credits for full citation.

33 "Yip Harburg, Speech at University of Vermont," pp. 19, 23, 24, YHF.

34 Ibid.

35 "Yip Harburg, Lecture at Northwood Institute, 1978," pp. 9–14, YHF.

36 Ibid., pp. 17–19.

37 Ibid.

38 "Yip Harburg, Speech at University of Vermont," pp. 25–26, YHF.

39 "Old Devil Moon," lyrics by E. Y. "Yip" Harburg, music by Burton Lane, 1946. See lyric credits for full citation.

40 "Yip Harburg, Speech at University of Vermont," pp. 26–28.

41 Ibid., pp. 28–30.

42 "Yip Harburg, Lecture at Northwood Institute, 1978," pp. 20–21.

43 E. Y. Harburg, Draft of Speech, December 4, 1949, YHF.

44 "Yip Harburg interviewed on Chappell's Broadway, February 27, 1970," p. 1.

45 "Lena Horne interviewed by Ernie Harburg and Deena Rosenberg, November 20, 1992," typed transcript, p. 8, YHF.

46 E. Y. Harburg Transcript. Courtesy of the City College of New York.

12. A PAUSE FOR BURTON LANE

1 Max Wilk, *They're Playing Our Song: Conversations with America's Classic Songwriters* (New York: Da Capo Press, 1973, 1991; reprint 1997), p. 210.

2 Ibid., p. 206.

3 "Burton Lane interviewed by Bernard Rosenberg and Ernie Harburg, April 11, 1983," typed transcript, pp. 22–23, Yip Harburg Foundation (YHF).

4 Ibid., pp. 22–23.

5 Ibid., p. 24.

6 "Burton Lane interviewed by Brad Ross, Ernie Harburg, and Art Perlman, July 10, 1984," typed transcript, p. 19, YHF.

7 Ibid., p. 24.

8 Ibid.

9 Wilk, p. 209.

13. ANGER, FRUSTRATION, AND PERSISTENCE DURING THE MCCARTHY YEARS

1 "Yip Harburg interviewed by Jack O'Brien on 'Critic's Circle,' WOR Radio, New York City, May 21, 1977," typed transcript, pp. 4–8, Yip Harburg Foundation (YHF).

2 Ibid.

3 "Chappell's Broadway, April 2, 1971–Guest: Yip Harburg," typed transcript, 1-10-17, p. 1, recording 7-10-400, YHF.

4 E. Y. Harburg to J. Robert Rubin, December 25, 1950, Series II, folder 23/196, MSS83. The E. Y. Harburg Collection in the Irving S. Gilmore Music Library of Yale University.

5 "Yip Harburg interviewed by Celeste Wesson of WBAI, Autumn, 1976," typed transcript 1-9-3, pp. 5–15, tape 7-1-10, YHF.

6 "Something Sort of Grandish—Paul Lazarus, WBAI-FM, March 2, 1980," typed transcript 1-9-8, p. 15, recording 7-1-100, YHF.

7 Harold Meyerson and Ernie Harburg, *Who Put the Rainbow in The Wizard of Oz?* (Ann Arbor: University of Michigan Press, 1993), p. 275.

8 "Chappell's Broadway, Discussion of *Flahooley*, 1969, with Yip Harburg and Sammy Fain," typed transcript, pp. 1–5, YHF.

9 "Yip Harburg interviewed by Celeste Wesson," pp. 3–5, YHF.

10 Ibid.

11 "Yip Harburg interviewed by Deena Rosenberg, November 22, 1976," typed transcript, p. 5, archive tape 7-1-70, YHF.

12 "You Too Can Be a Puppet," lyrics by E. Y. Harburg, music by Sammy Fain, 1951; *Flahooley*, 1951, typed manuscript of lyrics, pp. 1–2, YHF. See lyric credits for full citation.

13 "B. G. Bigalow, Inc.," lyrics by E. Y. Harburg, music by Sammy Fain, 1951; *Flahooley*, 1951, typed manuscript of lyrics, p. 7, YHF. See lyric credits for full citation.

14 "Flahooley," lyrics by E. Y. Harburg, music by Sammy Fain, 1951; *Flahooley*, 1951, typed manuscript of lyrics, pp. 15–16, YHF. See lyric credits for full citation.

15 "Chappell's Broadway, Discussion of *Flahooley*," pp. 5–6, YHF. "The Springtime Cometh," lyrics by E. Y. Harburg, music by Sammy Fain, 1951; *Flahooley*, 1951, typed manuscript of lyrics, pp. 30–31, YHF. See lyric credits for full citation.

16 Meyerson and Harburg, p. 295.

17 "Reminiscences of E. Y. 'Yip' Harburg," (February 1959) on pp. 40–52 in the Popular Arts Project through the Columbia University Center for Oral History.

18 Ibid., pp. 60–61.

19 "Push De Button," lyrics by E. Y. "Yip" Harburg, music by Harold Arlen, 1957; *Jamaica*, 1959, typed manuscript of Karamu Production, pp. 1-1-3 to 1-1-5, YHF. See lyric credits for full citation.

20 "Canadian Broadcasting Company interview with Yip Harburg, November 26, 1979," typed transcript, p. 37, tapes 7-1-60 and 7-1-80, YHF.

21 "Yip Harburg, Mark Taper Forum, February 5, 1973," typed transcript, p. 18, tapes 7-2-70, 7-2-80, and 7-2-90, YHF.

22 "Monkey in the Mango Tree," lyrics by E. Y. "Yip" Harburg, music by Harold

Arlen, 1957; *Jamaica*, 1959, typed manuscript of Karamu Production, pp. 1-7-32 to 1-7-33, YHF. See lyric credits for full citation.

23 "Yip Harburg, Mark Taper Forum," p. 30, YHF.

24 "Something Sort of Grandish—Paul Lazarus," p. 16, YHF.

25 "Canadian Broadcasting Company interview with Yip Harburg," pp. 36–37, YHF.

26 "Leave De Atom Alone," lyrics by E. Y. "Yip" Harburg, music by Harold Arlen, 1957; *Jamaica*, 1959, typed manuscript of Karamu Production, pp. 2-1-2 to 2-1-4, YHF. See lyric credits for full citation.

27 *The Happiest Girl in the World*, book by Fred Saidy and Henry Myers, story by E. Y. Harburg, lyrics by E. Y. Harburg, music by Jacques Offenbach, 1961, typed manuscript, title page, YHF.

28 "Something Sort of Grandish—Paul Lazarus," p. 17, YHF.

29 "Reminiscences of E. Y. 'Yip' Harburg," pp. 45, 46, 53, 57.

30 "Yip Interviewed by Jack Sterling: The Jack Sterling Show, WCBS Radio, New York City, Spring: 1961," typed transcript, pp. 1–5, YHF.

31 "The Glory That Is Greece," lyrics by E. Y. "Yip" Harburg, music by Jacques Offenbach, 1961; *The Happiest Girl in the World*, 1961, typed manuscript, pp. 1-2-9 and 1-2-10, YHF. See lyric credits for full citation.

32 "Chappell's Broadway, April 2, 1971," pp. 8–10, YHF.

33 "Adrift on a Star," lyrics by E. Y. "Yip" Harburg, music by Jacques Offenbach, 1961; *The Happiest Girl in the World*, 1961, typed manuscript, pp. 1-6-48 and 1-6-49, YHF. See lyric credits for full citation.

34 "Chappell's Broadway, April 2, 1971," p. 10, YHF.

35 "Something Sort of Grandish—Paul Lazarus," pp. 18–19, YHF.

36 "The David Frost Show—February 23, 1972, Guest: Yip Harburg," typed transcript 1-9-25, pp. 12–13, VHS 185, audio cassette 7-1-260, YHF.

37 "Yip Harburg interviewed by Michael Jackson, KABC Radio, California, post-1976, n.d.," typed transcript 1-9-1, p. 12, tape 7-1-20, YHF.

38 "E. Y. Harburg, Lecture at UCLA on Lyric Writing, February 3, 1977," typed transcript, pp. 11–12, tape 7-3-10, YHF.

14. A PAUSE FOR FRIENDSHIP DURING HARD TIMES

1 Burton Lane to E. Y. Harburg, November 22, 1950, Series II, folder 23/196, MSS83. The E. Y. Harburg Collection in the Irving S. Gilmore Music Library of Yale University.

2 E. Y. Harburg to Burton Lane, November 28, 1950, Series II, folder 23/196. MSS83, Yale University.

3 "A Conversation with Burton Lane by Deena Rosenberg, April 29, 1985," typed transcript, pp. 17–18, edited version of interview on VHS 5-1-74, Yip Harburg Foundation (YHF).

15. THE NEW OLD YIP

1 E. Y. Harburg to Student Mobilization Committee, New York City, July 2, 1968, Series II, folder 23/196, MSS83. The E. Y. Harburg Collection in the Irving S. Gilmore Music Library of Yale University.

2 "Yip Harburg interviewed by Studs Terkel, undated—probably January or February, 1977; Topic: Yip's New Book, *At This Point in Rhyme*," typed transcript 1-9-23, p. 2, tape 7-1-50, Yip Harburg Foundation (YHF).

3 "Yip Harburg, Mark Taper Forum, February 5, 1973," typed transcript, pp. 34–35, tapes 7-2-70, 7-2-80, and 7-2-90, YHF.

4 "Yip Harburg interviewed by Studs Terkel, undated," p. 8, YHF.

5 "Yip Harburg interviewed by Maurice Levine, Lyrics and Lyricists series, March 23, 1977," typed transcript, p. 5, tape 242C, side A, YHF.

6 "Yip Harburg interviewed by Studs Terkel, undated," pp. 4–5, YHF.

7 Ibid., pp. 16–17, YHF.

8 "Yip Harburg, Mark Taper Forum," p. 37, YHF.

9 E. Y. Harburg, "Black Night at the White House," circa 1964, Series I, folder 20/154, MSS83, Yale University.

10 "Yip Harburg interviewed by Studs Terkel, undated," pp. 20–21, YHF.

11 Ibid., p. 25, YHF.

12 "Yip Harburg, Mark Taper Forum," p. 38, YHF.

13 "The David Frost Show—February 23, 1972, Guest: Yip Harburg," typed transcript 1-9-25, VHS 185, audio cassette 7-1-260, YHF.

14 E. Y. Harburg, "Anything Goes" in "Yip Harburg—Parodies and Others, n.d.," typescript, p. 1, YHF.

15 E. Y. Harburg, "If This Isn't Peace," ibid., pp. 1–2, YHF.

16 E. Y. Harburg, "I've Grown Accustomed to Disgrace," ibid., pp. 2–3, YHF.

17 "Yip Harburg radio interview with Jinx Falkenberg and unidentified male interviewer, n.d., ca. 1951," typed transcript, p. 1, YHF.

18 John Lahr, "The Lemon-Drop Kid," *New Yorker*, September 30, 1996, p. 73, accessed August 11, 2010. http://archives.newyorker.com.

19 "Canadian Broadcasting Company interview with Yip Harburg, November 26, 1979," typed transcript, p. 22, tapes 7-1-60 and 7-1-80, YHF.

20 "Yip Harburg interviewed by Studs Terkel, June 1978," typed transcript, p. 21, YHF.

21 "Yip Harburg on the *Great American Dream Machine*, WNET-TV, New York City, 1971," typed transcript 1-10-7, p. 1, recording 7-2-210, VHS 5-1-90, YHF.

22 "A Visit with E. Y. 'Yip' Harburg: A Musical Life in Concert, from CBC Television Broadcast, ca. 1979," typed transcript, p. 1, VHS 5-1-95, cassette 7-2-220, YHF.

23 E. Y. Harburg, "Look to the Rainbow," in "Yip Harburg—Parodies and Others," possibly 1972, pp. 9–10, YHF.

24 "Speech by Yip Harburg, Horatio Alger Awards, 1979," typed transcript, pp. 2–3, YHF.

25 E. Y. Harburg, *At This Point in Rhyme: E. Y. Harburg's Poems* (New York: Crown Publishers, Inc., 1976), back page.

Bibliography

Because the purpose of this book was to present E. Y. "Yip" Harburg's work primarily through interviews, the sources I used were, of course, decided by that task. However, I did use other sources to fill out the story. As this rather unconventional bibliography will show, many of these sources represent Yip's own work.

ARCHIVAL SOURCES

My primary archival source was the Yip Harburg Foundation. The small foundation office has a wealth of information and provided me with almost all of the interviews used. The foundation's website can provide the general audience with a great deal of information about Yip, from news of events to works written about his life to archival material. A portion of the material can also be found in the E. Y. Harburg Papers at the New York Public Library for the Performing Arts at Lincoln Center, but I did not have to use that source. I did use the E. Y. Harburg collection in the Irving S. Gilmore Music Library of Yale University. Much of the material at Yale involves the evolution of each of Yip's musicals and songs. I was most interested in documenting his political work and found a small cache of items in that collection. I also had access to the registrar's records of City College of New York, which supplied me with Yip's college transcript. Otherwise, all of my material was obtained through the Yip Harburg Foundation (www .yipharburg.com).

YIP HARBURG'S UNPUBLISHED INTERVIEWS AND SPEECHES

I read well close to fifty published and unpublished interviews that Yip gave over the years. The following list includes all of the unpublished interviews and speeches I received from the Yip Harburg Foundation, which I edited and wove into a narrative about Yip's career. I have listed them here in chronological order, along with the names given on the cover sheet of each interview. These sources are also listed in the endnotes as they appear in the text.

"Yip Harburg interviewed by Deems Taylor, *The Kraft Program*, January 25, 1934," typed transcript.
"Yip Harburg radio interview with Jinx Falkenberg and unidentified male interviewer, n.d., ca. 1951," typed transcript.

"Reminiscences of E. Y. 'Yip' Harburg (February 1959), Popular Arts Project through the Columbia University Center for Oral History." Used by permission of the Columbia University Center for Oral History and the Yip Harburg Foundation.

"Yip Interviewed by Jack Sterling: The Jack Sterling Show, WCBS Radio, New York City, Spring: 1961," typed transcript.

"World of Music—N.E.T.—E. Y. Harburg: Lyrics for the Musical Theatre— Host: Morton Gould, January 27, 1965; broadcast March 10, 1965," typed transcript.

"Yip Harburg interviewed by Professor David M. Keller, 'The Dramatic Experience,' Program 1: The Musical Comedy Theatre, WNYC-TV, 1968," typed transcript.

"Chappell's Broadway, Discussion of *Flahooley*, 1969, with Yip Harburg and Sammy Fain," typed transcript.

"Yip Harburg interviewed on Chappell's Broadway, February 27, 1970," typed transcript 1-10-16, recording 7-10-390.

"Yip at the 92nd Street YM-YWHA, December 13, 1970," typed transcript 1-10-3, cassettes 7-2-10 and 7-2-20.

"Yip Harburg on the *Great American Dream Machine*, WNET-TV, New York City, 1971," typed transcript 1-10-7, recording 7-2-210, VHS 5-1-90.

"Chappell's Broadway, April 2, 1971—Guest: Yip Harburg," typed transcript 1-10-17, recording 7-10-400.

"Yip at the Y #2, February 1, 1972," typed transcript, archive tapes 7-2-50 and 7-2-60.

"The David Frost Show—February 23, 1972, Guest: Yip Harburg," typed transcript 1-9-25, VHS 185, audio cassette 7-1-260.

"Yip Harburg, Mark Taper Forum, February 5, 1973," typed transcript, tapes 7-2-70, 7-2-80, and 7-2-90.

"Yip Harburg at the 92nd Street Y, December 15, 1974," typed transcript, recording 7-2-110 (formerly listed as RR2 and RR5).

"Yip Harburg interviewed by Aljean Harmetz, Spring, 1975," typed notes.

"Yip Harburg, Speech at University of Vermont, April 21, 1975," typed transcript, recording 7-2-230 (formerly listed as RR9).

"Yip Harburg interviewed by Celeste Wesson of WBAI, Autumn, 1976," typed transcript 1-9-3, tape 7-1-10.

"Yip Harburg interviewed by Deena Rosenberg, November 22, 1976," typed transcript, archive tape 7-1-70.

"Yip Harburg interviewed by Michael Jackson, KABC Radio, California, post-1976, n.d.," typed transcript 1-9-1, tape 7-1-20.

"Yip Harburg interviewed by Studs Terkel, undated—probably January or
February, 1977; Topic: Yip's New Book, *At This Point in Rhyme*," typed
transcript 1-9-23, tape 7-1-50.

"E. Y. Harburg, Lecture at UCLA on Lyric Writing, February 3, 1977," typed
transcript, tape 7-3-10.

"Yip Harburg interviewed by Maurice Levine, Lyrics and Lyricists series,
March 23, 1977," typed transcript, tape 242C, side A.

"Yip Harburg interviewed by Jack O'Brien on 'Critic's Circle,' WOR Radio,
New York City, May 21, 1977," typed transcript.

"Yip Harburg, Lecture at Northwood Institute, 1978," typed transcript, tapes
7-3-30, 7-3-40, 7-3-50, 7-3-60, and 7-3-70.

"Yip on the Dick Cavett Show, WNET-TV, New York City, 1978," typed
transcript, audio cassette 7-1-240, video cassettes 5-1-23 and 5-1-24.

"Yip Harburg interviewed by Studs Terkel, June 1978," typed transcript.

"Speech by Yip Harburg, Horatio Alger Awards, 1979," typed transcript.

"A Visit with E. Y. 'Yip' Harburg: A Musical Life in Concert, from CBC
Television Broadcast, ca. 1979," typed transcript, VHS 5-1-95, cassette
7-2-220.

"Canadian Broadcasting Company interview with Yip Harburg, November 26,
1979," typed transcript, tapes 7-1-60 and 7-1-80.

"Over the Rainbow: Yip Harburg interviewed by Deena Rosenberg, 1980,"
typed transcript from video documentary, archive audio cassette 7-1-220,
archive video cassette 5-1-41.

"Yip Harburg at the Y—January 27 and 28, 1980," typed transcript 1-10-5, audio
recordings 7-2-140 and 7-2-150.

"Yip Harburg interviewed by Jonathan Schwartz, WNEW-FM, New York City,
February 17, 1980: Subject: Harold Arlen's 75th Birthday," typed transcript.

"Something Sort of Grandish—Paul Lazarus, WBAI-FM, March 2, 1980," typed
transcript 1-9-8, recording 7-1-100.

"Speech by E. Y. 'Yip' Harburg: Oral History Luncheon, Waldorf-Astoria,
May 17, 1980, Moderated by Martin Bookspan," typed transcript, recording
7-2-201.

"The Revue: Yip Harburg with Deena Rosenberg and Mel Gordon,
November 15, 1980," typed transcript 1-9-11a, tape 7-7-270.

"Brief interview with Yip Harburg: Canadian Broadcasting Company (not
confirmed), n.d.," typed transcript 1-9-22, tape 7-1-200; probably from the
late 1970s or 1980.

"The 20th Century: The Songs of Harold Arlen, Narrator/Interviewer: Walter
Cronkite," n.d., typed transcript.

OTHER UNPUBLISHED INTERVIEWS

The Yip Harburg Foundation also allowed me to use several interviews with people who had worked with Yip. Of those I read, I used long passages from the following.

"Burton Lane interviewed by Bernard Rosenberg and Ernie Harburg, April 11, 1983," typed transcript. Used by permission of Lynn Lane.

"Burton Lane interviewed by Brad Ross, Ernie Harburg, and Art Perlman, July 10, 1984," typed transcript. Used by permission of Lynn Lane.

"A Conversation with Burton Lane by Deena Rosenberg, April 29, 1985," typed transcript, edited version of interview on VHS 5-1-74. Used by permission of Lynn Lane.

I also used two sentences from the following interview.

"Lena Horne interviewed by Ernie Harburg and Deena Rosenberg, November 20, 1992," typed transcript.

PUBLISHED INTERVIEWS

A number of authors interviewed Yip and his collaborators, and either published the interviews as separate units or incorporated them into the narrative. I quoted from several of these works, including a few with long passages.

Harmetz, Aljean. *The Making of The Wizard of Oz*. New York: Alfred A. Knopf, 1977; reprint New York: Hyperion, 1998.

Jablonski, Edward. *Harold Arlen: Rhythm, Rainbows, and Blues*. Boston: Northeastern University Press, 1996.

Lahr, John, "The Lemon-Drop Kid." *New Yorker*, September 30, 1996, pp. 68–74, accessed August 11, 2010. http://archives.newyorker.com.

Meyerson, Harold, and Ernie Harburg. *Who Put the Rainbow in The Wizard of Oz?* Ann Arbor: University of Michigan Press, 1993. Used by permission of University of Michigan Press.

Rosenberg, Bernard, and Ernest Goldstein. *Creators and Disturbers: Reminiscences by Jewish Intellectuals of New York*. New York: Columbia University Press, 1982. Used by permission of Columbia University Press and Deena Rosenberg Harburg.

Terkel, Studs. *Hard Times: An Oral History of the Great Depression*. New York: Random House, Inc., 1986.

Wilk, Max. *They're Playing Our Song: Conversations with America's Classic Songwriters*. New York: Da Capo Press, 1973, 1991; reprint 1997. Used by permission of David Wilk.

CONVERSATIONS AND E-MAILS

Yip's son and president of the Yip Harburg Foundation, Ernie Harburg, was most generous with his time. The specific communications cited in the text are included here.

Author interview with Ernie Harburg, October 5, 2010, New York City.
E-mail from Ernie Harburg to author, February 28, 2011.

UNPUBLISHED MUSICAL SCRIPTS AND LYRICS

The Yip Harburg Foundation allowed me to use the original typescripts of several librettos of musicals that had not been published. In the case of *Finian's Rainbow*, I was able to use a more accurate copy than the one published in 1947. These librettos, in chronological order, included the following.

Hooray for What!, lyrics by E. Y. Harburg, music by Harold Arlen, book conceived by E. Y. Harburg, written by Howard Lindsay and Russel Crouse, from an idea by E. Y. Harburg, 1937, 1938.

Bloomer Girl, lyrics by E. Y. Harburg, music by Harold Arlen, book by Sig Herzig and Fred Saidy, based on the play by Lilith and Dan James, 1944.

Finian's Rainbow, lyrics by E. Y. Harburg, music by Burton Lane, book by E. Y. Harburg and Fred Saidy, 1947. Dialogue used by permission of Anthony Saidy and the Yip Harburg Foundation.

Flahooley, lyrics by E. Y. Harburg, music by Sammy Fain, book by E. Y. Harburg and Fred Saidy, 1951.

Jamaica, lyrics by E. Y. Harburg, music by Harold Arlen, book by E. Y. Harburg and Fred Saidy, 1957.

Jamaica, lyrics by E. Y. Harburg, music by Harold Arlen, book by E. Y. Harburg and Fred Saidy, 1959 Karamu Production.

The Happiest Girl in the World, lyrics by E. Y. Harburg, music by Jacques Offenbach, book by Fred Saidy and Henry Myers, based on Aristophanes' *Lysistrata* and Bullfinch's stories, music research by Jay Gorney, 1961.

Darling of the Day, lyrics by E. Y. Harburg, music by Jule Styne, book based on Arnold Bennett's *Buried Alive*, 1968.

What a Day for a Miracle, lyrics by E. Y. Harburg, music by Henry Myers, Larry Orenstein, and Jeff Alexander, book by Henry Myers, based on Myers's novel *Our Lives Have Just Begun*, 1971.

"'Till We All Belong, n.d.," typescript.

"Yip Harburg—Parodies and Others, n.d.," typescript.

PUBLISHED WORKS BY E. Y. "YIP" HARBURG

Harburg, E. Y., *At This Point in Rhyme: E. Y. Harburg's Poems*. New York: Crown Publishers, Inc., 1976.

Harburg, E. Y., and Fred Saidy. *Finian's Rainbow: A Musical Satire*. New York: Random House, 1946, 1947.

Harburg, Yip. *Rhymes for the Irreverent*. Madison, WI: Freedom From Religion Foundation, Inc., 2006.

Harburg, Yip. *The Yip Harburg Songbook*. Milwaukee, WI: Hal Leonard Corporation, n.d.

MUSIC AND FILMS

I was raised on Yip Harburg's music and have seen several of his works, including productions of *Bloomer Girl*, *Finian's Rainbow* (three times), *Flahooley*, and the original production of *The Happiest Girl in the World*. Of course, I have seen *The Wizard of Oz* many times, and the film versions of *Finian's Rainbow* and *Cabin in the Sky*. Here I have listed those works specifically viewed or listened to during the course of writing this book.

Bloomer Girl. Original cast recording, Decca Broadway, remastered, Universal Classics Group, UMG Recordings, Inc., 2001. (CD)

Brother, Can You Spare a Dime? Yip Harburg Foundation, 2001. (CD)

Cabin in the Sky. Original soundtrack, Disconforme: Sound Track Factory, 1999.

Darling of the Day. Original cast recording, remastered, RCA Victor: Arkiv CD, 1998. (CD)

E. Y. Harburg: American Songbook Series. Smithsonian Collection of Recordings: Smithsonian Institution Press and Sony Music Entertainment, 1994. (CD)

Finian's Rainbow. Original cast recording, Columbia Masterworks, digitally remastered, Sony Music Entertainment, 1947, 2000. (CD)

Finian's Rainbow. Irish Repertory Theatre cast recording, Sh-K-Boom Records, 2004. (CD)

Finian's Rainbow. New Broadway cast recording, PS Classics, 2010. (CD)

Flahooley. Original cast recording, EMI Music Special Markets and DRG Records re-release of 1951 Capitol Records recording, 2004. (CD)

Gay Purr-ee. Warner Brothers Pictures, 1962, 1990, 2003. (DVD)

The Happiest Girl in the World. Original cast recording, Columbia Masterworks re-release by Sony Music Custom Marketing Group and DRG Records, 2002. (CD)

Jamaica. Original cast recording, BMG Music and Collectables, 2003. (CD)

Life Begins at 8:40. Recording of Library of Congress Concert Performance, PSC Classics, 2010. (CD)

"A Tribute to Blacklisted Lyricist Yip Harburg: The Man Who Put the Rainbow in The Wizard of Oz." Democracy Now!: DemocracyNow.Org Independent Radio & TV News, December 26, 2011 (DN2011.1226). (DVD)

A Visit with E. Y. "Yip" Harburg: A Musical Life in Concert. DRG Records and Sony Fox Production, 1981. (VHS)

The Wizard of Oz: 70th Anniversary Special Edition. Warner Brothers and Turner Entertainment Co., 2009. (DVD)

Yip Sings Harburg. Koch International Classics, 1996. (CD)

OTHER SOURCES

For years, I have been reading books on theater history. The books and articles that I used for this specific project include the following.

Alonso, Harriet Hyman. *Robert E. Sherwood: The Playwright in Peace and War*. Amherst: University of Massachusetts Press, 2007.

Atkinson, Brooks. *Broadway*. New York: Limelight Books, 1970, 1974; reprint 1990.

Bordman, Gerald. *American Musical Theatre: A Chronicle*. 3rd ed. New York: Oxford University Press, 2001.

De Mille, Agnes. *And Promenade Home*. Boston: Little, Brown and Company, 1956, 1957, 1958 by Agnes de Mille. Copyright renewed 1984, 1985, 1986 by Agnes de Mille. Used by permission of Harold Ober Associates Incorporated.

Duke, Vernon. *Passport to Paris*. Boston: Little, Brown and Company, 1955. Used by permission of Kay Duke Ingalls.

Engel, Lehman. *Words with Music: Creating the Broadway Musical Libretto*. Updated and revised by Howard Kissel. New York: Applause Theatre and Cinema Books, 2006.

Flinn, Denny Martin. *Musical! A Grand Tour*. New York: Simon & Schuster Macmillan, 1997.

Furia, Philip. *Ira Gershwin: The Art of the Lyricist*. New York: Oxford University Press, 1996.

Gershwin, Ira. *Lyrics on Several Occasions*. London: Redwood Burn Limited, 1959; reprint 1977.

Gorney, Sondra K. *Brother, Can You Spare a Dime? The Life of Composer Jay Gorney*. Lanham, MD: Scarecrow Press, Inc., 2005. Used by permission of Scarecrow Press.

Jones, John Bush. *Our Musicals, Ourselves: A Social History of the American Musical Theatre*. Hanover, NH: Brandeis University Press, 2003.

Knapp, Raymond. *The American Musical and the Formation of National Identity*. Princeton: Princeton University Press, 2005.

———. *The American Musical and the Performance of Personal Identity*. Princeton: Princeton University Press, 2006.

Lebow, Eileen F. *Bright Boys: A History of Townsend Harris High School*. Westport, CT: Greenwood Publishing Group, Inc., 2000.

Rosenberg, Deena. *Fascinating Rhythm: The Collaboration of George and Ira Gershwin*. Ann Arbor: University of Michigan Press, 1991, 1997.

Seers, Benjamin. "E. Y. 'Yip' Harburg," typed manuscript, 1999, accessed August 27, 2010. http://www.yipharburg.com.

Sheed, Wilfrid. *The House That George Built*. New York: Random House, 2008.

Sondheim, Stephen. *Finishing the Hat: Collected Lyrics (1954–1981) with Attendant Comments, Principles, Heresies, Grudges, Whines and Anecdotes*. New York: Alfred A. Knopf, 2010.

Stempel, Larry. *Showtime: A History of the Broadway Musical Theater*. New York: W. W. Norton and Company, 2010.

Stephens, James. *The Crock of Gold*. New York: Dover Publications, Inc. 1997; reprint of 1912 ed. .

Vogel, James. "*Jamaica* on Broadway: The Popular Caribbean and Mock Transnational Performance," *Theatre Journal* 62, vol. 1 (March 2010): 1–21.

Lyric Credits

I am extremely grateful to the copyright holders of Yip's lyrics who generously granted me permission to quote his words. At their request, I have listed the lyric credits *exactly* as they instructed. Therefore, there are some discrepancies between the punctuation and capitalization in these song titles and those that appear in the text. These are minor and caused by the various sources I used. Permissions to quote from other materials appear in the bibliography next to the entry for that source.

"Adrift On A Star"
Lyric by E. Y. "Yip" Harburg
Music by Jacques Offenbach
© 1961 (Renewed) Glocca Morra
    Music
All Rights Administered by Next
    Decade Entertainment, Inc.
All Rights Reserved
Used by Permission
Reprinted by Permission of Hal
    Leonard Corporation

"And Russia Is Her Name"
From *Song of Russia*
Words by E. Y. Harburg
Music by Jerome Kern
Copyright © 1944 Universal–
    Polygram International
    Publishing, Inc. and Glocca Morra
    Music
Copyright Renewed
All Rights for Glocca Morra Music
    administered by Next Decade
    Entertainment, Inc.
All Rights Reserved
Used by Permission

Reprinted by Permission of Hal
    Leonard Corporation

"April In Paris"
Words by E. Y. "Yip" Harburg
Music by Vernon Duke
Copyright © 1932 by Kay Duke
    Music, administered by Boosey &
    Hawkes: An Imagem Company
    and Glocca Morra Music
Copyright Renewed
All Rights for Kay Duke Music
    administered by Universal Music–
    MGB Songs
All Rights for Glocca Morra Music
    administered by Next Decade
    Entertainment, Inc.
International Copyright Secured
All Rights Reserved
Reprinted by Permission of Hal
    Leonard Corporation and Boosey
    & Hawkes

"The Begat"
Lyric by E. Y. "Yip" Harburg
Music by Burton Lane

"B. G. Bigelow, Inc."
From *Flahooley*
Lyric by E. Y. "Yip" Harburg
Music by Sammy Fain

"Brother, Can You Spare A Dime?"
Lyric by E. Y. "Yip" Harburg
Music by Jay Gorney

"Ding-Dong! The Witch Is Dead"
(From "The Wizard of Oz")
Music by Harold Arlen
Lyric by E. Y. Harburg

"Don't Look Now, Mr. Dewey (But
Your Record's Showing)"
Lyric by E. Y. "Yip" Harburg
Music by Arthur Schwartz

"The Eagle and Me"
From *Bloomer Girl*
Lyric by E. Y. "Yip" Harburg
Music by Harold Arlen

"Flahooley"
From *Flahooley*
Lyric by E. Y. "Yip" Harburg
Music by Sammy Fain
© 1951 (Renewed) Glocca Morra Music and Chappell & Co.
All Rights for Glocca Morra Music administered by Next Decade Entertainment, Inc.

"Free and Equal Blues"
Lyric by E. Y. "Yip" Harburg
Music by Earl Robinson
© 1944, 1947 (Renewed) Glocca Morra Music and Chappell & Co.
All Rights for Glocca Morra Music Administered by Next Decade Entertainment, Inc.

"The Glory That Is Greece"
Lyric by E. Y. "Yip" Harburg
Music by Jacques Offenbach
© 1961 (Renewed) Glocca Morra Music
All Rights Administered by Next Decade Entertainment, Inc.

"Gotta Get Out and Vote"
Lyric by E. Y. "Yip" Harburg
Music by Earl Robinson
© 1944 (Renewed) Glocca Morra Music and Music Sales Corporation
All Rights for Glocca Morra Music Administered by Next Decade Entertainment, Inc.

"Happiness Is a Thing Called Joe"
Words by E. Y. Harburg Music by Harold Arlen
Copyright © 1942 (Renewed) EMI Feist Catalog Inc.
Exclusive Print Rights administered by Alfred Music Publishing Co., Inc.

"Hooray for What"
From the musical production *Hooray for What!*
Lyric by E. Y. "Yip" Harburg
Music by Harold Arlen
© 1937 (Renewed) Glocca Morra Music and S.A. Music Co.
All Rights for Glocca Morra Music administered by Next Decade Entertainment, Inc.

All Rights Reserved
Reprinted by Permission of Hal
    Leonard Corporation

"Last Night When We Were Young"
Lyric by E. Y. "Yip" Harburg
Music by Harold Arlen
© 1937 (Renewed) Glocca Morra
    Music and S.A. Music Co.
All Rights for Glocca Morra Music
    Administered by Next Decade
    Entertainment, Inc.
All Rights for Canada Controlled by
    Bourne Co.
All Rights Reserved
Used by Permission
Reprinted by Permission of Hal
    Leonard Corporation

"Leave De Atom Alone"
From *Jamaica*
Lyrics by E. Y. Harburg
Music by Harold Arlen
© 1957 (Renewed) Harold Arlen and
    E. Y. Harburg
All Rights Controlled by Harwin
    Music Co. and Glocca Morra
    Music
All Rights Reserved
Reprinted by Permission of Hal
    Leonard Corporation

"Let's Take a Walk Around the Block"
Words and Music by Ira Gershwin,
    Harold Arlen and E. Y. Harburg
Copyright © 1934 (Renewed) New
    World Music Company Ltd.
Rights for the Extended Renewal
    Term in the U.S. controlled by

WB Music Corp., S.A. Music and
    Glocca Morra Music
All Rights outside of the U.S.
    controlled by WB Music Corp.
All Rights Reserved
Used by Permission of Alfred Music
    Publishing Co., Inc.

"Let's Take a Walk Around the Block"
From *Life Begins at 8:40*
Lyric by Ira Gershwin and E. Y.
    Harburg
Music by Harold Arlen
© 1934 (Renewed) WB Music Corp.,
    Glocca Morra Music, S.A. Music
    Co. and Arlen Music, Inc.
All Rights Reserved
Reprinted by Permission of Hal
    Leonard Corporation

"Look to the Rainbow"
From *Finian's Rainbow*
Words by E. Y. "Yip" Harburg
Music by Burton Lane
Copyright © 1946, 1947 by Chappell
    & Co. and Glocca Morra Music
Copyright Renewed
All Rights for Glocca Morra Music
    administered by Next Decade
    Entertainment, Inc.
International Copyright Secured
All Rights Reserved
Reprinted by Permission of Alfred
    Music Publishing Co., Inc. and Hal
    Leonard Corporation

"Lydia the Tattooed Lady"
Words by E. Y. Harburg
Music by Harold Arlen

"Man For Sale"
From *Bloomer Girl*
Words by E. Y. Harburg
Music by Harold Arlen

"Monkey in the Mango Tree"
From *Jamaica*
Lyric by E. Y. Harburg
Music by Harold Arlen

"Necessity"
Lyric by E. Y. "Yip" Harburg
Music by Burton Lane

"Old Devil Moon"
From *Finian's Rainbow*
Words by E. Y. "Yip" Harburg
Music by Burton Lane

"Over the Rainbow" (From "The
Wizard of Oz")
Music by Harold Arlen
Lyric by E. Y. Harburg

All Rights Reserved
Used by Permission of Alfred Music
    Publishing Co., Inc.

"Push De Button"
From *Jamaica*
Lyric by E. Y. Harburg
Music by Harold Arlen
© 1956, 1957 (Renewed) Harold
    Arlen and E. Y. Harburg
All Rights Controlled by Harwin
    Music Co. and Glocca Morra
    Music
All Rights Reserved
Reprinted by Permission of Hal
    Leonard Corporation

"Quartet Erotica (We're Not What We
    Used to Be)"
Words by Ira Gershwin and E. Y.
    Harburg
Music by Harold Arlen
Copyright © 1934 New World Music
    Company Ltd.
All Rights Administered by WB
    Music Corp.
All Rights Reserved
Used by Permission of Alfred Music
    Publishing Co., Inc.

"Right as the Rain"
From *Bloomer Girl*
Lyric by E. Y. "Yip" Harburg
Music by Harold Arlen
© 1944 (Renewed) S.A. Music Co.
    and Glocca Morra Music
All Rights for Glocca Morra Music
    administered by Next Decade
    Entertainment, Inc.

All Rights Reserved
Reprinted by Permission of Hal
    Leonard Corporation

"The Same Boat, Brother"
Lyric by E. Y. "Yip" Harburg
Music by Earl Robinson
© 1944, 1945 (Renewed) Glocca
    Morra Music and Music Sales
    Corporation
All Rights for Glocca Morra Music
    Administered by Next Decade
    Entertainment, Inc.
All Rights Reserved
Used by Permission
International Copyright Secured
Reprinted by Permission of Hal
    Leonard Corporation and Music
    Sales Corporation

"Something Sort of Grandish"
From *Finian's Rainbow*
Lyric by E. Y. "Yip" Harburg
Music by Burton Lane
© 1947 (Renewed) Glocca Morra
    Music and Chappell & Co.
All Rights for Glocca Morra Music
    Administered by Next Decade
    Entertainment, Inc.
All Rights Reserved
Used by Permission
Reprinted by Permission of Alfred
    Music Publishing Co., Inc. and Hal
    Leonard Corporation

"The Son of a Gun Who Picks on
    Uncle Sam"
Words by E. Y. Harburg
Music by Burton Lane

Copyright © 1942 (Renewed)
Chappell & Co., Inc.
All Rights Reserved
Used by Permission of Alfred Music
Publishing Co., Inc.

"The Springtime Cometh"
From *Flahooley*
Lyric by E. Y. "Yip" Harburg
Music by Sammy Fain
© 1951 (Renewed) Glocca Morra
Music and Chappell & Co.
All Rights for Glocca Morra Music
Administered by Next Decade
Entertainment, Inc.
All Rights Reserved
Used by Permission
Reprinted by Permission of Hal
Leonard Corporation

"Sunday in Cicero Falls"
From *Bloomer Girl*
Words by E. Y. Harburg
Music by Harold Arlen
© 1944 (Renewed) S.A. Music Co.
and Glocca Morra Music
All Rights for Glocca Morra Music
administered by Next Decade
Music Corp.
All Rights Reserved

"That Great Come and Get It Day"
From *Finian's Rainbow*
Words by E. Y. "Yip" Harburg
Music by Burton Lane
Copyright © 1946 by Chappell & Co.
and Glocca Morra Music
Copyright Renewed

All Rights for Glocca Morra Music
administered by Next Decade
Entertainment, Inc.
International Copyright Secured
All Rights Reserved
Reprinted by Permission of Alfred
Music Publishing Co., Inc. and Hal
Leonard Corporation

"There's a Great Day Coming
Mañana"
From *Hold on to Your Hats*
Words by E. Y. Harburg
Music by Burton Lane
Copyright © 1940 by Chappell & Co.
and Glocca Morra Music
Copyright Renewed
All Rights for Glocca Morra Music
Administered by Next Decade
Entertainment, Inc.
International Copyright Secured
All Rights Reserved
Reprinted by Permission of Hal
Leonard Corporation

"What Can You Say in a Love Song?"
From *Life Begins at 8:40*
Lyric by Ira Gershwin and E. Y.
Harburg
Music by Harold Arlen
© 1934 (Renewed) WB Music Corp.,
Glocca Morra Music, S.A. Music
Co., Harwin Music Co. and Arlen
Music, Inc.
All Rights Reserved
Reprinted by Permission of Alfred
Music Publishing Co., Inc. and Hal
Leonard Corporation

"When I'm Not Near the Girl I Love"
From *Finian's Rainbow*
Lyric by E. Y. "Yip" Harburg
Music by Burton Lane
© 1946, 1947 (Renewed) Glocca
    Morra Music and Chappell & Co.
All Rights for Glocca Morra Music
    administered by Next Decade
    Entertainment, Inc.
All Rights Reserved
Used by Permission
Reprinted by Permission of Alfred
    Music Publishing Co., Inc. and Hal
    Leonard Corporation

"When the Boys Come Home"
From *Bloomer Girl*
Words by E. Y. Harburg
Music by Harold Arlen
© 1944 (Renewed) S.A. Music Co.
    and Glocca Morra Music
All Rights for Glocca Morra Music
    administered by Next Decade
    Music Corp.
All Rights Reserved
Reprinted by Permission of Hal
    Leonard Corporation

"When the Idle Poor Become the Idle
    Rich"
Lyric by E. Y. "Yip" Harburg
Music by Burton Lane
© 1946, 1947 (Renewed) Glocca
    Morra Music and Chappell & Co.

All Rights for Glocca Morra Music
    administered by Next Decade
    Entertainment, Inc.
All Rights Reserved
Used by Permission
Reprinted by Permission of Alfred
    Music Publishing Co., Inc. and Hal
    Leonard Corporation

"You Gotta Get Out and Vote"
Words by E. Y. Harburg
Music by Earl Robinson
Copyright © 1944 (Renewed) by
    Music Sales Corporation (ASCAP)
International Copyright Secured
All Rights Reserved
Reprinted by Permission of Music
    Sales Corporation

"You Too Can Be a Puppet"
From *Flahooley*
Lyric by E. Y. "Yip" Harburg
Music by Sammy Fain
© 1951 (Renewed) Glocca Morra
    Music and Chappell & Co.
All Rights for Glocca Morra Music
    administered by Next Decade
    Entertainment, Inc.
All Rights Reserved
Used by Permission
Reprinted by Permission of Hal
    Leonard

Index

Page numbers in italics refer to illustrations.

Music:Interview

A SERIES FROM WESLEYAN UNIVERSITY PRESS

Edited by Daniel Cavicchi

Yip Harburg:
Legendary Lyricist and Human Rights Activist
by Harriet Hyman Alonso

Reel History: The Lost Archive of Juma Sultan
and the Aboriginal Music Society
by Stephen Farina

Always in Trouble: An Oral History of ESP-Disk',
the Most Outrageous Record Label in America
by Jason Weiss

Music/Interview is a book series featuring the best interviews with performers, producers, and other significant figures in the world of music, past and present. For updates and more information on the Music/Interview series, visit www .wesleyan.edu/wespress.

About the Author

Harriet Hyman Alonso is professor of history at the City College of New York (CUNY) and has an appointment at the CUNY Graduate Center. She holds a BS in English and American literature and dramatic arts from New York University, an MA in women's history from Sarah Lawrence College, and a PhD in history from Stony Brook University. Alonso taught history and women's studies at Fitchburg State University (Massachusetts) from 1989 to 1999. In 1992, the students at Fitchburg voted her Faculty Member of the Year. She received the same honor in 2008 from the students in the Division of Interdisciplinary Studies at the City College Center for Worker Education, where she served as associate dean and director from 1999 to 2002 and founding department chair from 2006 to 2009.

Alonso is the author of many articles and book reviews and four previous books, including *The Women's Peace Union and the Outlawry of War, 1921–1942*, the groundbreaking *Peace as a Women's Issue: A History of the U.S. Movement for World Peace and Women's Rights*, and the prize-winning *Growing Up Abolitionist: The Story of the Garrison Children*. Previously, she received an article prize for her work on Jane Addams and Emily Greene Balch, and was the recipient of a National Endowment for the Humanities research fellowship for her work on *Robert E. Sherwood: The Playwright in Peace and War*. She is a proud, longtime member of the Peace History Society.